MAVERICK
A Dissident View of Broadcasting Today

By the same author

Atlantean: Ireland's North African and Maritime Heritage
Smokey Hollow: A Fictional Memoir
Conamara, the Unknown Country

BOB QUINN

MAVERICK

A Dissident View of Broadcasting Today

To the memory of Patrick B. Quinn,
cooper and painter, 1902–1966,
who could not compete with the pram in the hall.

First published in 2001 by
Brandon
an imprint of Mount Eagle Publications
Dingle, Co. Kerry, Ireland

Copyright © Bob Quinn 2001

The author has asserted his moral rights.

British Library Cataloguing in Publication Data is available
for this book.

ISBN 0 86322 288 9

10 9 8 7 6 5 4 3 2 1

Cover design by id communications, Tralee, Co. Kerry
Typesetting by Red Barn Publishing, Skeagh, Skibbereen
Printed in Scotland by Omnia Books

CONTENTS

Acknowledgements

I thank Lelia Doolan, Michael Viney, Brian Mac Gabhann, Michael D. Higgins, Donncha Ó hÉallaithe, Patsy Murphy, Robert Quinn, Toner Quinn and Rod Stoneman, who each ploughed through different drafts and encouraged me to continue. Jonathan Williams taught me attention to detail, curbed my ramblings somewhat and guided the book into the hands of the indefatigable Steve MacDonogh.

Naming the many RTÉ friends who marked my card would be delicate because most of them still work there. They know who they are, and I am grateful to them. However, I can formally mention the professional assistance I got from RTÉ's new Freedom of Information department under its director, Peter Feeney; the RTÉ library under Con Bushe; and Lyric FM under its director, Seamus Crimmins. My interpretation of their facts is entirely my own. Muiris Mac Conghail, Joe MacAnthony, Maolsheachlainn Ó Caollaí, Dana Hearne, Nollaig Ó Gadhra, Tom Widger, T.P. O'Mahony, Gearóid Ó Murchú and Seosamh Ó Cuaig were erudite on historical detail. Eric Spain and Gillies MacBain were inspirational, and Séamus Ó Tuathail was generous with his advice.

For research and insight into child-targeted advertising, I relied much on the work of Ralph Nader, Gary Ruskin and Kalle Lasn, as well as Bairbre Quinn, Vicky Donnelly, Trócaire, the children of Kiltiernan N.S., Miriam Allen, Simon Rowe, Breda O'Brien, Rev. J. Carroll, Larry Hynes, Mary Owen, Ciara Ní Ghabhann. For lending me a white, quiet room, I am indebted to Pádraic Ó hAoláin and Seán Ó Coisdealbha of Muintearas.

For their sometimes heroic courtesy towards me during my tenure on the RTÉ Authority, I must pay tribute to Farrel Corcoran, Joe Barry, Bob Collins, Tom Quinn and Carmel O'Reilly.

This book would not have been written without the support of Aosdána.

THE LONE RANGER

Kemo Sabe?
The Lone Ranger

At 10 a.m. on the last Friday of June 1995, the nine members of the new RTÉ Authority, accompanied by their officers and servants, assembled round a polished oval table in the boardroom on the third floor of the administration block in Donnybrook, Dublin 4.

That morning marked the 541st meeting of the RTÉ Authority.

The new chairman sat with his back to the window, the director general and the assistant director general on his right. The director of corporate affairs and the recording secretary covered his left flank. Behind the five of them, through the plate-glass windows, full-grown sycamores and chestnuts luxuriated in their summer dresses. We eight ordinary members sitting opposite that window had the best view. Studying the movement of those trees, their seasonal greening, browning and shedding, would while away many a moment of ennui for me over the next four years. Peering over our own shoulders were portraits of past chairmen and directors general of RTÉ: Eamonn Andrews, Ed Roth, Kevin McCourt, Tom Hardiman, Todd Andrews, Donal Ó Morain, Sheila Conroy, P.J. Moriarty and company.

I felt as out of place as the Lone Ranger. Even as I had

approached the building, when I saw a besuited figure waving at me, I thought I was going to be told to leave the environs, that it had all been a mistake. In the sixties, some programme-makers called this building the Reichstag. Its symmetrical driveways were somehow reminiscent of a Nuremberg rally. The building then housed all those not at the coalface of programme-making. It still does. It is now known as the Montrose Hilton.

It was actually Tom Quinn, the director of corporate affairs himself, who was welcoming me and directing me towards a reserved parking space. I exchanged greetings and carefully backed my trusty banger in, wishing I had brought Tonto with me from the Wild West. My old compadre and his Indian friends were way out beyond the walls of Montrose, mercurial in their loyalties, malleable with liquor and trinkets, more or less pacified but still vaguely threatening. I was on my own now, pardner.

Once a month I would push through the same swing doors, take the same lift for a three-hour session of windmill-fighting followed by a sumptuous lunch. It should have been a five-year term. To avoid suspense you should know that after four years I decided that even one more year as a marginalised bit of a rubber stamp was too much and I resigned. The reason I endured it for so long was old-fashioned stubbornness; for historical reasons, many thought I would not last more than six months. The Lone Ranger was not known for lingering, even for the sake of his cherished cause of public broadcasting.

Broadcasting in Ireland has traditionally had a public service ethos. 2RN was founded in 1926 as a branch of the Department of Posts and Telegraphs. It begot Radio Éireann, which begot Radio Teilifís Éireann, a semi-state statutory body which was launched on New Year's Eve 1961 in the Gresham Hotel in Dublin. I was there, seconded with my fellows from the RTÉ sound department to help with seating in the Gresham for all the great and good of Irish society.

Outside in O'Connell Street, it snowed while tenor Patrick O'Hagan tried to entertain the great unwashed. Inside, the Gresham was luxury itself. Although I was not among those entitled to eat upstairs, I stole a menu to see what I was missing: Dublin Bay Prawn Cocktail, Filet of Sole Nantua with Vin Tourat, Supreme of Chicken Gourmet with Beaujolais, Petit Fours and Liqueur or coffee. (I still have the menu, which shows what an inveterate hoarder I am.)

In the Gresham that night the honoured guests – including, I believe, the young King Hussein of Jordan – resembled famine victims. We youngsters were astonished at the resulting chaos, at the undignified scrambling for seats, at the gluttonous and free scoffing and drinking by the cream of Irish society. We soon abandoned the distasteful scene, retreated to the basement of the hotel where there was free food and drink for us, too, possibly to reward us for our discrimination.

At midnight Charlie Roberts, the inimitable floor manager, clutching his headphones and clipboard and trailing a cable, dashed on stage and bellowed, "Cue 1962".

Teilifís Éireann was on the air, having been blessed on screen by President Eamon de Valera and the Primate of All Ireland, Cardinal D'Alton. Dev said the following:

> Never before was there in the hands of men [*sic*] an instrument so powerful to influence the thoughts and actions of the multitude . . . On the other hand, it can lead through demoralisation to decadence and disillusion. Sometimes one hears, when one urges higher standards in information and recreation services, that one must give the people what they want. And the competition unfortunately is in the wrong direction, so standards become lower and lower.

His words may have been prescient, but that was only Dev talking in the twilight of his career. We were young and optimistic. I had returned from a job teaching Berlitz English in Germany and was delighted to work in such an ambience of youth, energy and creativity.

Montrose, the new studio building designed by Michael Scott, was not yet ready, so we had beavered away for the previous six months stockpiling programmes in a warehouse in the centre of Dublin. A couple of streets away in Henry Street, the Senior Service (as Brendan Cauldwell named Radio Éireann), if a little apprehensive about all these new developments, continued on its solid reliable way in the GPO. The Tower Bar in Henry Street and Madigan's pub in Moore Street were still the most attractive aspects of work for some of those talented radio people.

But the atmosphere in television was youthful and ebullient. That phase actually lasted a number of years until the rot set in, and in 1969 I left the place. Shortly before I returned to join the RTÉ Authority, an old hand in the organisation said to me, "Bob, you thought it was bad when you left. That was paradise compared to now."

Contrary to the contemporary belief that RTÉ in the sixties was run by perverts and deviants – which earned the place the name "Fairyhouse" – we were actually, or at least relatively, innocent. The most daring breakthrough for many of us was an all-night drinking party on Good Friday, a day when all the pubs traditionally closed. I retain a copy of a page from an early *RTÉ Guide* because it lists my one and only play for radio, *The Image*, which starred a woman, Celia Salkeld, in the role of God. Overleaf there are more important details: the TV programmes on RTÉ's single channel. They begin at 5.30 p.m. and end at 11.30 p.m.

It starts with *Fadó Fadó* for children, has *Gaelic Report* at 7, *The Treaty Debates* at 8, *Féach* at 9.50, and ends with *Outlook* presented by Fr Leon Ó Morcháin. There were only fourteen minutes of cartoons, some of which, as I remember well, were incomprehensibly brilliant works from Czechoslovakia. Ah, the innocence and unchallenged Irishness of those days. Little vestige of it remains on television, but some gems like the *Thomas Davis Lectures* and *Sunday Miscellany* incredibly survive on radio, alongside the gentle dinosaur which is Ciarán Mac Mathúna's *Mo*

Cheol Thú. I can't imagine why, if our past is officially now a different country, we hang on for dear life to such relics of "aul' dacency".

My first job in television occasionally placed me in the small Studio Three where I would roll the prerecorded Angelus tape, followed immediately by the signature tune for the news – a version of "Baa Baa Black Sheep" by Dohnanyi. I would then feed in sound effects from the BBC library to accompany the (mute) film reports. I still remember the catalogue number of the most useful record: No. 3/6. It consisted of murmuring voices in an echoing room. From what one could decipher, they were all saying "rhubarb, rhubarb". The sound fitted most news reports perfectly.

In the two years I spent at this undemanding job, which also involved swinging a boom microphone on dramas and general cable-bashing, I would use up superfluous energy by writing short stories for the *Evening Press* and features for the radio service. In 1964 I was offered two jobs by RTÉ. One was as programme assistant for sponsored programmes in radio; the other was as producer/director in television. How different life would have been if I had chosen the first. But I spent several fulfilling years producing studio programmes and film documentaries, some of which were good enough to represent RTÉ at international festivals. By 1968 I had reached the conclusion, rightly or wrongly, that my work was only serving to ratify the commercial abuse of public broadcasting.

I formally resigned from my staff job in RTÉ in October 1968, bought an old car and drove to Tehran and back. Poverty then forced me to become a contract producer for RTÉ. That was a mistake. The following May, 1969, I did the unpardonable. I hijacked a crew, brought them across country to Clare Island and promptly sent them home with a short note denouncing all of RTÉ's commercial and organisational works and pomps. It prompted an upheaval in RTÉ which resulted in the resignations of Jack Dowling, producer, and Lelia Doolan, head of Light Entertainment, as well as a book entitled *Sit Down and Be Counted*. In his introduction to this "cultural evolution of a television station", Raymond Williams wrote:

> Consider also the contemporary events in Paris, wherein the attempted renewal of society, by students and workers, the well-trained radio and television service suddenly found its full voice and began speaking as it needed to speak and not as in expediency it had found convenient and manageable. With the failure of the general renewal, a serious revenge was taken on the professionals involved. Many of them were dismissed and, as in the case of Prague, too few of their colleagues elsewhere showed the necessary solidarity and support.

Then I became a dishwasher in London. Dowling, Doolan and myself briefly returned to RTÉ for an infamous appearance on *The Late Late Show* in November 1969. Afterwards I was singled out (by an anonymous caller) as "a rudderless intellectual who can't see the wood for the trees". This judgement may still be true. When Gay Byrne demanded, on air, to know why I had bothered to appear so broodingly on his show, I responded that he had offered me £25 and an air ticket from London; and that these were my only reasons. It was a great many years before I was invited back on the show.

However, if a character reference were needed for the three people who left RTÉ in that eventful May of 1969, one could do no better than quote the flattering memoir of the then chairman, Todd Andrews: "Sad to say, those who left the service were highly intelligent people, well informed and animated by the best of sociological and national convictions." Despite the headaches the event caused RTÉ, it did not prevent the station from involving itself in co-productions with me over the following thirty years.

I believe my unlikely appointment to the RTÉ Authority in 1995 was a product of the sense of humour of the minister responsible for broadcasting, Michael D. Higgins.

On 31 May the minister's adviser – Colm Ó Briain – had rung me at home to sound me out. In the light of my erratic thirty-five-year relationship with the national broadcaster, it was an astonishing invitation.

I thought for a moment and said yes. When the minister rang to confirm his decision, I told him it might be a mischievous appointment and warned that I might not express my opinions on such an Authority in as graceful a manner as he.

"That also has its value," the minister said.

When Louis Marcus, an ancient workhorse of a filmmaker like myself, heard of the appointment, he sent me a postcard saying: "Congratulations. The lunatics have taken over the asylum."

On that lovely June morning, before we entered the inner sanctum of the boardroom, I met old acquaintances: Joe Barry, the director general, had been the affable outside broadcast engineer when I produced *School Around the Corner* in the sixties. An outgoing Authority member, Gay Byrne, shook my hand and wished me all the best. I had been the youngest ever producer of his *Late Late*; indeed, the show first topped the audience ratings during my brief reign. I met Carmel O'Reilly, secretary to the secretariat and once a neighbour of mine in Terenure, Dublin, and Daphne O'Donnell, secretary to the Authority secretary and wife of a technical genius named Kevin, now a lecturer, with whom I cable-bashed in the sound department in the early days. In a sense we were all old friends, although we had not met for aeons. It was like coming home. Joe Mulholland, still head of News, when told that it had been nearly thirty years since I dramatically walked out of my job in RTÉ, said in his phlegmatic Donegal burr, "You never really left us." I realised I was seen as a kind of poltergeist returned to bump into furniture in the daylight.

Dr Garret FitzGerald flatteringly greeted me by my first name. The ex-taoiseach was described in the staff newsletter as having an interest in theology. It became clear that there was no better man to count the number of angels one could fit on the head of a pin. Des Geraghty was also there. He had once worked on studio cameras, and we had not met in all the years since Des played the tin whistle at a drunken barbecue in Dollymount. He was now, I gathered, a bigshot in SIPTU and president-designate of that organisation.

Bob Collins, the assistant to the director general, whom I had met in the context of TV for the Gaeltacht, answered succinctly when asked, in Irish, how he was getting on: *"Ag cosaint an rud do-cosanta,"* he replied. This could be translated either as "protecting what is hard to protect" or "defending the indefensible". I opted for the latter interpretation. Within eighteen months Collins would succeed Joe Barry as director general.

The other members of the cast were unknown to me: Bill Attley, soccer enthusiast and soon-to-retire general secretary of SIPTU; Anne Haslam, tax consultant from County Offaly and one-time Fine Gael election candidate, who would continually worry about my nicotine intake; Anne Tannahill, who, as befitted a canny Belfast publisher, rarely commented but made copious notes (when she resigned from the Authority in 1998, she was replaced by Pat Hume, a former teacher from Derry). There was a handsome woman, Maureen Rennicks, manufacturer of road signs in Mulhuddart, whom I can recall opening her mouth but once in my presence. She lasted six months, to be replaced by Patricia Redlich, an agony aunt from a Sunday newspaper. At her first meeting, she spoke on "creativity" to the assembled RTÉ Authority.

At least, I told myself, there is Betty Purcell, the staff representative. I knew her only by reputation. She had, with Seosamh Ó Cuaig of Raidió na Gaeltachta, taken an NUJ case against the disastrous Section 31 censorship to the Human Rights Court in Strasbourg. They lost, of course. As the only person besides myself with direct experience of programme-making, she would prove to be my sole ally on the Authority. This is not to say that Purcell did not have her own very distinct agenda. She had been elected by the staff on the promise of keeping them informed of the Authority's deliberations by means of a regular newsletter. One of the first things the new Authority did was to take this promise in its jaws, worry at it for a moment, then emasculate it. Result – no newsletter would be issued without official vetting.

The new chairman, Farrel Corcoran, professor of communications in Dublin City University, had invited me to meet him over a pint in Temple Bar a few weeks before. The professor seemed a nice man, and we had, not one, but two pints, after which I expressed the blunt opinion that RTÉ was out of control. The professor said he found the prospect of his new appointment intimidating, an attitude which, to my mind, he had difficulty shaking off. In the philosophic desert that was and is RTÉ, the professor's chairmanship has been described by a close observer as "an academic too late".

In this uncertain atmosphere began a period when I observed RTÉ trying to protect the elusive concept of public broadcasting from the attempts of certain politicians and huge financial interests to destroy it. In the process I also noted RTÉ's self-destructive contribution. It was a good microcosm of the parallel dissolution of that once-sovereign but increasingly confused entity known as the Republic of Ireland.

I admit to a moment of panic at that first meeting. I realised that I was in the company of people who measured their and others' every word; my natural mode of impatient rhetoric would have to be greatly tempered. I never achieved this ambition. It also briefly occurred to me that we, the RTÉ Authority, in this centralised state of broadcasting, might be considered to be the Politburo. It was a vainglorious idea. I soon found out that the real masters were the permanent officers of the Executive. I tried to imagine the jaundiced feelings of these veteran administrators as they viewed the motley collection of broadcasting amateurs and part-timers who had been foisted on them as "the Authority". There had been the tradition of overlapping Authority membership, to preserve some continuity of policy. But in 1995, the clean sweep of outgoing members meant that now there was an entirely fresh class of greenhorns to be slowly and painfully educated into the realities of modern broadcasting.

As I studied the faces around the table, an image of the pecking order came to my mind: a daily procession round the seven hectares of bog which constitute my garden in Conamara. I, the chairman, am conducting the regular inspection of tiny trees planted the previous winter. I am followed by Ceefor the cat, who is tracked by Beefor the bantam cock who fancies her; followed by Blackie the tomcat who is inscrutable, followed by a black puppy, Óiche, who is largely ignored by the others. One or other of my various children might also trail along, reluctantly. As in this boardroom their acceptance of leadership is based less on respect than on self-preservation. Though fate has imposed on them a shared and quite transient territorial imperative, each is preoccupied with its own deeply personal constituencies.

A late vocation to ecology had induced me to plant trees, to counter in a minuscule way the depredations of the increasing number of internal combustion engines on this planet. One must start somewhere, however small. As well as cleaning the air, my trees would in coming years also serve to clear my brain from the toxic residues left by meetings of the RTÉ Authority.

On this midsummer morning in 1995, not long after the deliberations of the Authority began, I asked to be supplied with a copy of the daily television log. This is a meticulous computerised record of everything transmitted, from presentation announcements to programmes to commercials. It gives the precise second at which everything begins and everything ends. It reveals exactly what constitutes the quantity of output from RTÉ television; the quality is obviously another matter. But to study exactly what we broadcast every day seemed a reasonable request from a member of the group that was statutorily responsible for every belch of such a formidable output.

The affable atmosphere on the other side of the boardroom table immediately froze. Director General Joe Barry knew exactly where I was heading: that it was not the programmes I wanted to study – I knew enough about them – but the commercial messages in between. He knew that, even after thirty years, my preoccupation with this aspect of broadcasting was unaltered and that my attention had increasingly become focussed on the commercial exploitation of children. He decided to cut me off at the pass.

"No, we couldn't possibly let you have the daily logs."

"Why not?"

"They are for internal consumption only."

"But I'm a member of the Authority responsible for this organisation. Am I not now vaguely internal?"

"We're in a very competitive business. Suppose our competitors got their hands on it? We couldn't have such delicate information floating around outside."

I ignored the implication that I might dash off to the nearest TV magnate and show him proof that RTÉ actually "broadcasts".

"The delicate information contained in the minutes and agendas, the bumf that pours out of this place – is that not floated through the post to me?"

"I'm afraid I couldn't approve of this. But we might arrange for you to study the logs in here." He looked inquiringly at Tom Quinn, the Authority secretary and director of corporate affairs. Tom nodded agreeably.

I pointed out to the chairman that if I had the patience to sit for hours in front of my television set at home, I could tediously record this precise information myself – and was already doing so; that by its very nature it was already available to the public, quite apart from the "competition", if they were interested enough. And the prospect of spending days in RTÉ studying logs under supervision was not one that appealed to me. I would feel like the journalist in *Citizen Kane*, reading archives under a gimlet eye in a bank vault. I asked the chairman if the nine assembled persons did not statutorily constitute the entity known as RTÉ? I had checked this out. Were we not, in fact, the RTÉ Authority, charged with hiring and firing officers and servants such as the director general and his staff, and therefore entitled to instruct them to do our bidding?

Sharp intakes of breath. It may have been the first and last time that the formal relationship between Authority and its officers was ever spelled out in this room. The chairman instantly deciphered the message. I got the logs. The interchange was recorded in the minutes thus:

> There was also the question of access of information from RTÉ to Authority members [implying that "RTÉ" existed autonomously from its Authority] and the need to strike a reasonable balance between members having access to information to facilitate policy-making and the possibility of *maverick* requests for various information [my italics].

I had already been earmarked as a maverick. But it was round one to me, and it taught me the first lesson: RTÉ is an organisation in the hands of a few dedicated semi-public servants who will fight tooth and nail to protect it from real or imagined attack from outside or inside. This means that even that body of temporary political appointees – the Authority that governs it – is a prime suspect. Todd Andrews, chairman in 1969, wrote "Clearly it was not within the competence of a disparate group of individuals such as constituted the Authority . . . to produce a serviceable broadcasting policy".

I recently checked my impression with John Carroll, ex-secretary of the then ITGWU, who had served fifteen years on the RTÉ Authority. He did not find my analysis of our insignificance at all fanciful, agreeing that three hours a month is inadequate to make informed decisions about such an organisation. I hope we were not quite as useless as the committee defined in the *New York Times* as "a group of the unwilling, picked from the unfit, to do the unnecessary". But we were not far off.

It is the nature of all organisations, public and private, to give information to the boards of directors exclusively on a need-to-know basis. I am sure that civil servants have the same attitude to those temporary occupiers of panelled offices of state: the ministers of government.

The loyalty to the organisation is admirable, but the siege mentality is worrying. This first round suggested to me that it was not considered good form to subject to close scrutiny the actual output for which we were responsible; alternately, that such output would not stand up to close scrutiny. Interesting times lay ahead. It helped greatly that I had studied the scripts of *Yes, Minister,* the BBC series about an analogous situation.

In retrospect, I must have been regarded with a certain suspicion. I was independent, had never been a member of a political party – although my class origin dictated that I should always vote Labour, for good and often for ill. I had no threatening personal ambitions, lived on an artist's stipend, had no need to touch the forelock or ingratiate myself with anybody, had been known to attack RTÉ publicly and trenchantly, often without premeditation. Worse, I was the only one on the new Authority who had ever directed a television programme or film (*pace* Betty Purcell who was hands-on editor of *Questions and Answers* and *Divided World* and whose efforts to become a producer/director had been regularly stonewalled), and I had practised this trade for over thirty years. Worst of all, as detailed above, I had been one of the original thirty trainees enlisted to put Irish television on the air in December 1961. I went way back. Neutralising such advantages in this arena was the fact that I am a fulminator rather than a debater; my thought processes operate in so jagged and short-circuited a way

19

that, having assumed that once is enough to express my point, I forget that people are only half-listening most of the time, being preoccupied with what they themselves are going to say next. I share this fault. But I also initially had the naivety to believe that if the truth of a situation is outlined and the remedy is obvious, something will be done. Ancient though I am, I have retained the idealism of a young politician who enters the system assuming that action will immediately follow a clear enunciation of the problems. This, as Sir Humphrey might say to Minister Hacker, is to assume that organisations or political systems behave in a logical way. Such an expectation is entirely optimistic and disproved by experience. As Garret FitzGerald once said in a pre-election situation, "If people evaluate our programme, in logic they will come to us – if there is any logic in politics, which I doubt."

After that first meeting, I bumped into one of RTÉ's finest Current Affairs producers, then strangely transferred to directing a soap opera. "What is to be done about the mess?" I asked him.

"It's too late, Bob," he replied mournfully. "Joshua has blown his horn and the walls have tumbled down."

My wilful interpretation of this was to decide that the walls of public broadcasting had been breached by the barbarians and that they were now inside, in control. I bore this analysis constantly in mind.

It was my first experience of moving in the so-called corridors of power, and my naivety was exceeded only by my desire to learn how things worked. Over four years I gathered a smattering of an idea of this convoluted process. Certainly I learned that knowing how to put a film or TV programme together was of absolutely no value. A background of horse trading or, better still, poker would have been invaluable. Since I have no skill in either of these vocations, I sought advice.

There is an old warrior of my acquaintance named Hugh Duffy, now-retired chief executive of the Irish Music

Rights Organisation. Duffy is a solid, phlegmatic pipe-smoker whose qualities of thoroughness, patience and attention to detail are exactly the opposite of mine. This may be why he has been a successful businessman all his life and also why we have remained good friends since childhood: there was never competition between us. He also once worked for RTÉ. When I asked his advice as to what to do in the new position, he said the following: "Concentrate on changing one single thing at a time. If we all did this, we could change the world."

Thus it was that the first simple thesis I experimentally nailed on the door of the RTÉ cathedral was this: TO TARGET YOUNG CHILDREN AS CONSUMERS IS CHILD ABUSE

The lunch that followed that first meeting, by the way, was superb. The manageress who supervised it was soon to leave RTÉ and start a restaurant in a Conamara village near me. She would not be alone. Some other RTÉ people were just buying or building weekend cottages in the area and pushing up the price of sites so high that locals could not afford to live there.

THE FIRST LANGUAGE

Mo chlann féin do dhíol a máthair.
Pádraic MacPiarais, "Mise Éire"

When Gay Byrne was safely off the previous Authority, he said in an interview: "Teilifís na Gaeilge! Sweet Jesus, did we talk about Teilifís na Gaeilge."

The new Authority continued the tradition. There was hardly a meeting over the next four years that the subject was not plonked in front of us. I have counted forty mentions in the minutes. I had to be restrained in my comments, having been a prime mover in the illegal origins of the project. All of the RTÉ Executive must have known of my original criminal involvement.

When Charles J. Haughey, then taoiseach, was emerging from the RTÉ studios in the late eighties after a not-too-friendly interview, he turned to his companions and said, "Never mind. We'll soon have our own fucking station." One of his ex-ministers reported that remark to three of us in Conamara in 1988 when we were still agitating for a community TV service in the Gaeltacht.

When Haughey made the remark, Bob Collins was RTÉ director of TV programmes and held the opposite view to us. In 1987, at a language conference in Dublin, he said he was opposed to the establishment of a TV channel devoted to Irish language broadcasting. It was a good idea in theory, he said, but to talk about it in present circumstances was *"craiceáilte"*, meaning crazy. An Irish language service would have to continue to be provided instead within the existing RTÉ framework.

That same autumn, oblivious to both RTÉ's position and the anti-RTÉ activities of Haughey's henchman Ray Burke, the people of Conamara were laboriously putting up a small and illegal TV transmitter.

It was erected during a windy and wet October night on the bleak slopes of Cnoc Mórdáin near Cill Chiarán. The transmitter had been built from scratch in my small back room by an electronic genius named Norbert Payne, son of the poet Basil Payne. He was assisted by Josie Mac Donncha, a local student of electronics.

Seventeen years previously the Conamara Gaeltacht civil righters had shamed the powers that be into setting up a community radio service, Raidió na Gaeltachta, by use of the same tactic. They called their achievement Saor Radio Conamara. We called ours Teilifís na Gaeltachta and hoped to have the same impact.

For one weekend everybody converged on the community hall in Rosmuc to celebrate this signal occasion. Mary Bergin came to play her tin whistle. Cór Cúil Aodha travelled from Cork to perform. Gearóid Ó Tuathaigh, an eminent professor from UCG and later chairman of Údarás na Gaeltachta, could be seen dancing on screen. A local garda hung around the door of the hall, but did not interfere. My partner Miriam rang excitedly from home, fifteen miles away: "We can see a picture," she screamed. "And there's sound, too!" We hardly believed it. It was as if we had invented television all over again – with two and a half cameras: one borrowed by Billy Keady, one brought on the bus from Derry by Tom Collins, and the other an antique resuscitated by Norbert Payne. Christo Mhaidhco's pub in Turloughbeg was jammed with happy punters seeing a live broadcast from a few hundred yards away. It was like the first moon landing. The transmitter lasted for just three days. In an effort to avoid interfering with RTÉ's signal, Norbert had incorporated a large number of transposers. They overloaded the apparatus, and on Sunday afternoon it emitted smoke and expired. That was the rather undignified end of that transmission. But the apparatus was briefly resuscitated, and in the next six months there were two more transmission, from Carraroe and from Clare.

The operation was seen by RTÉ as an "unfriendly act". We were treated as pirates, even pariahs, or at least seen as giving comfort to the real commercial pirates, not the least of whom was Ray Burke. Much hair was torn out in Donnybrook. I understand that Bob Collins, in his then role as programme controller, let it be known that none of the ringleaders was to be interviewed on RTÉ. And we were not. There even seemed to be a reluctance in the RTÉ newsroom to report that the event had actually happened. As an independent contributor to RTÉ's schedules, I received a warning to distance myself from the operation. A senior executive bluntly told me that if I did not abandon what was seen as a pirate operation, it might influence their commissioning decisions in the future.

An indefatigable member of our group, an employee of RTÉ, must have also had his card marked, because a few nights after the broadcast he turned 180 degrees and announced that he was formally distancing himself from the operation. It was a shock to our small group, because he and I had traipsed the mountains of Conamara looking for and choosing a suitable site for our amateur transmitter. It did not mean, however, that he and a couple of his RnaG colleagues did not continue informally helping us – which RTÉ must have guessed but could do nothing about. Naturally, there were some members of the NUJ who were vehemently opposed to our shoestring proposals for a community TV service.

This story is full of ironies – not least of which was the RTÉ *Cúrsaí* programme begging the Conamara pirates for a tape of their exclusive last interview with the suddenly deceased Donal Mac Amhlaigh, author of *Dialann Deoraí,* who had spent much of his working life as a labourer in Northampton.

The first positive result was that Charlie Haughey approved of our initiative and earmarked half a million pounds for a future Gaeltacht TV service. It was Lottery money; apparently Haughey never paid for anything himself. At a formal dinner in the Royal Hospital, Kilmainham, celebrating the tenth anniversary of the founding of Aosdána, I wore a T-shirt with "Teilifís na Gaeltachta" emblazoned on the chest. He pointed to it and said, "Beidh sé ann" (it will be there). Little did we know that we were pawns in the bigger war against RTÉ. Our field of struggle was local and linguistic; RTÉ's was national and economic; Haughey's was bigger than both.

This was part of the baggage which I brought to the RTÉ Authority. I was frequently reminded of these heady events in the boardroom. Discussions on the the proposed Teilifís na Gaeilge, now TG4, were rarely off the agenda. Although a wholly owned subsidiary of RTÉ – admittedly imposed on it by Minister Michael D. Higgins – TG4 has constantly been felt by RTÉ to be a thorn in its flesh, especially in the matter of the latter's obligation to provide an hour's programming every day. It was over inevitable squeals of pain that Michael D. Higgins in 1995 urged RTÉ to hasten the establishment of the station (in his first meeting with the new Authority, which I shall describe later), and a wonderful technical job RTÉ did in double-quick time! The snag was expenditure. Having had the residue of the £10 million CAP (see "Public Broadcasting") money which RTÉ had carefully squirrelled away (the bulk was appropriated by the Department of Finance), earmarked by the minister as capital to build the station, RTÉ was now ordered to supply 365 hours programming to the station per year! The cost to the beleaguered national broadcaster would be at least £5 million per annum.

The odium towards this venture displayed by many people was not dissipated by the RTÉ Authority of which I was a member. In press statements and annual reports, it consistently associated, almost in a cause and effect relationship, the burden of TnaG with its own straitened circumstances. It is still doing so. The best-selling magazine in Ireland, the *RTÉ Guide*, buried the TnaG schedules in obscure corners of its pages. I protested regularly about these matters. The only injustice eventually remedied was that in the *RTÉ Guide*.

Not all Conamara people were happy either. The reaction of one Fianna Fáil man was gleefully noted down for me by a RnaG broadcaster: *"Foc é Michael D . . . Ní dhearna sé foc-all don taobh seo anyways . . . EVER . . . Céard a rinne sé, an foc-dog bradach? Alright . . . thóig sé foc-in monstrosity sa ngarraí sin thiar . . . do shower cuntannaí . . . nach bhfuil béarla ná Gaeilge acub."*

Because minors may be reading this, I would rather not translate it. One does not have to be a sycophant to note the daring of Michael D. Higgins acting in the darkness of such a climate.

Nevertheless, most of us trooped over to Baile na hAbhann in January 1996 to witness the minister turning the first sod on the new station. He explained his personal sense of urgency in getting the station going: "This decision had to be taken now or a crucial moment affecting citizenship, the Irish language and democracy would be lost for ever. The debate about Teilifís na Gaeilge is about national self-respect." On the RTÉ Authority in the main there was a politically correct attitude to these efforts towards saving the first national language – as long as the Authority did not have to foot the bill! The government alone should do it. This meant foot-dragging by RTÉ until the financial i's and t's were respectively dotted and crossed, which made it impossible for TnaG to plan its programme schedules. Just four days after the sod-turning, there was a controlled explosion of anger in Donnybrook when the TnaG advisory committee (represented by Brian Mac Aonghusa and Cathal Goan) first met the RTÉ chairman and the chief executive. Recriminations were tossed back and forth. In the end both sides, because essentially they were in bed together, agreed that any blame for the contretemps could be laid at the minister's feet, and they ended up friends.

When I realised the sorry impasse into which our original idealistic effort had been led, I said to the RTÉ Authority that I almost regretted our piratical actions. The only one who nodded assent was Bob Collins. We had come to the same conclusion – for patently different reasons. On Halloween 1996, the occasion of TnaG's first transmission, we held our monthly Authority meeting in Conamara. I imagine that if TnaG had been established in the grounds of Montrose, there would not have been half the objections.

There was other opposition; it was not just political opportunists or even so-called "west Brits" who were against an Irish-language community TV service. As I suggested at the time of our piratical activities, in an article in *The Irish Times*, the real enemies of the project were the Dublin Gaelic Revivalists, who seemed to me to be saying, "Why should we have pictures of Conamara people gathering seaweed imposed on us sophisticated Dublin people?" It seemed not to occur to these critics that Conamara people for thirty years had had images, equally irrelevant to their lives, imposed on them. The revivalist mindset never lost sight of the goal of imposing a veneer of halting Irish on the entire nation. In seventy years of such a state-backed aspiration, they had utterly failed. The real losers were the Gaeltacht communities who actually spoke exquisite and fluent Irish. As Senator Joe O'Toole has recently said, "Isn't it daft to think that we have spent eighty years trying to get people to speak the language in the Galltacht while virtually ignoring the very people who speak and live the language daily in the Gaeltacht?"

The object of those who set up Saor Radio Conamara and Teilifís na Gaeltachta was to try to salvage something from the ruins of the national revival policy. Joe Steve Ó Neachtain, a popular Conamara poet, playwright and actor, sanely observed: "Let us not impose ourselves and our language on English speakers. Let us run a Gaeltacht TV service, and those interested can eavesdrop on us."

As the first person to subtitle an Irish film in English (in 1977), I was pleased with Joe Steve's sane observation. The richness of Gaeltacht life should be made available to, not imposed upon, the culturally impoverished monoglot people of the Galltacht.

In 1987 a local community television service for the Gaeltacht was our modest ambition. It was eventually distorted into a grandiose plan to have a national and linguistically based service. The latter would initially ignore or gloss over the geographical reality of the Gaeltacht. The result – nine years later in 1996 – was a compromise: the TV station would be physically located in Baile na hAbhann in the Conamara Gaeltacht, but its philosophy, outlook and physical transmission would be "national". Like many compromises in Ireland, it fell between several stools and satisfied few. It would be called Teilifís na Gaeilge (not "Gaeltachta"), thus emphasising its location in the ephemera of linguistics rather than in the flesh and blood of small Irish-speaking communities. Later it was rebranded as "TG4" to pragmatically enhance its position on urban cable TV as a mainstream rather than a community broadcaster.

Compromise spawned paradox. When the new TV station was being reluctantly planned by RTÉ, the decision was taken that it would broadcast on UHF transmitters. Now, the only sizeable communities in this island who speak Irish as a first language, those people in the Gaeltacht areas of Kerry, Galway and Donegal, had only a VHF reception capability. Obviously this meant they could not receive a UHF signal unless they put up new aerials.

Images of red-shawled *"mamós"* and becapped pensioners climbing up roofs all over Conamara occurred to us.

The rationalisations for this odd decision were explained to me many times on the Authority by engineers, senior executives et al. Even Joe Barry, an engineer by training, told me that the future would be on UHF, that VHF would be televisually obsolete, that everybody would have to change eventually on to UHF. The hope was that thousands of households would dash out and buy new aerials, then clamber on to their roofs and install them to get a couple of programmes in "book Irish". There was a further Alice in Wonderland touch expressed at an Authority meeting: it was hoped that the advent of RTÉ's new competitor, the commercial station TV3 – also scheduled to broadcast on UHF – would be an incentive for Gaeltacht people to take the soup and buy a UHF aerial. I still have no TV3 reception, for which relief I believe I am to be envied – TV3 has not bothered to extend its signal so far west. In desperation the Executive proposed that there might even be some small subsidy offered to Gaeltacht viewers to buy aerials and join this global village, this brave new world of UHF. Nothing came of that.

A government-appointed technical subcommittee had been set up to examine the situation. Michael Grant was the chairman. The committee got the impression that a VHF service for the Gaeltacht was impossible. But it was learned that an RTÉ internal report had shown that this was not quite accurate: it might be inconvenient but it certainly was not impossible. Bobby Gahan of RTÉ claimed that the report was confidential, but when it was pointed out by Michael Grant that all of the committee's dealings were confidential (until this moment), the report surfaced – thanks to Bob Collins' sensible intervention. It made no difference. The engineers' minds were clear: provision of a VHF facility for the Gaeltacht would disrupt their plan – as well as their plans for VHF-carried digital radio. It was intended that the whole TV network would be UHF based.

This systematic engineering perspective has dominated RTÉ for forty years, rather like Egyptian priests whose technical knowledge of the Nile's fluctuation enabled them to dominate millions of peasants. As Charles Curran of the BBC long ago pointed out, the BBC regional services are "the result of engineering requirements and not of the people of those regions".

Even though technology is never neutral, the engineers must not entirely be blamed. It was clear from the start that the priority audience was the cabled urban audience in the advertisers' prime category who might or might not have a smattering of what is laughingly called the first national language of the state. The viewers in the Gaeltacht were a poor last in this race. Eighteen months after the station's launch, only 50 per cent of Munster viewers had access to its programming.

One of the ironies of this decision was that with the advent of digital broadcasting – which will make community access broadcasting a serious possibility – it transpires that the VHF vehicle, whose obsolescence had been confidently predicted by the powers that be, would not be useless. When I asked Joe Barry from whence the original decision had emanated, I was told "the department". But an outside engineer then suggested to me that no engineers other than RTÉ engineers would have advised the department. This in turn suggested to me that a pragmatic decision had been taken by engineers, which suited the linguistic politics of urban *Gaeilgeoirí*, whose prime, if futile, ambition has always been to turn Dubliners into *Gaeilgeoirí*. Even if this meant that the baby – a community TV service for the Gaeltachtaí – was thrown out with the bathwater of VHF.

Our little adventure ultimately led to the establishment of Teilifís na Gaeilge (now TG4). But it was defined as a national service with little technological and not much other social relevance to the community from whose womb it was untimely torn. Ironically, thanks to the the careful steering of its baby steps by Cathal Goan, and recently by Pól Ó Gallchóir, TG4 has now emerged as the only Irish TV channel which, in my opinion, can unambiguously claim to represent the interests and tastes, as well as the intelligent idiosyncrasies, of the Irish people.

TG4 has survived everything and provides a crucial alternative to RTÉ – as well as being a useful stalking horse for the mother house in Donnybrook. It has been used as a laboratory to experiment with more efficient newsgathering practices, lack of familiarity with which in the first six months caused a series of appalling blunders and damaged the early reputation of the baby TV service. The station is also used – as independent programme-makers have found to their cost – as a means of RTÉ cherrypicking the TG4-commissioned programmes for next to nothing. Internal logic admits that RTÉ is entitled to such a concession: it makes its own superb archive freely available to TG4. That is little consolation to independent programme-makers who provide practically all TG4's nonnews output from which RTÉ can pick the choicest morsels.

I hope I may be pardoned for devoting so much attention to these matters. My view from the Gaeltacht periphery of this island informed much of my perspective on the RTÉ Authority. In the ecology of Irish broadcasting, RnaG and TG4 may be considered to be the only species that are unique to Ireland, and like any rare species whose cultural hinterland is ever diminishing, they are hanging on by their fingertips. In the ecosystem of sounds, images and ideas which broadcasting should be, there is presently a monocultural preponderance of weeds, choking all educative possibilities, asphyxiating our cultural life and slowly toxifying our imaginations. RnaG and TG4 are essential detoxifiers.

On a personal note: these past thirty years in the Conamara Gaeltacht have been the informative and educational part of my life. They have given me an insight into the political and social contradictions of Irish life which I would never have acquired in the protected environment of middle-class Dublin and RTÉ. It has also been the richest cultural experience I have encountered – and I have lived and travelled from Iran to Germany, from Canada to North Africa.

Best of all, the fresh air has kept me, a decadent drinker and smoker, relatively healthy. When I was a harassed RTÉ staff producer in the sixties, my life expectancy was actuarially assessed at forty-five years, which gloomy prognistication I have defied for over twenty years. If Montrose gave me heartburn, Conamara saved my life.

THE AGE OF EFFLUENCE
Shit happens.

B ecause I live in a rural area, my home is serviced by a septic tank. This fixture was originally badly constructed, developed severe transmission faults, and I never seemed to have the wherewithal to fix or replace it. Owing to faulty plumbing, its malodorous contents could occasionally back up into the bath. To protect my children from cholera or the black plague, I was obliged twice a year to open the access points and clear the sewage pipe that led to the tank. The task demanded a gas mask – alternatively, a windy day – and thirty feet of chimney-sweeping apparatus. This is a good exercise in humility, a pungent reminder of one of the fundamentals of human existence: at bottom, we are all equal. The job is analogous to that of certain monastic orders, each of whose members dig a little of their grave every day.

The lavatory on the third floor of the RTÉ administration building is also a great equaliser, a place where it is difficult for Authority members to maintain any natural or acquired pomposity. Real encounters take place here, and within this sacred portal one of my new colleagues, Bill Attley, told me a good story.

On a large building site in Donegal, the workers were all making solid money but found it hard to shed old habits like collecting unemployment assistance. The names under which they were employed on the building site were perforce all bogus, and this was a source of frustration to the local "gaugers", the agents of the social welfare system. However, the latter showed commendable and, according to Bill, unusual initiative when they hit on a bright idea to circumvent this fraud. They dressed one of their younger and prettier female employees in a tight miniskirt and sweater and sent her pedalling her endless legs out to the site on a bicycle. Armed only with a book of raffle tickets as bogus as the workers' assumed names, she charmed the birds off their scaffolding. Every single man Jack of them bought a ticket from the beauty and carefully wrote his real name and address on the stub. These stubs were carefully and pleasurably perused by the local office of the Department of Social Welfare. It was the end of that scam – and of the workers' dole.

Attley, a committed trade unionist and then secretary of SIPTU, was illustrating to me the fact that even he was not blind to the vagaries of human nature and did not believe that all workers were saints, particularly rural workers who were not unionised. However, when it came to union members in safe public employment, the ones who mainly paid his and Des Geraghty's salaries, he was utterly fearless in their defence.

This became clear when I initially put forward my objections to child-targeted commercials.

With the help of the daily TV log, I made a detailed study of their frequency. At our second meeting, in late July, under the umbrella of a discussion on the Green Paper on Broadcasting, I insisted that the Authority have piped through to them in the boardroom one of the commercial breaks at that moment being transmitted by our own Network 2. They were thus forced to watch the endless procession of seductive messages directed at their children and grandchildren. I doubt if they had ever paid attention to them before; adults do not bother to watch children's TV. Perhaps a domestic event the previous week had added an edge to my assault: Miriam had presented me with yet another bouncing baby boy – her second, my fourth – whom we named Dominic, after the Order of Preachers. Together with the two girls, I had altogether produced six young targets for commercial consumption.

Fuelled by this thought, I energetically pointed out to my colleagues the symmetry between the Third World exploitation of children as sweatshop labour and that of our own children being brainwashed to buy the toy products of the same sweatshops from Hawaii to China. Two years previously, the Kader toy sweatshop in Bangkok went on fire. Because its young workers were locked in, 148 of them were burned to death and 469 more were injured. Among the charred remains were scattered hundreds of soot-stained Bugs Bunnies, Bart Simpsons, the Muppets and Big Bird from *Sesame Street*. Claiming that RTÉ through its child-targeted advertising practices was encouraging this business, I formally proposed the following motion: "That we, the RTÉ Authority, cease treating children as targetable consumers, i.e. as a market, and forthwith remove commercial messages from the context of children's programming."

It was a crude tactic: to highlight the defencelessness of children, to make some kind of analogy between child abuse (which was all the rage in the Irish media at the time) and child-targeted commercials. Children are the soft underbelly. If I could achieve a questioning of the ethics of contemptuously treating them as consumers, perhaps adults might wake up and say, "Hey, I'm an advertising puppet, too!" The battlefield of child-targeted commercials was the front I had tactically – but with a certain amount of passion – chosen on which to combat the excesses of global consumerism and its pernicious influence on good broadcasting.

But initially, what was Joe Barry's reaction to the viewing of the commercial break? He sat back smiling and said, "I didn't think business was so good."

However, Joe did not get the job of director general for being a softie. One of the menacing phrases he used to me at the time in relation to this whole system of commercials was, "You poke at this at your peril."

Further, when he adroitly mentioned that the loss of revenue on curbing our child-targeted commercials could cost fifty jobs – which was an exaggeration – both trade unionists on the Authority were adamantly against such a step. Any reform, no matter how well-intentioned, that constituted a threat to jobs in RTÉ was absolutely out. Bill Attley was a man I would love to have had in my corner. Des Geraghty, too. But even the influence of these two powerful and articulate men was limited in RTÉ. Despite their suggestion that, proportionate to the attention given to agriculture on RTÉ, there might also be a programme devoted to normal trade union activities, no such step was ever taken. Gearóid Ó Tuathaigh of UCG had pointed out the same lack in RTÉ programming as long ago as 1984.

Following my line in practical terms, Betty Purcell proposed a moratorium on at least the Christmas toy advertisements which would lose the station not more than 1 per cent of its income. But the powerful worker voices on the Authority said we must first establish how the loss would be covered. This touch-kicking became a recurrent tactic when anything difficult was proposed.

The result of this first skirmish was that the director general promised a full examination of the problem and a detailed proposal within two months. My motion would also be discussed then. After these exertions, I retreated to the lavatory for a smoke.

Perhaps it was my familiarity with septic tanks, perhaps a throwback to schooldays, but as the months rolled by the lavatory would become my refuge. When Patricia Redlich was in full spate, droning on about the recalcitrance of RTÉ staff and boring at least me to tears with "nanny states" and "hush puppies" and a litany of Thatcherisms, I would rise and head for this retreat.

The *Phoenix* magazine had an interesting item on her at the time of her appoinment in March 1996. Being *Phoenix*, it may have been speculative. It said that she had been appointed to RTÉ directly by Taoiseach John Bruton, and she was reported as being close to Eoghan Harris, who had been an advisor to Bruton. This version, whether true or not, was never challenged. Realistically, Minister Michael D. Higgins would hardly have approved the appointment of a woman who shortly before had said in the *Sunday Independent* that the minister would not be unhappy if Saddam Hussein acquired a nuclear device! The *Sunday Independent* was forced to apologise.

Redlich brought to three the quota of Bruton appointees on the Authority, joining Anne Haslam and Garret FitzGerald, the first ex-taoiseach to be so appointed. When in power he had strongly advocated the depoliticising of such appointments (and did so as recently as September 2000 in his *Irish Times* column). However, in 1995 times must have been hard, particularly after his recent flirtation with GPA, AIB and the whole damn catastrophe in which he speculated and lost hundreds of thousands of pounds, as well as his home.

The lavatory was also the place where I found my secret weapon. There were at least three occasions when certain members of the Authority were outraged by my actions and demanded my resignation. To staunch my wounds, all I had to do was recall some early words of the chairman to me as we stood shoulder to shoulder in the urinal: "You know, of course, that it would take a vote of both houses of the Oireachtas to get rid of you."

I had not previously known that. Since then I have wondered if the chairman ever regretted giving me that invincible shield of burning brass. It had been forged by Conor Cruise O'Brien in an amendment to the Broadcasting Act in 1976: the solo power of a minister to sack either an individual member or the Authority as a whole was rescinded.

The subsequent frictions on this Authority, with which I admit having not a little to do, reflected the tensions within the organisation. A survey of staff attitudes two years previously – after a bitter strike of programme people about cutbacks in camera crews – revealed that 64 per cent of the staff thought management passed the buck, 59 per cent thought they were indecisive, 56 per cent said they were bureaucratic and 58 per cent said they were inconsistent. Sixty-four per cent thought RTÉ was clique-ridden, 69 per cent thought it secretive, 62 per cent said morale was low, and 75 per cent thought there was a chasm between management and the actual programme-making operation. Thirty-five per cent of the staff thought that RTÉ fulfilled its public service obligations "not at all".

One RTÉ producer sorrowfully expressed the situation to me: "RTÉ is like a dysfunctional family with alcoholic parents. The children run around lost and wild, not knowing where they are."

Since that survey was conducted within a year of the devastating 1992 strike of programme staff, and on the assumption that things must have improved, I suggested to the Executive that the survey might valuably be updated. A question I would have included was this: which TV channel do you most watch? I would have laid bets that the majority of RTÉ staff concentrated their viewing on cross-channel and satellite services – from which they could derive useful programme ideas – rather than their own home-produced stuff. That was left for us deprived people in three-channel land.

Incidentally, the only group in this survey which seemed to be happy was management, 78 per cent of whom thought RTÉ was a good place in which to work. To paraphrase Mandy Rice-Davies, "They would say that, wouldn't they?"

This was the atmosphere into which the new Authority

was launched. It was a perilous stage for an ingenue such as me. As in domestic circumstances, there is always something of a love-hate quality in such relationships. Never interfere in a husband-wife row. I knew that I had to tread carefully.

I sought further advice.

Ben Barenholtz is an independent New York producer who has survived in the jungle of film and theatre for many years. He has produced for, among others, the Coen brothers, so he is no slouch. *Barton Fink* and *Miller's Crossing* are on his CV. On his annual visit to the Galway Film Fleadh in July, I took the opportunity to explain my position and ask for tactical advice on how to get a director general to see things my way. Over our customary breaking of brown bread – washed down with a bottle of vodka – Ben said:

> Remember that a big shot has a job to keep, that he has an ego, that he has had to do awful things. Remember particularly that if he had any integrity he wouldn't be in that job in the first place. The tactic is to persuade the guy that his job will not be jeopardised by your proposal. Reassure him that he is great. Reassure him that everybody has to do awful things, that he shouldn't feel guilty. Certainly don't you make him feel any more guilty. Tell him what he wants to hear. Then tell him new ways of not losing money.

This was sound advice which was effectively transmuted by me into the following: tell the chief executive that his job is not the most important thing in the world and that I couldn't care less anyway; try to undermine his ego; make him feel as guilty as hell for the awful things he is doing. Finally, tell him he must lose money.

In defence I submit that as a member of Aosdána, the Irish parliament of artists, to which I was the first filmmaker elected, I was entitled to use artistic licence. Nobody is perfect. Joe Barry, the director general, understood this very well. The more I impetuously demanded action on child-targeted commercials, the more he retained his avuncular calm. Only once did he impatiently call me a crank and compare my unrelenting campaigning to that of a previous Authority member, Dr Bill Loftus. This good man, the coroner for County Mayo, daily witnessed the bloody result of alcohol-induced carnage on the roads and incessantly called for the abolition of advertisements for drink. He, too, was ignored.

In a manipulative mediocracy, the standard defence against "novel" thinking is to call for a report or to invoke oracles called consultants. The advantage of these is that, like royal commissions and Irish tribunals, they enable decisions and retribution to be postponed. Moreover, when their expensive advice proves worthless, they can be blamed. This tactic is a catch-all for indecisiveness. It produces what F.R. Scott has called "the rain of facts which deepens the drought of the will". Handling the demands of people like Loftus and myself was easy: the Executive would simply promise a report on the financial implications.

John Horgan of DCU, an experienced broadcaster, wrote about this time: "If RTÉ stays much the same and tries to muddle through, the chances are it will be overwhelmed. There is not likely to be a second chance."

Those were my sentiments entirely. I had, therefore, circulated a three-page list of direct questions for the Executive. They were designed to underline for the greenhorns on the Authority the rationalisations behind what appeared to me to be contradictions in RTÉ's financial, programming and scheduling strategies. Ben Barenholtz once said to me that when somebody asks a simple question and somebody gives a simple answer, God is listening. My questions were obviously not simple enough and went unanswered. God developed wax in his ears.

The worst thing I suggested was that the members of the Authority have five minutes on their own after each session: no Executive present, no note-takers, no record, to give the Authority the opportunity to discuss informally its officers' and servants' performances. That suggestion was not even allowed to reach the starting post. Neither did my later proposal that the highly paid senior executives should have temporary contracts similar to those they imposed on producers and directors.

It was high summer in Conamara. In July it was a relief to escape from the sogginess of Dublin to the sweet air of the West. The spiralled yellow cores of ox-eye daisies lined the roadsides, and puffs of bog cotton exploded all over the marshes. On my personal bog, purple was the dominant colour: loosestrife, marsh orchid, spiraea and heather carpeted the place. Meadowsweet was the perfume. Here, like the Prince of Wales, I could resume my dialogue with trees. RTÉ was also getting out of the city, its programmes following staff and management to their holiday hideaways round the country. After August it is assumed that when they return from Kerry, Conamara and Donegal, nobody is left in these desolate places and RTÉ can revert to being Radio Teilifís Dublin again.

To further educate its new Authority into the nature of broadcasting reality, the Executive arranged an informational weekend for September.

THINK TANK

When you feel too small to make any difference,
think of a mosquito in a closed room.
African proverb

August 1995 passed away in a dead heat, disturbed only by a noisy strimmer with which I scythed bicycle paths for a bunch of nine-year-olds through the grass and heather.

With pieces from a large and broken mirror – kids again! – I cemented the image of a gleaming tree on an old wall. There was a burnt, hazy look about everything. We inspected the compressed 4,000-year-old vegetation at the bottom of a dried-out pond. The mud in the gullies shrunk, cracked and became crazy paving. Even the rampaging green stars of pondweed looked distressed. Meanwhile, I was making photographic portraits of my neighbours for a book. The darkroom was a refuge from the heat. It was a relief to feel the first cool airs of September.

I had to prepare for the September Authority meeting. I sensed this would be decisive for RTÉ's child-targeted commercials policy. As part of my research, I tried to demystify TV ads for the children; I got them to count the fast picture cuts and rewarded the first correct answer. Fortunately, I would have a dry run for my ideas at a broadcasting seminar in the Irish Film Institute in Dublin, to be chaired by none other than Professor Corcoran, chairman of the Authority.

On the evening of 7 September, in front of a respectable public audience, I launched as ferocious an attack as I could on the child-targeting techniques of advertisers and, by implication, on RTÉ policy. My research was over-extensive and not marshalled succinctly, but I felt the subject was too serious for clever soundbites. I assume my long-windedness was the reason the chairman felt impelled to cut me short.

In the crowded bar after the meeting, the chairman and I met again. He said he had been taken aback by the pre-cipitateness of my motion at the previous, July, Authority meeting. He told me it might be wise not to alienate man-agement, that he had found persuasion was better than confrontation in getting things done, and that an adver-sarial approach led to reluctance, passive aggression, foot-dragging, grudging tokenism and the marginalisation and non-adoption of good ideas. I deduced that, like Ben Barenholtz, he had absorbed that principle in his earlier thirteen-year career in the jungle of American academe. He was actually prophetic in his analysis.

A couple of weeks later came our next, two-day session. Outside the Cedar Room in Jurys hotel in Ballsbridge, I passed through a group of RTÉ senior managers. They were poised on the edge of the think tank, ready to dive in and give us our first major briefing. We exchanged friend-ly greetings.

I had soldiered with some of them thirty years before and, frankly, I would have preferred to sit with them rather than join the Authority in the Cedar Room. Through infor-mal conversation I might have learned more about the warp and weft of the RTÉ organisation. They might have admitted privately that there was complacency and feather bedding in their ranks; that programme content was being dictated by a commercial environment and its output was almost indistinguishable from its commercial competitors;

that its so-called "editorial board" was impotent; that there were two classes in the station – "those who wanted to make programmes and those who wanted to stop them"; that there hadn't been an original programme idea in ten years nor any attempt at talent development; that the organisational structure had hardly changed in forty years; that some people at the top were less of a help than a hindrance. As it happened, over the next couple of years, those judgements would all be conveyed to me – privately.

Yet there was no stinting of ideas as they entered, presented their statistics, answered our naive questions and departed. Members of the RTÉ Authority are supplied with mountains of documents. Every month a bulky envelope is delivered by courier. It contains details of most aspects of the national broadcaster's current activities, with the emphasis on how the budget stands and what plans the Executive wishes to have approved. It can never be said that the Executive was parsimonious with paper. I wondered how close we were to the comic *Yes, Minister*, James Hacker, who, when he demanded to be briefed fully, was snowed under with despatch boxes. (Coincidentally, as I write these words, RTÉ is retransmitting this twenty-year-old BBC masterpiece.)

I doubt if the busy people on successive RTÉ Authorities ever have time to read and digest all of the documentation. A quick look at the minutes of the last meeting to make sure they are themselves correctly quoted, a glance at the agenda to see if there is a particularly critical issue must often appear to suffice. Down through the years there must also have been a few Authority members who never read the bumf at all, but relied on their own native wit and cunning to be brought up to speed at the monthly meetings.

For the first time in my life I became the school swot, forcing myself to read and reread almost everything I was sent – except, initially, financial reports, which sent me into a coma. Policy decisions which appeared to impinge directly on programming were my prime interest. It took a while to realise that the financial engine drove everything and that the petrol for that engine was considered to be, in the main, television advertising, with the licence fee consisting of a politically crucial but diminishing reserve tank. That is when it became hard work.

I found the senior managers of RTÉ to be frank and personable, keen that we be familiarised with the complex political depths as well as with the shoals and shallows through which they steered the tanker. They had a dispassionate, rueful and almost resigned air, as if to say: here is the situation; we do our best but the universality of the problems makes our task very tough. Maybe you can do better? One could not but have sympathy for their plight.

At this September think-in, we learned that RTÉ managed over 2,000 souls (1,400 of whom were permanent and pensionable) and paid them £60 million a year – which sum almost equated with the licence fee. They put out 10,000 hours of TV every year, ran three radio channels and had a commercial income twice the amount of the licence fee.

They ran symphony and concert orchestras, a string quartet, choral groups and a radio service in Irish, and contributed to many festivals and cultural events in Ireland. It was a large and complex operation, critical to the cultural life of this island. And we were reminded that it had been undernourished by successive governments which constantly deferred or refused a necesssary increase in the licence fee. Government also insisted that An Post continue to collect this licence fee, probably because that body deducted £7 million in "collection costs" before it passed the remainder on to RTÉ. There was an evasion rate of 13 per cent. To me the greatest surprise was learning that 20 per cent of all licence fees was paid by the Department of Social Welfare – and the government even took a commission on that! It did not take genius to work out that here was the clear fiscal expression of an otherwise muddy government control of broadcasting.

Problems, problems, problems. RTÉ's radio audience was being eroded by local independent radio. Its TV audience was under siege from cable, satellite and MMDS sources of cross-channel services. Ironically RTÉ was the principal technical facilitator of its own competition because it had set up and owned the entire transmission network in the state; it had even developed and still held 40 per cent of the shares in Cablelink, which efficiently distributed the competing channels in urban areas. But it could not influence the content of cross-channel services plus satellite TV which beamed in its 57 varieties unchecked. Rupert Murdoch (after whom playright Denis Potter named his fatal disease) was vacuuming up sports programme rights and viewers indiscriminately, like a factory ship. Dim and distant were the days when RTÉ had a near-monopoly of viewing and listening on the island.

It was a litany of despair. It did not take much savvy for me to realise that curtailing the commercial abuse of children would be the last bead on management's rosary.

What reassured me about this September session was the apparent conformity of mine and Garret FitzGerald's approaches. Time and again we seemed to anticipate each other's questions and observations. This seeming telepathy indicated that at least initially we shared similar perspectives on broadcasting. For instance, at one stage in the debate I interjected, "When the radio commercials come on, I just turn them down and then don't bother to turn up the programme again." Garret nodded sadly. "I do the same," he said.

But as time went on, marked differences emerged between the two of us. These arose from our respective prioritising of problems, our distinct political and especially geographical perspectives and our separate remedial proposals.

I had already decided that the first step for the patient in this complex and depressing diagnosis was to invoke the fundamental basis of the Hippocratic Oath: "First, do no harm." In other words, at least stop exploiting children. By this I meant that although thirty-five years ago RTÉ may have been statutorily forced by Seán Lemass and T.K.Whitaker to function as a semi-commercial, semi-state body, it was never intended to embrace the grosser indecencies of commercialism to survive – specifically, the commercial targeting of infants. How a nation or organisation treats its children is a pretty good litmus test of its civilised behaviour. Being a programme-maker, my ultimate concern was the corrosive impact such an activity was having on the general scheduling environment and on programme quality itself.

FitzGerald, while having a patrician distaste for the excesses of commercialism and a keen sense of "good" current affairs programming, seemed always to regard our relationship with Northern Ireland to be the most pressing matter for RTÉ. I was more concerned with RTÉ's impact on our own citizens. I could quote Bob Collins who in 1996 stated:

> It is not desirable therefore that 64% of RTÉ's income would come from commercial sources. It is not that there is any correlation between sources of income and editorial decisions [!], but that sort of imbalance is not desirable because if that process continues it doesn't take long before commercial considerations become the dominant forces, and determine, tend to determine, or seek to determine, how editorial decisions are made.

Henry David Thoreau anticipated this: "After the first blush of sin comes its indifference; and from immoral it becomes, as it were, unmoral, and *not* quite unnecessary to that life which we have made." Collins' long-departed predecessor, Muiris Mac Conghail, had been more direct: "Commercial policy to do with the placement of advertising is also a primary consideration in scheduling: perhaps the ultimate consideration."

In the Cedar Room in Jurys, the management's solution

to all problems seemed to be more money, specifically an increase in the licence fee. Debate on the subject could be summarised as follows:

> "RTÉ cannot remain a marginalised regional broadcaster; it must break out of its territorial confines and conquer the world with the help of the Irish diaspora, perhaps taking as a model the success of *Riverdance*."
>
> "How will this be financed?"
>
> "Well, firstly by increasing our commercial income."
>
> "But you already expressed concern about our growing dependence on such income, higher than at any time in the organisation's history."
>
> "Quite. In fact, absolutely. All the more reason why the licence fee should be increased, ideally to match the commercial income, 50/50, like it used to be in the good old days." [In 1983 Con Bush, then head of RTÉ Young People's programmes, delivered a fine paper to the Celtic Fim and Television Festival in which he said that "more than 45% revenue from advertisements would be a threat to public interest".]
>
> "What about, for a start, going halfway, by reducing our reliance on commercial income and acquiring some street credibility for our pious aspirations?"
>
> "Your point is well taken. But if we could bring the licence fee up somewhere near it, all would be well. Besides, the licence fee endorses public broadcasting's place in Ireland's democratic fabric. It is an investment in the integrity of public service broadcasting; it confers responsibilities on us, and it requires concomitant accountability to all the children of the nation, blah, blah, blah."

I imagined hollow laughter from the children of the nation in both the inner city and the regions, those areas within and without the Pale which were long resigned to the fact that RTÉ is, was and always will be a predominently middle-class, Dublin-based and Dublin-oriented organisation.

But what upstaged all these discussions – and certainly my child-centred concerns – and was dropped with a splash into that September 1995 think tank was what was considered by all to be the most serious challenge to RTÉ: the Green Paper on Broadcasting.

This was prepared under the aegis of a FineGael/ Labour/Democratic Left coalition, but it had the unmistakeable imprint of the minister in power, Michael D. Higgins. Unusually for a government utterance, it lucidly and with no holds barred described the crisis in modern society, and especially in public service broadcasting.

It decribed broadcasting as potentially destructive by pitting profit motive against collective rights, deterritorialising imperialism against minority cultural needs, disfiguring us politically, homogenising us linguistically and depressing our inclination for cultural expression.

Political and economic forces were threatening the relative autonomy of broadcasting from government and the market; young people were subservient to fashion generated by the cycles of industrial production; citizens could, in a culture of narcissism, become mere instruments in the reproduction of a triumphant global culture, dependent on imported goods and imported images; there was a tendency towards nostalgia in tourism and the "museumisation" of heritage. My reaction to this was like that of the projectionist in the film censor's office who remarked to W.B. Yeats after the poet's impromptu and particularly impressive analysis of a particular film, "I couldn't have put it better myself, Mr Yeats."

One thing I liked about the introduction to this Green Paper was the defiant rejection of a historical revisionism that had undermined and made shameful to its citizens the possibility of a national Irish identity. But what particularly pleased me was that one of the co-authors of the Green Paper was none other than our new chairman, Professor Farrel Corcoran. With such an ally, I thought, reforming RTÉ was going to be a piece of cake.

Again what I forgot was that the description of a problem, no matter how well-meaning and intellectually qualified its authors are, has nothing whatsoever do with the realpolitik of attempting to solve it.

For a start, the only proposal in the Green Paper that seemed to reverberate among the dovecotes was the suggestion of a full-time Super Authority to replace the Independent Radio and Television Commission and to be responsible for all broadcasting matters, including RTÉ. The rationale was that RTÉ had done a good job overseeing the development of broadcasting when the national broadcaster was the only game in town. With the proliferation of broadcasting channels inside and outside the island, the scene needed a more focussed and professionally qualified Authority. It made sense to me. The advantage that I could see was that a professional Super Authority might be a buffer zone between the national broadcaster and the government and its civil servants.

But the reaction of our Executive – which convinced everybody else on the Authority – was that RTÉ would be "humbled, shrunken and demoralised" by such a body. There were two terrifying prospects for the managers of the flagship of Irish broadcasting: one, they would have to define RTÉ's public broadcasting role and the way it spent its money more precisely to a hands-on board of full-time professionals; two, they could no longer confine their policy explanations to a bunch of broadcasting amateurs and political appointees who met once a month for three hours and a slap-up lunch.

The RTÉ managerial hegemony would be shattered. The Chinese curse was laid upon the Executive: it would henceforth live in interesting times. Predictably, when the Green Paper became a White Paper, little attention was paid to the RTÉ advantages in the proposed legislation. For instance, it would declare sporting occasions such as the All-Ireland Finals to have cultural importance and to be beyond the reach of the Murdoch empire, thus maintaining

such events "free-to-air" and incidentally saving RTÉ infla-
tionary fees. The legislation would index-link the licence
fee, a boon RTÉ had long sought. It would repeal the Section 31 directive (that did not happen until 2001). But the
terror inspired by a Super Authority which could investi-
gate RTÉ structures and finances overshadowed everything
else. It is extraordinary that, due to a change of government in 1997 and the "slow learning curve" (as sources in
RTÉ, whether fairly or not, described it) of Michael D.
Higgins' ministerial successor, it took six years to finally
put the new legislation in place.

However, these vague immensities were at the time secondary to my prime concern: child-targeted commercials.
Eventually our think tank got around to them.

True to his word, Joe Barry had included in the agenda
a forty-page summary of the situation. He also made some
practical proposals.

I had already learned that word of my Children's Cru-
sade had swept through the corridors of Montrose. Even
before this Authority had a chance to debate the matter, it
was raised informally at the RTÉ Staff Participation Forum
and the implications were briefly discussed. Many staff
members are also parents, so a delicate balance was
required between their protective instincts towards their
children and the hard facts of their personal economic survival. The idea of abolishing child-targeted commercials
was rejected. One of the comrades was alleged to have
remarked as they emerged, "The little bastards got short
shrift there." For my part I thought of Stephen Dedalus'
description of Ireland as the old sow that eats her farrow.

Joe Barry had to be more circumspect in his presentation. But his preparations included a pre-emptive strike
and a sop to other Authority members – Purcell, Fitz-
Gerald and Tannahill – whom he realised were also
uncomfortable with RTÉ's child-targeting activities. The
first two even agreed with me that RTÉ was breaching its
own ethical guidelines on this matter. At this meeting the

director general proposed to abolish commercials during pre-school children's TV time, that is, between the hours of 2 p.m. and 3 p.m. (when advertising revenue was minimal, by the way). Sponsorship would be withdrawn from all children's programmes, and the incidence of commercial breaks in such programming would be reduced to a maximum of two in any clock hour. It was a decent gesture from a well-meaning man – the proposal was actually drafted by his then assistant, Bob Collins – and it opened a tiny slit of opportunity in admitting that, yes, there are questions to be asked about commercially exploiting the natural credulity of small children.

When Barry launched this brave plan, I imagined the trade unionists on the Authority heaving a sigh of gratitude at how their chief executive had gently levered them off the hook. After all, several hundred members of their union worked for the Hasbro toy-making subsidiary in Waterford whose sales depended exclusively on TV advertising. Typically and ungratefully, I thought the offer was inadequate, not to say derisory, and said so. I was overruled, of course.

However, Purcell and FitzGerald were still concerned about the intensity of toy advertisements during the Christmas period. Even Tannahill wanted them banned all year round. Purcell again proposed a six-week moratorium on them. Tactician that she is, she suggested that the director general's plan should not be announced until we made up our minds about the more immediate problem of Christmas toy advertising. It was no good. A majority agreed that the director general's appeasement tactic could be publicly announced and we could discuss the Christmas market later. My own motion did not even get a seconder.

What was significant about even Joe Barry's small compromise was that the advertisers were just beginning a campaign of lobbying the European Court to force Greece, Sweden, Finland, Germany, Belgium and Austria to allow them to target children as consumers, just as they were already doing in the rest of Europe and most ruthlessly in the heart of this darkness, the United States.

The director general's mild proposal caused alarm among these vested interests. As a result, Pat Kenny asked me on to his radio show.

On 18 October 1995, on RTÉ Radio 1, I again spoke forcibly about the decision and referred to RTÉ's commercial irresponsibility towards children. What emerged in that radio debate was that Irish manufacturers (as distinct from multi-nationals) and advertising agencies had little to lose if the proposal to ban Christmas toy commercials was adopted. Both the commercials and the toys were imported. The frail indigenous Irish toy industry had long been decimated by the multinationals. (Toys made by Hasbro's subsidiary in Waterford were actually exported to the UK to acquire export relief tax and promptly imported again.) Salesmen from London treated Ireland as a market on a par with Manchester, hopping across the Irish Sea for a day to take orders from the bigger supermarkets and hopping back home again the same evening.

But the phenomenon of the global market made this more than a storm in a teacup. And the fact that several prominent Irish ad agencies and public relations firms increasingly front for New York agencies was not irrelevant. I can name some of them: Bates, Irish International, QMP D'Arcy, FCC Shandwick, McCann-Erickson, Fleishman-Hilliard Saunders, Park Communications, Edelman, TDI. Not surprisingly then, Steve Shanahan, chairman of the Institute of Advertising Practitioners of Ireland, was reported to be astonished by Joe Barry's proposal: "Helping the nanny state is certainly not the media's role," he declared. "The whole thing is unbelievable."

Ian Fox – also an important figure in IAPI as well as being a classical music expert on RTÉ – said, "It's a madcap idea." Even a disloyal senior RTÉ executive was quoted as saying (anonymously and patronisingly): "You can't just unilaterally do these things. It's a new Authority and it just has to find its feet." This comment made me consider the possibility that the public row was actually "allowed" to happen so that the new Authority would be intimidated into fear of the advertisers.

But the tiny gesture from a tiny island sent ripples across Europe. Already a "war chest" was being organised by confectionery companies and toy manufacturers to fight the example of Sweden, which was the staunchest opponent of commercials during children's programming. In October, Joe Barry said he had received worried inquiries from near and far. David Hawtin, director general of the British Toy and Hobby Association, complained in writing to Chairman Corcoran about my broadcast remarks. But he directly confirmed RTÉ's pivotal function in this industry when he said that it was "unlikely that a major retailer will make a commitment to buy a new toy unless that retailer can be guaranteed that the toy manufacturer will advertise it on television". He also poo-poohed Trócaire's allegations about labour and working conditions in Asia.

This proved to me that RTÉ was, after all, not such a small fish in the big broadcasting sea; we could actually make a difference. Peter Waterman, vice-president of Britain's biggest toy manufacturer Hasbro, said: "The decision is totally unnecessary. All the evidence shows television advertising is harmless to children." He did not quote such "evidence". Clearly he had never heard of Consumer International in his own country which pointed out that of the £418 million spent there on advertising, half of the advertisements directed at children involved food items that were high in sugar, fat and salt.

Betty Purcell's motion about Christmas toys was deferred until November. One dark afternoon, after a heavy and liquid lunch which reduced the Authority to a bare quorum, the proposal about banning such commercials was pushed to the end of the agenda and summarily kicked out. To copper-fasten the matter, Joe Barry extracted a commitment from the few remaining members that the subject would not be discussed again for at least eighteen months "to restore the confidence of advertisers in RTÉ".

At this point I have to mention my suspicion that Barry's proposal, besides being an attempt to quieten me, was also aimed at buying a little peace for his remaining stint as director general. When he requested that the subject not be reviewed for eighteen months, I noticed that it coincided with the date on which he was due to retire. I did not blame him. Barry had been appointed to bring peace to the organisation, and even though some considered it the peace of the mortuary or the kind of ceasefire where knee-cappings continue, he was held in genuine affection by many RTÉ people. He deserved a relatively peaceful exit period, and I suspended my attacks on this front for some time. After his retirement from RTÉ in 1997, in a brief telephone conversation with me, he graciously confided, "You know, Bob, you'd be surprised how many people agreed with you." Barry was unprecedentedly appointed to the new RTÉ Authority in June 2000, and at time of writing he is back in the boardroom, this time as a passenger.

Three days after that September think tank, I was a thousand miles away introducing a film of mine to an audience in Moscow. In the following days and on subsequent visits to Russia and Tatarstan, I witnessed what a disaster the embrace of the "market economy" had been for the citizens of the former Soviet Union and its capital, Moscow. Mafia thugs ran the city, and it was not safe to be on the streets after 10 p.m. It felt slightly familiar, as if I were back in Dublin city.

FREEDOM OF INFORMATION

A thought that sometimes makes me hazy:
Am I – or are the others crazy?
Albert Einstein

A lthough I was reluctantly prepared to suspend my fire on Joe Barry's compromise, the matter was not allowed to rest there.

My speaking on the Pat Kenny radio show caused alarm among the higher echelons of management. If I were allowed to get away with that, what other breaches of security might I attempt? As Bill Attley once said to me in the third floor lavatory, "This place is tighter than the KGB."

Very soon after the broadcast there was the expected telephone call from the chairman. Professor Corcoran expressed concern about the matter. He said that we must work out the parameters of free expression, that individual members commenting on live issues was a problem, that good public relations were critical, that a clear and unified presentation of the Authority's view was essential to avoid cock-ups, and so on and so forth. I mentioned my suspicion that the controversy might have been welcomed by the Executive in order to frighten the new Authority into line. He dismissed this conspiracy theory, implying that simple incompetence in public relations was the cause. On balance, he was probably right.

For those interested in the psychology of internal politics, here is a point for noting. Based on the idea that the chairman's contribution to the Green Paper reflected a similar viewpoint to mine on broadcasting in general, my assumption was that our views on the critical condition of RTÉ also coincided. During one of his mildly rebuking phone calls, I reassured him that I understood the restrictions on him speaking plainly, but that I felt no such restrictions. Therefore, I could spell out crudely what he might articulate more reservedly. In other words, I saw myself as his ideological hitman and in this respect was at his service. The poor man must have shuddered at this offer. What I overlooked was that whatever about the possible similarities of our views, our respective tactical approaches were diametrically opposed. It was obvious that I was the only person on the Authority utterly devoid of diplomatic skills.

The Executive realised this, as well as the fact that mine was a mouth that never refused words. And the chairman was their hitman. In November 1995 he was induced to bring in a list of new rules governing members' access to the media. The chairman was cruelly described in *Phoenix* as having already gone native.

The new document was an impressive argument for self-censorship, to which each Authority member was required to subscribe. Essentially it supported the principle of *uno duce, una voce*.

At great and, I fear, rhetorical length, I refused my assent to the proposals, invoking various principles of freedom of speech, precedents from all over the world and throughout history: everything from Tom Paine's *Rights of Man* to sources such as Benjamin Franklin's "they who would remove liberty to increase their protection deserve neither liberty nor protection". I would hate to have been at the receiving end of my rhetoric. Admittedly most of my quotes came from the United States, but since we were now well on the way to being a cultural and economic colony of that great country, why not invoke some of the principles upon which its greatness was founded?

It was ironic that the national broadcaster which so constantly demanded openness and transparency from state and Church was itself inclined to behave like an ostrich when hard questions were asked of it. I pointed out that because broadcasting was one of the few activities in which I had some experience, to be gagged on this subject would be ludicrous. Further, I reminded them that the chairman himself had a few months earlier said that "the Authority members were present in their personal capacity to defend the public interest".

A few of the Authority members saw other dangers and agreed with Betty Purcell that there should be a lessening of the draconian measures demanded by the chair. She suggested that in a sentence that urged us to "collectively and cooperatively communicate with the other media", there be added the phrase "where possible". It was exactly the phrase used two years later by the European Union – and welcomed by RTÉ – which enabled European public broadcasters to ignore film and programme-makers' pleas to include at least 51 per cent of European-produced programmes in their schedules.

I also saw it was the kind of loophole through which one could drive a coach and four, and so I immediately agreed. With one bound I was free. Purcell was wonderful at defusing explosive situations in my favour. I hope it was because she also saw me as her main ally on the Authority.

This was not simply a matter of limiting the garrulous indiscretions of a person like me. We were negotiating deeper waters. A couple of years ago a photographer named Jacqueline Hassink wrote to forty of the biggest private and public corporations in Europe and requested permission to photograph their boardrooms. No directors, no chairmen, no staff, no people; just the inanimate room and its impressive table. The corporations included household names like BP, Volkswagen, Renault, Unilever.

The subsequent exhibition in Dublin's Gallery of Photography included nineteen framed, glossy, entirely black prints. These represented the corporations that had refused her simple request. Ms Hassink's question was equally simple: what had they got to hide?

There is a secret document in the RTÉ archives dated 12 June 1969 and called "Agenda Item No. 4". It was written by the director general of the time, Tom Hardiman, as a special report for the eyes of the RTÉ Authority and their eyes only. It took this member of the RTÉ Authority three years to extricate that sensitive document from the RTÉ secretariat – exactly the same length of time that it took individual Romanian citizens to get access to the personal files kept on them by the Ceauşescu secret police.

It is an odd fact that no sitting RTÉ Authority is allowed access to minutes of the deliberations of any previous Authority. Thus the neophytes go into an apparently greenfield situation, virgin territory in which they can create a fresh broadcasting culture without precedent. *Mar dhea*! In fact RTÉ is such a labyrinth, constructed through forty years of political and commercial wheeling and dealing, that the only way of constructively approaching it might be to examine a previous Authority's deliberations and discover what on earth they were thinking. But that is out of the question. What we have in this rule is the permanent staff's secret weapon against the temporary intruders – the Authority.

The Official Secrets Act, imposed by Britain in 1889, was strengthened in the sixties by no less than C.J. Haughey when he cited the theft of Leaving Certificate papers as a justification. Even the menu in the Dáil restaurant was guarded by the Official Secrets Act. In RTÉ's case, the official theory proferred to justify its own opaqueness was that Authority members would not feel free to speak frankly at meetings if they thought their sentiments were for public – or any other – consumption.

It is considered reasonable for Irish citizens to have

access to County Council meetings or to the deliberations of Dáil Éireann; the latter are actually televised. It is all right for RTÉ reporters like Charlie Bird to publicly challenge politicians, company directors and bank chairmen, even a former chairman of RTÉ, Jim Culliton, to come clean and tell the truth. But records of the delicate negotiations keeping afloat that flagship of public communication, RTÉ, were on the Index, as tightly locked up as the Vatican vaults.

From the start I displayed gay abandon towards this encrusted custom. That soul of courtesy, Garret Fitz-Gerald, possibly imagining that he was still in Leinster House, used indignantly to throw the terms "solidarity" and "cabinet confidentiality" at me. In response I suggested that Garret might have illusions of grandeur about our role as an Authority. The cabinet meets at least once a week. We met once a month. We were a temporary collection of political appointees who were discouraged by our own officers from studying minuted precedents which could conceivably make our deliberations more focussed.

Ironically it was FitzGerald's daughter-in-law, Eithne FitzGerald of the Labour Party, who finally succeeded in having her Freedom of Infomation Act adopted by this closed society.

Long before this window was opened, pushing my luck, I tried to make a bargain with my colleagues. I offered to keep my public mouth shut for the time being on one condition: that I be given access to the minutes of previous Authorities, to establish if there were precedents for such points of principle, i.e., a clash between individual rights and membership of RTÉ. I even offered to write a paper on the subject for the Authority. Tom Quinn said that in seventeen years experience he had never come across such a contretemps; as director of corporate affairs, he should know. There were no takers to my proposition, so I said "all bets are off", meaning that I retained the right to speak out when and wherever I chose.

The trouble for the mandarins was the looming Freedom of Information Act. On the face of it, a public communication enterprise such as RTÉ – when it was brought into the net – would have to give pretty good reasons to refuse information. In fact, as originally drafted, there were sufficient qualifications in the proposed act to facilitate the continuation of the RTÉ culture of secrecy. The Authority listened carefully as I – apparently the only one to study the matter in detail – listed the comforting exemptions such as meetings of the government, deliberations, functions and negotiations of public bodies, parliamentary, court, law enforcement and public safety and so, protectively, on and so forth. RTÉ could easily drag its feet; however, as primarily an information purveyor, it would be expected to set an honourable example. For RTÉ, I urged the Authority, it should be a matter of energetically applying at least the spirit of the forthcoming act to our dealings. In fact, the eventual legislation was considerably liberalised: the main thing protected in the context of broadcasting was – very properly – the information sources of programme-makers.

My request for permission to study the minutes was rejected by my colleagues. It was not until February 1997, after constant pressure from me and with the shadow of the act hovering over him, that the chairman finally authorised my studying – within the confines of RTÉ – those specific minutes which had relevance to my research. These would be identified in a preliminary search to be conducted by Tom Quinn.

This was a bit like Catch 22. How could I pinpoint precedents without studying all the minutes? To overcome this obstacle, I asked for copies of all agendas. Agendas give absolutely no secrets away. They simply list subjects for discussion. They might give me clues. Although the chairman agreed to this, there was a condition: I must study them in Montrose itself. These innocuous lists could not be let out, even though every week I had confidential documents delivered to my door! It was clearly a measure to make it as difficult as possible for me. These people fought hard and probably took no prisoners, I thought. Then the chairman relented and said I could take the agendas home. But the director of corporate affairs again had a word in his ear; the chairman changed his mind. It was a minor example of where the real power lay. As a matter of principle, when I was thus denied permission to read these agendas at home, I declined the offer to study them at Montrose.

But like a dog with a bone, I buried the problem, brooded over it, and the following year excavated it again. In the New Year, 1998, I came up with a test case. I requested access to all minutes from May to December 1969, a period in which I knew the question of authority versus the individual must have been aired at at least one Authority meeting. This was one of the advantages of my having a long memory and a chequered history. They must have realised there was no way out of this; three months later Tom Quinn formally handed me the minutes in question – to be read in his office, of course. I sat down feeling that I had won a small victory. In a very short while I arose, defeated.

Not only were these minutes useless; in comparison to the excellent and detailed minutes which the present secretariat kept of our proceedings, those 1969 minutes were a disgrace to a public body, both in their skimpiness and in their concealment tactics. A brief, standard phrase was used to cover discussions: "Observations made by the Authority Members were noted for action by the DG, where appropriate."

Worse, anything worthy of special attention was covered in "Reports" which were not attached to the minutes. The mandarins had won again.

I made a note of the particular report in which I was interested and requested it in writing. More delaying tactics ensued. The chairman wrote to me, expressing worry about the "vast archival spirals" into which I might be leading them. I replied:

> You refer to possible "vast archival spirals" resulting from my request for the "report" referred to in the above minutes. Either such a report exists as part of the minutes or it does not. Without it the minutes are an insult to archivists or historians or even Authority members.

I finally extricated the report in question for the simple reason that it had to refer, among much else, to me. Further, the thirty-year statute of limitations on such material would soon expire.

This is the relevant extract. It refers to the *Sit Down and Be Counted* controversy in 1969 when I walked out of RTÉ and, as earlier mentioned, provided the spark that soon led to another producer, Jack Dowling, and a department head, Lelia Doolan, resigning from their jobs.

> Although not itself the real issue, the letter of resignation (copy attached) written by Producer Bob Quinn triggered off the recent unrest. Bob Quinn is a competent film director who joined the organisation as a Trainee Sound Operator in 1961. He is a restless individual who twice left the organisation and was re-engaged. He had suffered from an on-going illness and his letter of resignation appeared to be an emotional outburst which may have owed much to his ill-health.

Although I am aware of the principle of "damning with faint praise", even I was taken aback at this version of events. The only undeniable assertion is that I joined RTÉ in 1961.

I formally resigned – only once – from my staff job in RTÉ in October 1968. I then bought an old car and drove to Teheran, returning at Christmas. The exertion of this experience may have caused the minor illness referred to by Hardiman. The ailment was epididymitis – a form of TB of the testicle – which streptomycin easily cleared up.

Apart from it I was, according to a doctor, "as healthy as a young trout", and I am happy to report that it did not stop me fathering six healthy children. There is not even the remotest medical association with emotional states. This "competent" film director was recognised (even personally by Tom Hardiman) as producing work so excellent that it won a Jacob's Award and consistently represented Ireland at international festivals. As Gerry McLaughlin, the legal officer who handled these occasions, once said to me, "Isn't anybody else making programmes in here?"

Finally, the letter written by me and referred to above was not at all a formal resignation. It was requested by my nervous production assistant who wanted to be exonerated from complicity in my act of freedom in hijacking a film crew to the West of Ireland. It was a personal letter addressed to friends and colleagues, and I specifically asked the assistant that a copy should be sent to Tom Hardiman. The fact that my letter was developed into a huge political row was actually none of my direct doing. I had the perfect alibi: I was busy snagging turnips on Clare Island and conceiving my first son there.

Having got this bit of petulance off my chest, may I point to the significant facts.

In May 1969 the director general of RTÉ was confronted with a revolt in the station. He had lost two producers and a department head. The three issued a clarion cry to battle against a systems management which was militating against creativity. Tom Hardiman had to dampen the fires and reassure the Authority that he was in full control of the situation. His tactic was to isolate the prime mover – my good self – as a disturbed personality and the others as simple troublemakers. As it happened, Hardiman sent Maeve Conway, my erstwhile department head, haring across Ireland to plead with me to return to the fold, which unflatteringly suggests that the director general thought I was really only a harmless poor divil on a skite. By contrast, when the other dissident producer, Jack Dowling –

who actually knew what he was talking about – sent in a
formal resignation, Hardiman is reported to have said, on
the advice of Todd Andrews, "This is one cheque I'll cash."

The insight into how far a chief executive will go to preserve his organisation, his personal authority and his job
was of great value to me on the RTÉ Authority on which
I served. It also proved comforting as I experienced the
process of being marginalised as the months and years
went by. Professor Corcoran refused my request to bring
this ancient minute to the attention of the Authority, on the
grounds that it was purely a personal matter between
myself and Tom Hardiman. I thought of Santayana's comment about those who, being unable to remember the past,
are doomed to repeat it. But the chairman did agree to put
a copy of my refutation on the files. Because I still did not
want to undermine his chairmanship, I let it pass. That was
a mistake.

In Defence of the Realm

*A government only needs to leave uncertain what treason
is and it becomes despotic.*
Montesquieu

If I were to choose the single most destructive imposition
on RTÉ in its history, I would opt for the directive under
Section 31 of the Broadcasting Act of October 1971.
Twenty-four years later the mindset it induced still occasionally echoed through RTÉ Authority discussions.

One day in May 1996, a photograph in *The Irish
Times* of an anti-drugs community march in Dublin
prompted comments from the Authority members. Des
Geraghty said he was dubious about the leadership of this
campaign in that he recognised some of the front
marchers in the photograph as members of Sinn Féin. Old
attitudes die hard. He was originally a member of that
party before it split in two, producing on the one hand
his Official Sinn Féin and on the other Provisional Sinn
Féin. Geraghty and some of his colleagues later meta-
morphosed into a new party called Democratic Left
which would soon be subsumed by the Labour party. The
main principle that seemed to be retained by them was an
unrelenting distaste for Provisional Sinn Féin. Geraghty
has since (June 2000) been reappointed to the RTÉ
Authority for a second term.

At this brief discussion in May, there was thus an air of doubt about the bona fides of these anti-drugs community groups. If there were to be programming on the drugs issue, Geraghty urged that care be taken in the selection of participants. This sensitivity towards desperate inner city people's attempts to salvage their communities by accepting help from whatever source had once, I deduced, been shared by the authorities who had dragged their feet in helping such communities. They were initially reluctant to cooperate with community workers like Christy Burke because he was a Sinn Féin elected representative. In May 1996, Mr Burke was awarded £15,000 against RTÉ for repeating the *Sun* newspaper's libel that his meeting with Dr Ian Paisley could be described as "Shake Hands With the Devil". What was interesting to me was that even after the ceasefire in the North, Sinn Féin still attracted such unqualified odium.

Long ago, in October 1971, I was oblivious to Gerry Collins, the Fianna Fáil minister for posts and telegraphs, and his vague directive under Section 31. It stated that RTÉ should "refrain from broadcasting any matter calculated to promote the aims or activities of any organisation which engages in, promotes, encourages or advocates the attaining of any political objective by violent means". In those early days I had no interest in this Section 31. I was too busy surviving in Conamara. Even the measures that Gerry Collins introduced in 1971, which were endorsed by Labour's Conor Cruise O'Brien in 1974, hardly cost me a thought. Apparently the object of these was to avoid giving the IRA and Sinn Féin what Margaret Thatcher called "the oxygen of publicity". But Conamara was off the map in such matters, and Dublin was now a different world, a different country, a past I had abandoned. Indeed, my only reaction to these was to complain that Minister for Posts and Telegraphs O'Brien, in his obsession with the IRA, was neglecting his duties as mastermind of our appalling telephone service which impinged directly on my film-making activities in Conamara. Perhaps complaining was my undoing. But the professionals in RTÉ were also horrified. One spirited reaction against the ministerial directive was voiced by an RTÉ producer:

> Section 17 of the Broadcasting Act obliges us to cater for the Irish language. It is a statistical fact that members of the Republican movement tend, on balance, to speak Irish fluently. Thus they tend to appear on Irish language programmes. Likewise members of the Republican movement tend to be at the centre of trade union or community controversies. It is impossible to know at what stage they are promoting the aims of an illegal movement. Prudential decisions are accordingly made by broadcasters on a minute-by-minute basis. These decisions [i.e. consequent on the Section 31 directive] . . . will be impossible to carry out. The practical result will be censorship of news and information.

How times and people change. The writer was Eoghan Harris.

When in November 1972 the entire RTÉ Authority refused to go belly-up to the government in the matter of transmitting the paraphrase of an interview with an imprisoned Provisional IRA leader, Dr Conor Cruise O'Brien said, in opposition: "Surely it is more dangerous to leave these people [the IRA] in the shadows. In a modern democracy, the autonomy of radio or television is as vital as the freedom of the press or Parliament." On 8 June 1973 he said, "I intend to take out Section 31 of the Broadcasting Act and remove altogether, and deprive any future minister of, the power to issue the kind of directions we have."

But, on 25 April 1974, when he was in power, he announced:

> I am allowing the directive issued by my predecessor to stand, forbidding representatives of paramilitary groups to broadcast on RTÉ . . . I am determined to ensure, as far as I can, that while armed conspiracies continue to exist in this country, their agents shall not be allowed to use the

> State broadcasting system for a systematic propaganda effort.

In 1976 O'Brien introduced legislation to copper-fasten the measure and, in fairness to him, he spelled out precisely the offending matters to which the order applied. He also explained clearly his reasons and introduced measures to ensure that the order could not be imposed at a single minister's whim. As Muiris Mac Conghail, press secretary to O'Brien's government at the time, pointed out in 1984, "Dr O'Brien put a better face on it but he was at one with Mr Lemass on the matter of government supervision [of RTÉ] when he saw it as necessary."

In fairness also to O'Brien, in the same 1976 legislation he introduced measures to protect the RTÉ Authority or any of its members from being summarily dismissed by any minister without consulting both houses of the Oireachtas. As I have said, I had reason to be grateful for that measure. In mitigation also, when the Fine Gael/Labour coalition took power in 1973, they were amateurs, not having been in government for the previous sixteen years. They landed in the middle of the oil crisis of 1973, inherited a dreadful economic situation and were also confronted with a full-blown war in the North of Ireland. They were so panicky that when the Dublin/Monaghan bombs went off in 1974 – an atrocity even worse than Omagh – they were less than enthusiastic about finding the loyalist perpetrators. This, according to Don Mullen's recent book on the subject, seemed to be because they wanted there to be only one set of villains pilloried in the North – the Provisional IRA. If the Provos had not planted the bombs, the Irish government was not in a hurry to find out who did.

The Section 31 rule prohibited RTÉ from transmitting "anything which may reasonably be regarded as being likely to promote, or incite to, crime or as tending to undermine the authority of the State". And who would ultimately decide what constituted such incitements? Not the professional broadcasters, but the politicians. The snag was that the broadcasters had to make the mistakes first, then the politicians could jump on them. There was again spelt out what successive governments believed: that broadcasting was too important to be left to the broadcasters. And every year the rule was renewed.

Even in 1997 – three years after the IRA ceasefire – powerful members of the RTÉ Authority were fretting over "interviews with Sinn Féin representatives who were merely repeating the same clichés and adding nothing by way of information to the public". I repressed a grin in the RTÉ boardroom when I heard this. It was a perfect description of most of our own political representatives' tactics when they were in interview mode. The irony was not seen by all the members; nor did they see that the Authority was actually expressing a lack of confidence in its own reporters' ability to extricate information from political figures. In fact, both trade unionists as well as the ex-taoiseach specifically expressed doubt that RTÉ journalists could "handle" Sinn Féin spokespersons – a backhanded compliment to Sinn Féin. Redlich even said that she believed RTÉ was steeped in a republican agenda. It was interesting for me to see the director general also falling in line with the heavyweight point of view.

As usual it was left to Betty Purcell and myself to object to these assertions and to defend the staff.

The Section 31 straitjacket on RTÉ had not been loosened until 1994 when Minister Michael D. Higgins declined to renew the directive. But this blot on our democratic escutcheon had lasted for over twenty years and had affected even political innocents like myself. Garret FitzGerald certainly regretted the lifting of the Section 31 directive. "It flushed them out," he said to me one day in January 1996 when we were on our way to a lunch with the staff. He must have forgotten that in 1972 he had said, "The real threat to the country was not the IRA but the threat to freedom of speech." But in his autobiography he wrote:

> Of the ban itself [Section 31] it is sufficient to say that there are two sides to the argument about it . . . The claim, frequently made, that if free expression were allowed, the potential damage from the publicising of extreme views would be countered by skilled journalistic handling, including interviews with IRA spokesmen, has no obvious foundation.

I understand that to mean that he trusted neither the principle of free speech nor, as it now happened, the competence of the journalistic staff under his authority in RTÉ to interrogate people with "extreme views".

In the twenty years previous to this Authority's appointment, it was not the "simple" prohibition or the powers of interpretation assumed by the minister that directly infected RTÉ; it was the theological examination of conscience, the self-censorship and the ensuing timidity on the part of its employees that damaged not only RTÉ's reporting facility, not only its public reputation, but the pride that good journalists took in their work. It inculcated despair in their profession, and that can lead to a kind of laziness: when in doubt, leave it out.

It split the organisation into those who favoured Section 31 and those who opposed it. I was present in Jurys Hotel, Ballsbridge, in 1985 when one of the more courageous RTÉ journalists, Brendan O'Brien, used the live televised occasion of his (and my) Jacob's award to launch an attack on the legislation. There were others like him in the RTÉ newsroom. The NUJ (the journalists' London-based union) frequently complained about it. But the policeman had taken up residence in the skull of many an RTÉ staff man and woman.

How many promising careers in RTÉ this sickening imposition impaired is impossible to tell. How many mediocre apparatchiks it advanced is equally imponderable. Anybody who achieved promotion in those years should now be examining their conscience. Indeed, the damage of such a measure – which was completely contrary to the norms of public broadcasting in a free society – is immeasurable. Like nuclear waste dumped in the deep, it has an invisible afterlife and lies in wait to pollute objective broadcasting for years afterwards. In the seventies the insult to the intelligence of the Irish public was compounded by the fact that on the east coast those viewers and listeners with access to cross-channel services could at one stage hear and see people who were banned from the national airwaves. When I first heard Gerry Adams' voice on radio, I was taken aback. Somehow I had never imagined a West Belfast accent – which illustrates how disinformed I was by our national broadcaster. This feeling was shared by the millions of southerners whose understanding of the North had been lobotomised by Section 31. What must northern nationalists have thought of us? We already knew the despite northern unionists had for us.

At a meeting of the Celtic Film Festival in County Down in the mid-eighties where I served on the jury, I was present when Seán Ó Mordha, still an RTÉ producer, was asked from the floor why the RTÉ staff did not strike against Section 31. He shrugged and said, "We'd simply be closed down." The voice from the floor – a northern voice – asked a rhetorical supplementary: "Would that be a bad thing?" Seán did not respond further, seeming to realise there was no point in defending RTÉ.

It has been argued that this legislation caused the prolonging of the northern war and can therefore be blamed for increasing the number of victims. As Ed Moloney, Northern Ireland editor of *The Sunday Tribune*, said at a conference organised by the Irish Council for Civil Liberties in February 2000:

> I believe people died unecessarily because of this type of behaviour. They died because the media were not allowed to explain events properly and therefore people, especially in this State, did not understand as well as they could and should have. Was this responsible for lengthening the Troubles unnecessarily? I believe it could well have been.

Moloney also illustrated well the climate in RTÉ:

> For most of the time that I practised journalism for outlets in the South, the prevailing prejudice was this: if you wrote or wanted to broadcast about the IRA or any related issue, such as the claims of innocence made by the Birmingham Six, the Guildford Four and others, then you were in fact what was then called a fellow-traveller.

If what journalist Ed Moloney has said is correct, that such an imposition may have extended the war in the North and cost lives, our politicians also have blood on their hands.

The grotesqueries of the Section 31 legislation emerged regularly. Once a shop steward for Gateaux employees, Larry O'Toole, was banned from arguing his colleagues' industrial case on RTÉ because in his spare time he was a supporter of Sinn Féin. He successfully challenged the ban.

Though, as I have said, I had a disinterested view of the politics of the time, that black science inevitably impinged on me. In 1975 in our new home – an old Congested Districts Board factory in Carraroe which we converted every weekend into a fleapit cinema – my then wife and I had been showing feature films: films like *Man of Aran, Dr No,* even *Enter the Dragon*. There were few other recreational facilities for young people in the area. One weekend I showed my own film, *Caoineadh Airt Uí Laoire*, which featured the people of Conamara and which, admittedly, had originally been commissioned by Eamon Smullen of Sinn Féin. It was described by Ciaran Carty of the *Sunday Independent* as "the Irish film I for one have been waiting for". The following weekend a young local garda landed on my doorstep with a summons. He said that I had no licence to show films. I pointed out that no such licence existed in Ireland. All we had was an obsolete 1904 direction about nitrate film inherited from the British, together with an inapplicable Dance Hall Act.

The garda said that there was impression abroad that I was showing films to raise money for Sinn Féin! It would have been beyond his superiors' imagination to realise that the pittance the locals paid as admission fee to my "cinema" was entirely devoted to feeding my family. The projection box was in fact our bedroom, in one wall of which I had cut a hole through which to project the 16mm films. Besides, the implication of my toeing any political party line was incompatible with my mercurial instincts.

The case actually went to the local court in Casla, where I shared the defendants' bench with *poitín*-makers and TV licence defaulters. The judge summarily dismissed the charge – much to the disappointment of film archivist and maker of *Mise Éire*, George Morrison. George, delighted to illuminate the general ignorance about film, had prepared some old nitrate film which he intended to let off as a stinkbomb in court. He would thus graphically illustrate the difference between the nitrate material which was governed by the ancient British act and the new safety film, which was not. Colum Kenny, now of Dublin City University and Independent Newspapers, was my (unpaid) lawyer. It may have been his first and only case as a would-be barrister, and I think he was delighted to succeed in having the charge dismissed. But the mud stuck to me. Some of my neighbours ever afterwards thought I was a kind of subversive.

I doubt if the RTÉ Executive and Authority would have shared this opinion; they may have simply regarded me as not quite a safe pair of hands in matters of state.

I have few fond memories of that black period between 1973 and 1977. In 1976 I was invited by Dr Eoin McKiernan, at short notice, to show and talk about my films in fourteen American cities to members of the Irish-American Cultural Institute. I was delighted to accept, not least because I knew my old friend Desmond Fennell was also going on the tour. The title of his lecture was to be "Irish Proposals for Peace in Northern Ireland".

Just before I left for the States, Fennell told me he was pulling out of the tour. He would give me no specific reason, which I thought strange, but I embarked on the odyssey. At the end of the tour, in Washington, I learned the real reason. The Irish Ambassador in Washington had pressurised Dr McKiernan to withdraw Fennell's invitation. This appeared to be on the grounds that the writer was seen as a Provo fellow-traveller. Dr McKiernan had explained his problem to Fennell, pointed out that the Institute's valuable work was greatly dependent on official Irish government support. He asked Fennell to keep the matter quiet as it would jeapordise McKiernan's relationship with the government. When I finally learned of this in Washington, I was indignant that a writer and social philosopher – whatever one thought of his views – should be censored in the land of the First Amendment. In Washington I took the opportunity of my last lecture to publicly denounce our government's act of censorship. I was taken quietly aside and more or less asked by Dr McKiernan not to shout too loudly.

Recently Fennell told me the full story. He had written to his old school friend Garret FitzGerald, who was minister for foreign affairs at the time, asking for an explanation for the ban. The reply was a blah-blah letter from the department, but FitzGerald also conscientiously handwrote a postscript to Fennell. He reminded Fennell of the famous Amherst, Massachusetts, conference where Fennell had participated in an informal conversation in the late hours. In the context of the Heavy Gang and other state bullying, Fennell had imprudently used the phrase "your tyrannous government" to a staff member of the Department of Foreign Affairs. The woman duly reported this expression back to her employers. It was the excuse the department needed to prevent Fennell from exercising his right to free speech in the home of free speech, the United States of America.

These incidents seem to be carefully noted in the Kafkaesque circles that guard the security of a state. In 1984 I had a reminder of my peripheral involvement in such matters during the manhunt for Dominic McGlinchey when I was visited in Carraroe by two local gardaí. They were effecting the well-publicised government (also a Fine Gael/Labour coalition) policy of searching every house in the country for the so-called "Mad Dog". Then RnaG rang to ask why my house was surrounded by Special Branch cars! I looked out the window and ascertained that this was indeed so. The gardaí found a child's pellet gun whose barrel was blocked and took it away, never to be returned. It did not even belong to me.

I learned later that, rather than this being a house-to-house search as publicly announced by the government, mine was one of only four houses searched in south Conamara. I suppose it was a compliment to me, a free-thinking artist who was by nature a pacifist, in an atmos-phere of continuing state paranoia about paramilitarism. It was really something to brag about and finally distin-guished me from those harmless people in the sixties and seventies who were hurt because they, too, were not harassed by the Special Branch.

I suppose the authorities had cause to be suspicious. Anybody vaguely engaged in media activities who did not loudly and publicly utter an *auto-da-fé* condemning the actions of "terrorists" was automatically assumed to be a fellow-traveller. In a civil war situation there is only one question: on whose side are you neutral? And, indeed, I must be suspect. Was I not willing, along with my local curate – and very good novelist – Fr Pádraic Standún, to actually meet Gerry Adams, once and very briefly, when he visited Carraroe? Section 31 was still in full flight, fright-ening everybody in RTÉ. But novelist Standún, who had previously gone on a lone Christmas fast to protest against republican brutality in the North, and myself were invited to address the gathering. He and I simply showed our faces at the meeting. We said we had turned up because no Sec-tion 31 would ever prevent us from talking to anybody we pleased. We even shook Gerry Adams' hand as we left – as did Presidents Mary Robinson and Mary MacAleese on later occasions. John Hume implied more or less the same as us when he negotiated with Adams. But John Hume was braver; he had much more to lose. Since then Gerry Adams' hand seems to have been shaken by everybody in the world except Gay Byrne.

This was more of the baggage I carried with me on to the RTÉ Authority. It did not mean I was "political". I hope it had produced in me a kind of Beckettian sense of the absurdity of all pretension and a realisation that I.F. Stone was right when he said that all governments lie.

When I examine my conscience, there were other reasons for me to be viewed suspiciously by state paranoiacs. In 1982 I became acquainted with a young man who at the age of seventeen had joined the IRA in the aftermath of Bloody Sunday. Within six months of that event, he was arrested and served ten years in Long Kesh. On release he took up film-making, which was how I met him. He decided when marrying an English girl that it would be prudent to have the ceremony in the Republic and have Fr Pádraic Standún officiate. I was invited, too, even played the church organ, and a good time was had by all. Some years later he and I were having a quiet drink. We had never previously seriously discussed the northern troubles or his specific involvement in them. On this occasion my curiosity overcame me. I innocently asked my friend, "Tell me, who are the IRA? What kind of people are they?"

"I'll put it like this," he said. "Half the Derry Brigade was at my wedding."

I remembered those joyful, happy-go-lucky youngsters and was astonished. Those were the fiends, terrorists, thugs, godfathers of crime, criminals, subversives that our media had encouraged me to loathe and despise? Now that was what I call a political education. On the RTÉ Authority, it enabled me to decipher many coded references.

In the *Crane Bag* in 1984, Peter Feeney (head of RTÉ Current Affairs from 1990 to 1997 and now running the Freedom of Information unit in RTÉ) wrote the following:

Censorship can be overt, as in Section 31, or covert, as where dishonest programme-makers transmit the kinds of programme they expect their political masters would prefer. My judgement is that RTÉ has been singularly unsuccessful in resisting the overt censorship, but has been reasonably successful in resisting covert censorship. *The latter resistance is often achieved without a significant input from the Authority.* [my italics]

THE OLDEST PROFESSION

Advertising is the rattling of a stick inside a swill bucket.
George Orwell

I have been planting trees for the past eighteen years. I started with tiny pines, stragglers that had wandered out from the Seana-Pheistín woods and needed a loving home. They were easiest to "liberate". I transplanted them to the thin soil round my leaky Congested Districts Board home in Carraroe. There was barely sufficient space around the walls to plant them. Still they thrived. Those evergreens now almost completely protect the old building and its new owners from curious eyes and Atlantic storms.

In 1994, in our new home a few miles further west, I had more space and could more easily pursue what had become an obsession. I was deriving more satisfaction from planting trees than from film-making, and I was learning the truth of the adage: to be happy for a month, find a wife; for a year, find a mistress; but for life, cultivate a garden.

In my new "garden", in truth a bog, I had to probe for tiny pockets of soil which might have a depth of more than eighteen inches; gales and turf-cutting had stripped the surface. So far I have found about 1,000 such niches and patiently filled them with individual trees. At the last count 563 survived. Of the fourteen "Lords and Commoners" i.e. trees of the woods described in the eighth-century *Bretha Comaithchesa* (judgements of neighbourhood), the only one I have not acquired and planted is the elm. Gradually I am camouflaging – but I hope also preserving – the grass-covered potato ridges that the late Mike O'Toole, his wife and his children labored over since 1937 when the Land Commission granted him this cottage and strip of bog for an annual repayment of 7/6d. My early period of residence here coincided roughly with my time on the RTÉ Authority and provided a perfect antidote to the stresses of that involvement.

One bleak January morning I looked out of my kitchen window at the muddy grey landscape and said: "This will not do. I must have colour."

Most of the trees I had planted were deciduous. Their leaves might be glorious in summer, but in winter their still immature branches made little impact on the grey sky. Subsequently, on the way home from an RTÉ Authority meeting, I stopped at White's garden centre in Ballinasloe and bought a dozen Sitka spruce, the breed whose intensive cultivation on our hillsides has become the bane of the ecologist's life. I did not care. A small touch of year-round green would cheer us up and provide some further protection from Atlantic gales. At worst I could cull them as Christmas trees. Their excesses would be controlled. As in broadcasting, one can rationalise anything.

Since the early nineties the only thing under control in RTÉ seems to me to have been the temper of professional programme-makers who saw their best efforts trivialised by the context and schedule in which they were increasingly forced to work. It is remarkable how few outbreaks of the broadcasting version of road rage there have been. Perhaps blood has actually been spilt, but in the closet of RTÉ it has been discreetly mopped up.

In 1995 an RTÉ press advertisement featured, in colour, the staff identity cards of Gay Byrne, Gareth O'Callaghan, Ian Dempsey, Ronan Collins and Mike Murphy, with the slogan: "More of Your Sales Team". There were no women featured. As if this did not spell out the message clearly, the text said: "Every weekday six out of ten adults in Ireland listen to our team of professionals – adding weight to your advertising. When people tune in to their favourite RTÉ Radio programmes, they're also tuning in to your advertising message."

None of these personalities was embarrassed to be used as salesmen and, in at least my opinion, to have their work thus trivialised; it must have been made worth their while. It was an indication of how far RTÉ and its stars had been pushed down the greasy pole of commercialism, further into a situation of entrapment between public service and private enterprise. I once asked an executive in the RTÉ sales department – who also happened to be the wife of the director of corporate affairs – why radio programmes had to be interrupted so frequently by single commercials. She told me, "That's what the advertisers want, more individual impact, not to be clustered or cluttered with other ads."

One has to be more than a channel-hopper to see the occasional fine work that RTÉ does in current affairs, news and documentary. It has to do these things in order to justify a public licence fee which represents one-third of its income. The trouble is that its blatant commercial approach – as indicated above – makes it easy for other commercial TV and radio interests to demand, as they are increasingly doing, some of RTÉ's public money.

These interests are inadvertently aided and abetted by RTÉ "stars" such as Pat Kenny, who proudly proclaim that the public does not pay their fees, that they are paid from the commercial income they attract. With such spades do myopic "stars" dig their own public broadcasting graves. Perhaps they are sufficiently insulated not to care.

However, here is a paradox. If one asks the question, whose, traditionally, have been the best-known voices on RTÉ, the answer will be predictable: Gay Byrne, Pat

Kenny, Marian Finucane, Gerry Ryan, Mike Murphy, Joe Duffy and the litany that never seemed to change over the years. But the answer would be wrong.

The most frequently heard voices on RTÉ radio and television over the past twenty years have belonged to less familiar names, like Jonathan Ryan, Bill Golding, Alan Stanford and company. Who are they? They are the voices on the ads. They are the real stars. Together, they soothe the fevered consumer mind hundreds of times a day with advertisers' exhortations and placebos. In the past I have met the above men, have even employed the skills of two of them. They are undoubtedly three of the most talented people I have known. Jonathan is a musician, architect, photographer, actor and a brilliant mimic; Bill is an excellent straight actor and had one of the finest operatic baritone voices in Ireland – I once saw him playing Mephistopheles in Gounod's *Faust*; Alan is of the pure cream of the Gate theatrical tradition. But they make much of their money from voice-overs. As Jonathan long ago explained his latest acquisition, a brand-new Volvo car: "Voice-overs, lots of voice-overs."

Therein lies their tragedy and the tragedy of the supporting actors, the best of Irish talent, who have been reduced to using their undoubted skills to sell everything from soap powder to tampons, from alcohol to bottled water (an odd phenomenon in this land of unlimited rain!), from newspapers to toilet paper: Maureen Potter, Niall Tóibín, Frank Kelly, John Kelly, Dustin, Barry McGovern, even the late and great Donal McCann, Claire McKeon, John Kavanagh, Ronnie Drew, Gerry Daly, Paddy Cole, *Glenroe's* Mick Lally, Mary McEvoy, Thelma Mansfield, Twink, Dave Fanning, Rosaleen Linehan, Bosco Hogan, *ora pro nobis* – it is a list of housebroken names. The late and also great Siobhán McKenna absolutely refused to yield to this temptation.

And what is wrong with it, one might ask? Laurence Olivier did it. Stephen Hawking advertises spectacles.

Pierce Brosnan flogs watches. Rowan Atkinson even does it. Sporting businessmen are at a premium: the likes of Jack Charlton, Mick McCarthy, Johnny Giles, Eamonn Dunphy, Eddie Irvine, Roy Keane, Ciaran FitzGerald, Jimmy McGee and the entire national rugby and soccer squads are for sale. Even star GAA players are cashing in. There was some excuse for the late Stanley Matthews endorsing Craven A cigarettes. He worked for a minimum wage of £10 per week! What excuse have our modern millionaire jocks?

And is theirs really a hanging offence? What is so terrible about people making money like this?

It is understandable if one is "resting", i.e. an unemployed actor whose only other recourse is the dole and who is at least practising his or her craft. Ironically, it is mainly the best-known and presumably most constantly employed actors who are offered these commercial gigs. But do unthinking showbiz or sports moneymakers – not to mention high academics – actually need this extra income? One really could not expect "jocks" to agonise over their part in the remorseless drive to brainwash the rest of us into a state of inadequacy when prominent intellectuals like Professor Brendan Kennelly and Senator David Norris, two Trinity academics, also became not-at-all hidden persuaders.

There seems to me to be little moral or philosophic difference in the motivations of the above and those of, say, a toyboy band like Westlife, whose manager, Louis Walsh, proudly says, "If there's a good deal and there's money on the table, I'll take it." Contrast the British pop group Chumbawumba who refused $1.5 million dollars from Nike for the use of a song during the World Cup; contrast poet Martin Estrada who refused £2,500 from the same company for the use of a poem during the 1998 Winter Olympics; or Ralph Nader, who refused $25,000 from the same global brand. In the nouveau Irish culture those principled people would be regarded as losers.

It might be considered tasteless to postulate an analogy of prostitution. But taste is not my strong point and I have sympathy for real prostitutes. There is certainly a difference between, on the one hand, the tragedy of an impoverished mother of four being forced to hire out her rather commonplace body to feed her children and, on the other, the sordidness of well-heeled public personalities lending the uniqueness of their voices, faces, talents and, to be old-fashioned about it, souls, for vastly greater sums of money. The difference may simply be hypocritical definitions of social acceptability, i.e. the weakness of taboos about greed relative to the strength of sexual taboos.

It is remarkable that while Irish personalities are shameless about exploiting their names for money, many Hollywood film stars are demure about such activity. Madonna is happy to sell vodka in Japan; Sylvester Stallone appropriately sells Japanese ham; Harrison Ford advertises beer there. The likes of Keanu Reeves, Sean Connery, Jodie Foster, Paul McCartney all add to their earnings with million-dollar appearances in ads for schools, banks and cigarettes in the mysterious Orient. What is significant is that many of their contracts specify that these ads must not be shown in the West. It would be bad for their images. It is all right to exploit impressionable Orientals, but their fans in the West might not approve.

Back home in the US, the Screen Actors' Guild maintained a long-running strike in protest about commercials. Unfortunately, it was not an ethical stance that was taken by the likes of Tim Robbins, Tom Hanks, Nicholas Cage, Richard Dreyfuss, Paul Newman and Harrison Ford. They had no objection to working on commercials; it was part of their culture. They just wanted to be used more and to be paid more. So bitter were Guild members that when Liz Hurley did a commercial they described her as "a scab". The strike was described as a matter of survival for the 80 per cent of their 135,000 members who earned less than $5,000 a year. But very few of those bit players would ever be asked to make a commercial; the poor were again being used as cannon fodder by the rich.

Packaging and marketing add at least a third to our household bills and perpetuate the swindle that commercial TV is free. The swindle approaches human beings cynically in terms of Super-haves, Have-somes, Never-haves and Have-nots. But who is to argue with this culture of opportunistic consumerism when the Irish national broadcaster endorses it and spends £190 million a year keeping it going, more than two-thirds of which comes directly from commercial activities? Despite all our reservations about American broadcasting, we are dedicated to copying it.

Here, it seems to me, is the kernel of the argument. Once you embrace and welcome a bit of commercialism and sponsorship as a respectable ingredient of public broadcasting, rather than a necessary evil, you are in that precarious state known as being only a little bit pregnant. If the US Communications Act of 1934 defined the soul of American broadcasting for ever as commercial, then the 1960 Irish act defined the soul of Irish broadcasting to be for ever semi-commercial. Bob Collins frequently had to remind me of this fact. But the present situation goes far beyond the dual mandate that was envisaged by Seán Lemass and Ken Whitaker and the committee they set up in 1958 to examine the televisual possibilities for this island. Even Síle de Valera, the current minister with responsibility for broadcasting, in one of her less confused elaborations of the embryo 1999 Broadcasting Bill, said, "Broadcasting in its totality is much more than a commercial activity where the object of the exercise is to *simply deliver the biggest audience at the lowest price.*" (my italics) The evolved RTÉ culture is dangerously close to being defined by the last nine words of that statement.

In fact RTÉ is frank about the necessity – as it sees it – of "using commercial means to advance public broadcasting". Adrian Moynes, the special assistant to the RTÉ director general, said as much in a thoughtful address to the Cleraun (Opus Dei) Study conference in February 2000 (which I attended and at which I actually called for a doubling of RTÉ's licence fee). In a fine paper entitled "Abuse, Advertisement and the Social Purposes of Broadcasting", Moynes reassuringly suggested that the phenomenon of the modern marketplace had much in common with the innocuous commercial context in which James Joyce's Leopold Bloom moved in 1904. Considering the modern development of the electronic bazaar, I disagreed profoundly with his comparison, and we had a gentlemanly correspondence about the matter. I suggested that his was special pleading, making a virtue of RTÉ's present contretemps. We agreed to disagree. But what it made me realise was that some of the minds that shepherd RTÉ are not exclusively those of careerists and marketeers, but of subtle and cultured men and women. This, paradoxically, worries me even more.

I would not go so far as to suggest a *trahison des clercs*; rather, the accommodation of the educated to what they perceive as the exigencies of political and economic reality. In his presentation, Moynes described the international context precisely, made a point of excluding particular reference to immediate Irish circumstances and did not take the opportunity to attack the years of incoherent public broadcasting policy by successive governments, which have contributed inexorably to the RTÉ impasse. I suspect he is too much of a gentleman to do this.

Nevertheless, I interpreted it as an acquiescence to realpolitik and market forces: reluctantly bowing to the will of both Caesar and Mammon. I can state categorically that RTÉ, since its inception seventy-five years ago and its incorporation as a semi-state entity forty years ago, has hardly been able to break wind without permission from its political masters and their civil service mandarins. I have found encouragement for this view in a fine chapter by RTÉ's Peter Feeney prepared for a *Festschrift* to honour

Brian Farrell, doyen of RTÉ current affairs broadcasters. To oppose and change this culture was the second reason I joined the RTÉ Authority.

First I had to discover how we had got into the mess in the first place, how we became embroiled in a system about which Joe Barry warned me, "You poke at this at your peril." What was Joe Barry talking about? Well, for a start: the official if unadmitted policy of the state since the depressed years of the 1980s.

With a demonstrably failed industrial policy, government resolved to gamble its few remaining ideas on Ireland's becoming a kind of fancy telephone exchange between the United States and Europe, a Trojan horse with which American telecommunications capital would intensify its cultural domination of Europe. It was logical. Ireland had already experimented with selling itself as an "offshore manufacturing location" based on generous capital grants and effectively nil corporation tax on export profits. As long as jobs could be created by multinationals, we did not care what they manufactured. The courting of essentially American telecommunications conglomerates followed this matrix of initiatives.

It actually began in 1985, according to Desmond Bell and Niall Meehan of the then NIHE, now Dublin City University, in a paper read at the International Television Studies Conference, 1988.

The Fine Gael Minister for Communications Jim Mitchell awarded Ireland's first DBS (Direct Broadcasting by Satellite) franchise to a private company called Atlantic Satellites. RTÉ had also lobbied for the right to develop this facility, to no avail. The winning company was now ostensibly controlled by a Wexford businessman called James Stafford – he of the later Century Radio fiasco – but it soon became clear that the Irish company was connected to the giant American corporation, Hughes Communications, which did most of the serious talking to Irish department officials. Hughes soon took an 80 per cent share in Stafford's company. Thus, as Bell and Meehan put it, Ireland's satellite share became the telematic gateway between Europe and the US, between places as distant as Athens and Denver.

This explains some of the the minor incongruities of our modern communications culture. When my wife recently rang the Radisson (Scandinavian-owned) Hotel in Booterstown, Dublin, her enquiry was serviced by a pleasant young man in California. Conversely, when a friend in New York directed a technical enquiry to an American computer firm somewhere in the States, his problem was solved by a technician located in Blanchardstown, County Dublin. My French-speaking daughter recently worked in a United Airlines call centre in Dublin, supplying flight information to callers from the US about flights to Europe. Strange times we live in.

When I think of it, this whole intricate techno-cultural American mesh in which Ireland joyfully finds itself may have been sensed by Joe Barry. With £16 billion flowing out of the country annually to the foreign corporations operating in Ireland, and 80 per cent of our recent economic growth dependent on them, who would be insensible to our dependency on the crumbs from the American table? An island which represents 1 per cent of the population of the EU and yet is the location for 27 per cent of the movable subsidiaries of US industry has to tiptoe carefully through the global tulips. To object to the cultural baggage (e.g., McDonalds, Kellogg's, Nike) that is inseparable from such investment might be considered an unfriendly act.

Barry may simply have been reacting in the standard RTÉ way to any suggestion of change. This reaction can be traced back as far as 1966 when Bobby Gahan, then director of sales, said that the station could not afford the kind of truth which the programme *Home Truths* was transmitting, that there was pressure from an advertisers' advisory council, and that RTÉ had a duty to its advertisers.

But my personal belief was that RTÉ had almost given up on the attempt to maintain an individual Irish voice and were finally conceding that centuries of indoctrination had worked: that the Irish were not only incapable of governing themselves, of thinking independently, but that "Ireland" itself was no longer a reality. It was more like a dead Sitka spruce around which we had draped Christmas lights and tinsel – all imported.

RADIO TEILIFÍS TONGA

Consumption is the sole end and purpose of production.
Adam Smith, *Wealth of Nations*

Tonga is an island in the Pacific. Older readers may remember that its Queen Salote upstaged Elizabeth II at the latter's 1953 coronation in London. The island produces excellent rugby players.

In 1993, when Tonga's Public Broadcasting Commission was told by government to go out and earn its keep, it was reduced to selling torches and batteries when cyclones were threatening; to make ends meet, it also ran an electronics shop and repair facility. That entered the folklore of Pacific public broadcasting. As reported in 1996 by Bob Makin, coordinator of the Pacific Islands Broadcasting Association: "No longer are broadcasters just broadcasting and programme-makers just making programmes; they are making money, too. Or trying to."

It is a reminder of what may be the ultimate fate of that other island public broadcaster, RTÉ, when only the climate may distinguish it from Tonga.

I recall a wintry day in February 1996 when the gale outside the RTÉ boardroom window was distracting me, the chestnuts and sycamores throwing their naked limbs about in a frenzy, their creaking and shrieking rendered mute by the double-glazing. I was miles away, thinking of the three eucalyptus trees, the four hazels and the seven birches that I had planted in the previous couple of weeks. Did I stake them firmly enough? Would they survive the present country-wide storm?

With some effort I concentrated on the storm within. The long-suffering director of programmes, Liam Miller, was defending himself from the attacks of the RTÉ television producers. There were sixty of these talented people, and an unstated number of them had had the temerity to publish a reaction to the Green Paper on Broadcasting, quite independently of RTÉ's official response. That in itself must have seemed like mutiny on the good ship RTÉ; nay, a hanging crime. We had the producers' document and Miller's response on the table in front of us.

The producers said:

> We believe the Irish viewing public are poorly served by RTÉ. The quality, diversity and independence of programming has been seriously damaged by the policies pursued by previous RTÉ Authorities and implemented by the station's management over the past ten years . . . a deliberate policy which has chosen to dilute programme policy and to replace it with quantity of programme hours produced from RTÉ.

When I read this I was heartened; it was not just a maverick like me saying these things. As an outsider, I had come to the same conclusion. But these were the staff producers, the people responsible for the *raison d'être* of RTÉ, which is programmes.

> The RTÉ schedule can best be described as a series of low-cost, formula programmes, many of them merely imitating what has been commercially successful elsewhere.

Oh dear, I thought, and at the same time: Hear, hear!

> The view from programme personnel within RTÉ is that it now resembles a factory, churning out the product day in, day out – with success or failure measured primarily in terms of output and market share.

In order to sustain this policy, control of the output became increasingly centralised, with decisions as to what programmes were made and how they were to be made being taken by an ever-decreasing number of management at the top of the TV programmes division. As the power has become more centralised, producers and even heads of programme departments have less and less input into the creation of the schedule.

In RTÉ, scope for creativity and innovation is curtailed by a policy that places quantity as its primary goal.

One of my first questions to the director general the previous summer had been why a relatively small organisation like RTÉ extended itself so thinly over such increased broadcasting hours. In 1984–85, with a TV programmes staff of 303 persons, RTÉ TV broadcast 975 home-produced hours (excluding news, sports and repeats). In 1996 it was planned to produce nearly double the amount of hours with a staff of 375. Joe Barry simply said, "We have to keep the shop open." So now I knew: RTÉ had been redefined as a kind of high street outlet, rather than a public service.

The producers raged on:

> The greater part of the budget of each programme is . . . controlled by labyrinthine departments of engineering and technical facilities, who consequently wield very considerable power over how programmes are made.

It was ever thus. But there were attempts to involve producers in shaping the schedule:

> . . .most notably an invitation in 1992 from the Director of TV programmes to submit programme ideas for the following year . . . the many programme proposals submitted were not even granted the politeness of reply, let alone acceptance or refusal.

Since April 1994, the producers wrote, the programmes management division had refused to meet the producers' group to discuss any system for the generation of programme ideas and proposals.

Their document also suggested that producers and programme-making staff should be assigned to regional studios, which made me cheer, too. Still, what a mess. And how could the unfortunate director of programmes defend this onslaught to his new bosses?

Liam Miller stayed cool under fire. He mentioned that all of the programme production departments – Entertainment, Features, Current Affairs, Young People's, Daytime and TV Sport – were headed by experienced former producers. So what had happened to these people, I wondered? I imagined them all standing in a row singing a chorus of the "*Internationale*" to the words "The working class may kiss my ass, I've got the foreman's job at last."

But Miller also admitted that more than half the total home-produced TV output was the work of producers from "other cultures and traditions", i.e. British freelancers fresh from directing *EastEnders* and the like. No wonder RTÉ was increasingly resembling its cross-channel counterparts. Miller had had a number of meetings with programme-makers in the past two years, but these meetings were, he said, not entirely satisfactory since the debate had tended to focus on programme-making (of all things!) and the needs of programme-makers, rather than addressing RTÉ's obligation to and relationship with the TV audience.

Miller referred to some good things like our responsibility as a public service broadcaster, acting *in loco parentis*, to regulate programme influences, and said that to slavishly follow the content of our competitors' output would be a disaster.

I thought of *Don't Feed the Gondolas*, *Crimeline*, *Challenging Times*, *Pot Luck*, *People in Need* – all cogs from across the water – and said to myself, *You are right, Liam, it is a disaster*. I had some sympathy for the man in the light of the fact that the most watched programme on RTÉ in spring 1996 was a cash giveaway horror called *Fame and Fortune*. What respect could a director of programmes retain for an audience who would suffer such trivia! Whether the audience was given much of a choice is another matter.

What was disturbing to me was the cold water thrown on producers' talent, creativity and motives by their own director of programmes. The only thing that distinguishes "creative" people from others is that they more desperately try to break through the inviolable core of human solitude. They need the backing of their superiors in these attempts. Questioning how representative the producers' reactions were, Miller described their response as a highly simplistic and misleading analysis, and suggested that they seemed alienated from other members of RTÉ.

But he got one valid blow home. He pointed out that when RTÉ invited producers to go to the studios in Cork to develop regional programming, there was not a single application from inside Montrose, "due to the marked reluctance of staff producers to accept assignments outside Dublin". I could have told him that beforehand. When Raidió na Gaeltachta was set up in Conamara in 1972, none of the Irish-speaking Donnybrook-based staff would initially agree to work there, even though some of them were from the Gaeltacht.

Finally, Miller said that their proclaimed anger and disillusionment was not truly representative of all producers. (Joe Barry also confirmed this personally to me.) But one of those producers, Tony MacMahon, said to me, "If the producer/director response to the Green Paper is not 100 per cent representative, it is because new, young hirelings will do anything to avoid offending management which butters their short-term contract bread." I could understand that.

Under the enormous and accelerating pressures of a changing Irish society, the cracks in RTÉ were widening. The two main tectonic plates, management and creative staff, which traditionally brushed against each other to produce containable and sometimes creative tensions, were now separating dangerously. In some airy space between, the Authority hovered uselessly. At all costs, our direct encounters with a rumbling staff must be contained in the context of polite monthly lunches. No wonder management was hypersensitive about my personal attempts to talk to employees. My choosing to have lunch in the canteen with trade unionists like Tom Gormley and Olly O'Farrell, rather than up on the third floor with the Authority, caused a certain frisson. Before one of our monthly meetings, I had ascertained that the people invited to the customary Authority lunch were the stars of our radio and screen services whose faces and voices, frankly, I had seen and heard enough over the previous thirty years.

Before I left home this time I checked by phone with the late saintly Monica Clune in RTÉ administration. How many of these invitees, I asked, were actually on the staff as distinct from contract personalities, businessmen and women whose faces and voices represent the image of RTÉ? Her answer made me decide that I would be better occupied meeting the ordinary staff in the canteen. Within minutes, the corporate sheepdog, Tom Quinn, was on the phone to Conamara asking, "What are you at, Bob?" Monica, dutiful servant to the last, had checked with him.

It transpired that I was not encouraged to have personal dealings with staff, that all contacts should ideally be channelled through the secretariat. If this is not paranoia, I fail to see what is.

I once wrote a long list of questions for Colm Molloy, director of sales. He never replied because, as the director general of the time said, "I have a problem in Authority members sending such detailed questionnaires to individual executives." I dutifully sent the questions through the secretariat to the Authority. I still got no reply from the man, perhaps because my questionnaire detailed how RTÉ was infringing its own guidelines on advertising. Then, what hope had I got when Professor Corcoran himself wrote a personal reply to me saying he thought these guidelines were "antediluvian". The guidelines had actually been recently updated in the light of the 1989 directives on the subject from the EU.

The truth was, I guessed, that apart from the inevitable mercenaries in a bunch of 2,000 people, there were few in RTÉ who did not simply want to do their work well. Most would have had the basic human instinct to think well of, and do well by, their fellow citizens. Many of the people there had a sense of public service. But, as a junior doctor once said of his profession, they were wounded healers. The country was in a crisis of growing affluence, together with the calculated destruction of "moribund" ideas and particularly the erosion of its traditional concept of an Irish identity. RTÉ was reflecting this crisis – and in my opinion, willy-nilly exacerbating it – while competing with the Goliath of broadcasting, Rupert Murdoch, and his agents on the island. The trouble was that RTÉ was accepting the Murdoch rules of warfare. They would have been better occupied practising the use of a slingshot, perhaps even applying guerrilla tactics.

At this particular time, money was not the real problem for RTÉ. It early emerged that RTÉ was cash rich, rolling in money, looking desperately for profitable or even vaguely broadcasting-related mattresses in which to hide its surplus. The *RTÉ Guide*'s profits were in millions. RTÉ's £200,000 stake in *Riverdance* was producing a small fortune for the station. As Kevin Healy, then director of radio, said to me, "The money is rolling in." We had the lion's share of the national advertising budget – which could partially account for much of the fire we attracted from the print media. We also had 80 per cent of the broadcast advertising expenditure.

RTÉ had even proved too clever for Ray Burke's 1990 diktat that there be a cap on advertising income. RTÉ had continued the intensity of its advertising policy exactly as before, but it now simply opened a new bank account and put the outlawed earnings into it. Bob Collins described RTÉ's tactic to me as not so much machiavellian as "Jesuitical". The same technique was previously used to defend RTÉ's alcohol advertising: "We are not advertising alcohol per se; we are advertising brands."

What seemed to be lacking was not money but direction. It was headless-chicken time – the same phenomenon that seems now to be shrouding the entire country in a fog. I took the opportunity – as I invariably did when I saw an opening – to suggest that if we were so rich we could afford to completely get rid of my *bête noir*, child-targeted commercials. This opportunism of mine became a joke on the Authority. One day in 1995, the director of programmes reported to the members that "the advertisers are unhappy because we are failing to deliver the young people to them". I expressed my customary outrage at this bald admission that (a) the emotional state of advertisers should be of concern to the public broadcaster and (b) that young people were seen as no more than an item on a delivery list.

After one of these interventions, Joe Barry kindly took me aside and said, "Bob, you pushed the boat out there. Don't expect it to go to America on the first push."

Joe was a wise man and fond of marine similes. Trying to rein in my naive enthusiasm for change, he pointed out that RTÉ was like an oil tanker: it takes a long time to change its direction and even longer to stop it. But at least there was an admission that something needed to change.

Quite early in the game I sat down and laboriously outlined for the Authority and the Executive what I thought might be a survival tactic for RTÉ. I sent it to the chairman on St Patrick's Day 1996. If the Executive read it, they ignored it. If the Authority members received a copy, they never commented. It disappeared into that specialised department, a feature of all large organisations, which is devoted to suggestions and which might well carry the cryptic title YMBJ, which stands for You Must Be Joking.

Chairman Corcoran himself wrote a fine paper in autumn 1996 which was, because of his position, included in the agenda. It was written in exactly the same spirit as mine, urging RTÉ to do what was obvious: to tap into the spirit of creativity in RTÉ; to listen to the audience; to provide a platform for new writers; to build a creative environment; to decentralise broadcasting and build on the base of existing production centres; to address complaints about "the liberal agenda"; to extend the range of documentaries on television; to make Network 2 risk-taking, innovative and experimental etc. etc. etc.

I could imagine RTÉ management also reading this with wry expressions that reflected the organisation's guiding principle: the force of inertia. As Emil Cioran once earthily observed, "Habit is the ballast that chains a dog to his vomit."

By the way, in November 2000, the island of Tonga sold the rights to the genetic information of its 108,000 citizens to an Australian company, Autogent Ltd, for an undisclosed amount. Previously, Tonga's economy had focussed on fishing and tourism and relied heavily on foreign aid.

PUBLIC BROADCASTING

It is a general error to imagine the loudest complainers
for the public to be the most anxious for its welfare.
Edmund Burke (1769)

The national public broadcaster of Ireland has not created a single permanent job since 1986.

This little-known fact emerged one day in a discussion about, appropriately, the staff pension fund which amounted to a half billion pounds! Term contracts – for which the euphemism is "continuous employment" – had become the norm in a national organisation as influential as the Department of Education. It had been such a well-obscured statistic that the members of the RTÉ Authority now learned it for the first time. Even trade unionist Des Geraghty expressed surprise. Obviously nobody on the Authority and its antecedents had "asked the right question" before. It must be one of the few modern "human resource" practices that RTÉ has adopted to match the strange times in which we live. The Microsoft organisation has the same proportion of permanent and temporary staff as RTÉ. This imposition of successive government/big business policy – hire only temporary staff – has produced problems of continuity and loyalty with which the station has to live but whose full drastic effect will not be felt until a huge bloc of experienced people have to retire – and very soon.

99

Such economically driven disregard for continuity in public broadcasting (and many other public services like health and education) is not new to Ireland. In 1950 the Department of Finance refused to sanction the sum of £150 requested for the purchase of a television set by the secretary of the Department of Posts and Telegraphs.

The latter, a far-seeing civil servant named Leon Ó Broin, wanted to buy the apparatus so that he could find out what was happening in this new industry. Already, BBC signals were seeping into a closed Irish society. But for the next ten years, the Department of Finance simply did not want to know and fought tooth and nail against Ó Broin's proposals for an Irish public television service. Finance said, "No charge must fall on the Exchequer," and did not conceal its derision for the new medium, describing it as a "luxury". But these keepers of the public purse gradually and reluctantly lost ground in their fight against the introduction of Irish television. It is clear that they considered that the pittance they were already spending on Radio Éireann was money wasted. Lest taxpayers' money be further sullied in what they thought should be a simple commercial activity, they favoured giving the TV franchise to a commercial outfit such as Pye (Ireland) Ltd or the London-based Finance Trust Company. In this sense the Department of Finance was fifty years ahead of its time, and Charles McCreevy would have felt perfectly at home there. Further, in the fifties, the above two companies paid Dáil Deputies Seán Mac Eoin of Fine Gael and Erskine Childers of Fianna Fáil to lobby for them – which suggests that brown envelopes are not at all a new phenomenon in politics.

Eventually, as we know, a compromise was found in 1960 which consisted of a mongrel arrangement between public service and commercial enterprise: in my opinion, the worst of all possible worlds.

What is this strange animal called public service broadcasting that is tossed about like a rag doll between squabbling children? Implicit in the description is the decent idea of serving all citizens equally, that is to say, non-exclusively.

The European Broadcasting Union maintains that the operation of the free market alone is incapable of meeting individual and collective aspirations. Can public service broadcasting do so? The BBC once aspired to, in the days of Lord Reith, when only the state had control of the airwaves and possessed the resources to develop the new and expensive electronic media. At least the concept of public service broadcasting has honourable intentions, whatever about their realisation. It is driven, as Michael Tracey (professor of mass communications at the University of Colorado at Boulder) observed in *The Ceremony of Innocence*, "by the desire to make good programs popular and popular programs good: it understands that serving the national diversity of a society is not the same as 'giving people what they want' ".

The initial commercial offers to set up Irish television proposed to confine the service to Dublin – "to see how it goes". Fortunately, the much maligned politicians and a few dedicated public servants like Leon Ó Broin knew that this was a non-runner. Seán Lemass and T.K. Whitaker – undoubtedly influenced by Éamon de Valera's wishes – finally decided that it would have to be a full-blown national service.

Most of us waste little time in agonising over the background to our principal entertainment and information medium. But if one is curious to know what is happening, the best principle is to "follow the money trail" – advice I first heard from Bill Attley. Since he said this, I have taken to reading the financial pages before I look at the book reviews in newspapers.

In the new and complex world of information technology, a few focussed people concentrate on making either a personal career or a personal fortune out of what seems to the average person to be an incomprehensible muddle. The

101

converging activities of TV and telephony are wide open for speculation. When the licence for a second national mobile telephone service was offered for sale in 1995, even RTÉ joined with a US cable corporation, Comcast, to bid for the licence which could cost as much as £40 million. RTÉ was in the media/communications field, had transmission sites and spare cash. It was statutorily entitled to do so. They were turned down. Instead the licence was awarded by Minister Michael Lowry of Fine Gael to Denis O'Brien's company, Esat Telecom, for the relative pittance of £15 million. (Two months later, O'Brien's 40 per cent shareholder Telenor arranged a donation of $50,000 to Fine Gael. One of Esat's advisers was Fine Gael TD Jim Mitchell.) At least, the public thought, the licence has been retained in Irish hands. In January 2000, O'Brien had no hesitation in selling his company, licence and all, to British Telecom. He became a national media hero for making a private fortune of £230 million from a public asset. The development of this asset had been helped in 1997 by Iarnród Éireann – also the property of the public – giving precedence to Esat's cable-laying requirements over the railway company's own urgent plans to lay cables for a safer signalling system. Denis O'Brien recently gave £50,000 to each of the four leading political parties. The Labour Party returned his money.

This is the atmosphere in which a public utility like RTÉ tries to diversify in order to survive.

A US secretary for labor, Robert Reich, has said that without national attachments people have little inclination to make sacrifices or to accept responsibility for their actions: "We learn to feel responsible for others because we share with them a common history . . . a common culture . . . a common fate." The late Christopher Lasch, historian author of *The Culture of Narcissism* and *Revolt of the Elites*, wrote in the latter that the denationalisation of business enterprise tends to produce a class who see themselves as "world citizens, but without accepting . . .

any of the obligations that citizenship in a normal polity requires".

We have a current example of this process in Ireland.

Cablelink was developed as RTÉ Relays in 1970 by the national broadcaster. Ironically, this system brought in the cross-channel TV competition to confront RTÉ itself; but at least RTÉ shared in the ensuing profits. In 1990 RTÉ divested itself (willingly or unwillingly, I cannot say) of 60 per cent of its 80 per cent shareholding in Cablelink to the national telephone service, Telecom Éireann. Five years later, when times were hard, it sold another 15 per cent to the same national telephone monopoly. But in 1999 the Irish government forced both Telecom and RTÉ to sell their entire remaining shares in Cablelink to a multinational corporation called NTL. The news was not altogether bad: RTÉ earned a nest egg of £123 million from the sale of its asset.

Immediately afterwards, Telecom Éireann was euphemistically privatised into a "public" company called Eircom. The Irish government spent £70 million successfully persuading the public to buy overvalued shares in their own property – since 1982 the Irish taxpayer (helped by German taxpayers through the EU) had spent £1.5 billion modernising the telecommunications system. To increase the confidence in its shares, Eircom then decided to offer its mobile phone subsidiary, Eircell, for sale to a multinational specialist in this field (Vodaphone). To complicate the matter, the above Mr Denis O'Brien also bid for control of the landline part of Eircom's business. Presuming these sales go ahead, it means that control of all telecommunication in the Republic of Ireland will soon be in the hands of people whose only responsibility is to global speculators and shareholders. Does this matter? Certainly not to stock exchange gamblers.

Meanwhile, the new majority controller of cable TV in Ireland, the octopus NTL, worked fast and stretched its tentacles. This specialist cable company, normally depending on

Sky Television for much of the programme content it delivers, is in bed with the Hollywood Universal studios, owns British Eurosport, has the rights to pay-per-view Premiership football and is a shareholder in the ITN twenty-four-hour news channel. At the time of writing, it is negotiating with Sky Digital, ONdigital and Telewest for further content. Having absorbed Cablelink, NTL instantly began developing a threefold service for Irish households: an integrated TV, internet and telephone service to its cabled urban customers, launching a pilot version of this in Tallaght, Dublin, in September 2000. It was, therefore, now in direct competition with both RTÉ, the national broadcaster, and with what once was the national telephone service and is well in advance of both these entities in capital and technical resources. As the population becomes increasingly urbanised and therefore amenable to cabling, this is a logical move. But the playing field is not level. According to financial journalist Matt Cooper (*The Sunday Tribune*, 20 October 2000), the state telecom's regulator actually prevented Eircom from offering TV services and thus competing with multinational NTL for three years from the date of the Cablelink sale! At the last count, NTL was pulling in its horns, having seriously overstretched its resources.

As it happens, this information technology South Sea bubble has recently become seriously deflated. But things are unlikely to revert to the pre-internet stage, and the pressure on public broadcasting will not diminish. The playing field has not been level for at least fifteen years. Historically, RTÉ has been at every stage discouraged by the state from taking steps to secure its future. The European Commission increasingly approves of this "rolling back of the State frontiers".

Meanwhile Minister Síle de Valera, nominally entrusted with national broadcasting (the real power was her colleague, Minister for Trade and Employment Mary O'Rourke), also told RTÉ in 2000 to sell its physical transmission network to the highest bidder. Ms de Valera's predecessor, Michael D. Higgins, dramatically described this decision as "treason". RTÉ became reluctantly resigned to the decision on the understanding that it would control 40 per cent of the proposed new digital broadcasting organisation, Digico. There followed a row about the actual sale value of the transmission network. A major arbiter in this squabble, appointed by the government, was the Allied Irish Bank group, which in recent years had conspired with its customers to defraud the state of £100 million in tax revenue. At one stage Minister de Valera was, according to newspaper reports, threatening that RTÉ would have no shareholding at all in Digico. Eventually RTÉ salvaged a 28 per cent share in the digital future.

It has seemed since 1985 that anything not tied down in this island is up for sale by government – an asset-stripping policy pursued so avidly since 1997 that the Irish economy in 2001 could boast a surplus of £6 billion while its public services expenditure was verging on the anorexic and had been reduced to the lowest percentage in Europe! "A country that cut down all its trees, sold them as wood chips and then gambled the money away playing tiddly-winks would appear from its national accounts to have got richer," as the *Economist* said in 1989 (quoted by Richard Douthwaite).

The only rationale I can think of to explain the social pathology of destroying the national broadcaster is that "golden circles" in the areas of finance and government hope they will be subject to less scrutiny from a rabble of competing broadcasting interests than from a coherent national broadcaster. The deregulation of Italian television produced the convicted criminal, Berlusconi. There is the possibility that the wholesale auctioning of public assets in Ireland may still be delivering quiet multinational pay-offs to ambivalent public representatives. My heart goes out to honest people in Dáil Éireann.

Whenever I criticise RTÉ, I also sympathise with its hobbled nature; my actions on the RTÉ Authority would have been much more drastic if I had not always borne in mind that such actions would give comfort to the enemies of public broadcasting.

What I have less sympathy for is its officers' craven fear of openly and publicly confronting successive governments on the state of broadcasting. RTÉ has prudently confined itself to working by stealth: polite press releases, lobbying in the Dáil, the deep briefing of selected journalists. These tactics have never worked to acquire the enthusiastic support of the public, which can judge RTÉ only by the dross served up on its screens. Furthermore, RTÉ's cat-and-mouse game with successive governments has led only to its present piecemeal deconstruction by disdainful masters.

What is remarkable, as Erik Svendsen's research in Denmark (also according to Professor Michael Tracey) shows, is "the remarkable persistence of attention to the national broadcasting system". In Ireland, for instance, when TV3 acquired the triumph of the European Champions League from under the nose of RTÉ it created hardly a dent in RTÉ's viewing figures, nor much of an audience boost for TV3. It seems that, like children in relation to their parents, no matter how much they are maltreated, Irish viewers still hope against hope that their national broadcaster will behave decently towards them. This is the real capital that RTÉ inherited in 1961 and which it seems to me to have squandered in recent years. Instead of treating the audience as an intelligent citizenry, it has allowed itself to play the game by the rules of other forces, to "see people as no more than statistics in skins, with a definable value captured in the most desirable rates, demographic buys, and cost per thousand". Hence RTÉ's pathetic adoption of a crude money-spinner, *Who Wants to Be a Millionaire?*, and the disinterment of an ageing ex-star to present the programme. This makes a lot of money for Tyrone Productions, Gay Byrne, RTÉ, the National Lottery and, above all, Eircom. The losers will be a public further encouraged to be materialist, money-grabbing, get-rich-quick wannabees who have never been educated to the idea of a public service style of broadcasting, never mind the concept of *civis*.

The process started a long time ago.

In the depression of the mid-eighties, the pirates were not just in business on the airwaves; some of them were in power. In 1985, accountants Stokes Kennedy Crowley prepared a report on RTÉ, commissioned by Fine Gael's Jim Mitchell. It was a devastating analysis of RTÉ's shortcomings and was politically designed as such.

On the basis of the report, Mitchell, encouraged by his party leader Garret FitzGerald, prepared broadcasting legislation. RTÉ wanted to be involved in local radio, but because the bill would give it only a minority share, the proposal was objected to by the RTÉ trade unions and by Labour's Toddy O'Sullivan and Frank Cluskey. As a result, RTÉ lost even this involvement in local radio. But that coalition government fell before it could introduce the new bill. On the change of government in 1987, the bill fell into the lily-white hands of Fianna Fáil's Ray Burke, who since 1974 had been secretly distinguishing himself in private enterprise, especially that which required land rezoning in north and south County Dublin.

Burke – a self-confessed lawbreaker – took the bill and made it worse. He played to the crowd by declaring that the state monopoly of broadcasting was over. The context was perfect for Burke. Monetarist thinking was in the ascendant: as usual, it claimed that competition would produce greater choice and variety. In broadcasting the reverse has been proved to be the case. All television now relies on a staple diet of soaps, sit-coms and soundbites. Besides, with the deregulated advent of pay-per-view and satellite broadcasting, the reality is that freedom of choice will be available only to those with the ability to pay. Freedom for the pike is death for the minnow.

Burke's proposed measures in 1987 included licensing twenty private local radio services, a national radio channel, a national TV channel – all to be supported by advertising, and all in the name of "independent" operators. He refused a modest £2 increase in RTÉ's licence fee, eventually limited its advertising income drastically, and he ordered RTÉ not to participate in local radio other than its existing commitment to Cork Local Radio – which has recently been closed down. To make the pill more bitter, Burke ordered RTÉ to actively facilitate commercial radio interests in setting up the latter's transmission network, even insisting that the national broadcaster should similarly help its other proposed competitor, a third TV channel. It was like telling Aer Lingus to provide jets for Ryanair.

Alan Dukes described Burke's measures as "a sordid affair", as having "the smell of sharp practice and corruption". Even Burke's own Senate colleagues were "appalled" by his "scandalous" proposals. An economic journalist, Jim Dunne, wrote: "What Mr Burke is doing is handing what amounts to a subsidy to RTÉ's competitors. What sort of free enterprise is that?"

Astonishingly, Burke seemed to be flying without the navigational aid of his own civil servants. They all subsequently denied knowing where he had got his ideas. From the Flood Tribunal have emerged curious accounts of the occasion in January 1990 when Burke's department officials and their RTÉ counterparts met over dinner, trying collectively to divine what on earth was in the minister's mind. They failed.

Without the hindsight of investigations like the Flood and Moriarty Tribunals, they and we could only speculate about the degree to which money in 1989 was influencing broadcasting policy as well as stimulating building activity in north Dublin.

Indeed, it has emerged that, three weeks before the 1989 general election, Ray Burke received a "political donation" of £35,000 from impresario Oliver Barry (who knew his way around, having been a member of the RTÉ Authority from 1982 to 1985, and of whom Gay Byrne, in the context of his own increased earnings from RTÉ, wrote in 1989: "God Bless Oliver Barry!"). Barry, with James Stafford of Atlantic Satellites fame, was part of a consortium which, with the blessing and help of Burke's machinations, was awarded the franchise for the new national channel, Century Radio. When the new station was in difficulties in 1990, Burke "capped" RTÉ's advertising revenue to give his patrons in Century a helping hand. During this period, after a tough RTÉ interview, Burke had the bit so firmly between his teeth that he could openly warn Peter Feeney, current affairs producer, that the RTÉ man's career would go no further! Burke forced RTÉ to reduce by two-thirds its fee for providing transmission facilities for its competitor. The kiss of life did not work. Century nosedived in November 1991. It would be four more years, in 1995, before the licence for a national commercial channel was taken up again, this time by Radio Ireland, now Today FM.

In the late eighties RTÉ was swimming in a cesspool. Henceforth, the only way was down. For eight years after 1986, out of thirteen European public broadcasters, RTÉ was the solitary one that was not granted an increase in its licence fee.

In mitigation, the instinct to reform RTÉ was not entirely unjustified. The organisation was overstaffed in many of its activities. It was certainly overcentralised and, in my opinion, still is. The idea of local radio stations outside the capital was also a reasonable reaction to the Dublin bias of the "national" broadcaster.

But the general thrust of Burke & Co.'s actions appeared to be to destroy, not just RTÉ, but the very concept of a publicly accountable broadcasting service and to give their business friends assistance in the lucrative business of local and national radio and TV. RTÉ was forced to reinterpret itself as a "company" rather than as a public broadcaster.

The radio pirates gained respectability from the Burke machinations – as did some of their presenters, who subsequently joined RTÉ. One irony is that when Today FM – successor to Century and now RTÉ's only national radio rival – was suffering from a cash flow problem in 1998, the RTÉ Authority approved an Executive proposal to defer some of the transmission fees due to it from its rival. Now that Síle de Valera's decision to sell the RTÉ transmission network has materialised, it is hard to imagine the successful purchaser – say the equivalent of Rupert Murdoch – being so charitable to a commercial rival.

To return to my earlier point about RTÉ's contractual hiring policy:

In 1996 I suggested to the chairman that, since RTÉ was now cravenly reinterpreting itself as a commercial company, then the short contractual basis on which RTÉ was hiring talented staff should be applied to its top executives. For example, if a new top executive were to be appointed from the ranks of staff, he or she should resign their permanent, pensionable status in RTÉ, throw away the parachute and take the risks commensurate with their vaulting ambitions. It would be a test of their self-confidence; sort out the men from the boys, the women from the girls. On the grounds that this proposal would convey a sense of mistrust by the Authority in its higher executives, engender resentment and antagonism, my suggestion was dismissed by the chairman.

In other words, whenever I suggested a defiant public broadcasting approach, my ideas were dismissed as running counter to commercial wisdom; when I applied the logic of commerce, there was a retreat to the protective shell of public broadcasting. The RTÉ Executive always wanted it both ways. And they got it.

BIO-DIVERSITY

I think that I shall never see
A billboard lovely as a tree.
Indeed, unless the billboards fall
I'll never see a tree at all.
Ogden Nash, "Song of the Open Road"

My bog was once a forest. Four thousand years ago, the climate changed, the rains poured down and the tree roots rotted. I still find traces of this petrified *giúsach* or bog oak in my garden. The blanket bog which gradually resulted has one significant property: its anaerobic layers preserve living matter from being eaten by bacteria. Perfectly preserved bodies are found in such places; Tollund man in Denmark is the best known. But on the surface of this apparently inhospitable environment, there is an astonishing variety of animal and plant life to which Tollund man is sadly oblivious. Snuggling up to my growing mass of alder, birch, willow, pine, beech, sycamore, maple and poplar is a profusion of small native plants. They are a bastion against the ecological threat of monoculturalism.

In the man-made ecology of broadcasting, the concept of "bio-diversity" is vanishing. All its expressions are acquiring a dead conformity. Homogenisation or "dumbing down" has been precipitated by so-called "competitiveness". Throughout the world this phenomenon is

111

developed and serviced by the equivalent of Tollund men, and they know it; they look human, but their spirit has long departed. In RTÉ the term "dumbing down" was one to which the Executive always objected, certainly when I used it. It was too close to the bone.

In December 1995, a few months after our appointment, the minister responsible for broadcasting, Michael D. Higgins, finally met the RTÉ Authority. All the members and the Executive turned up. The minister had also with him a team of three. The boardroom on the third floor was crowded, and as the meeting progressed it became quite stuffy. What the Executive and the Authority most urgently wanted to hear was when and by how much the minister would increase the licence fee. He quickly took us out of our agony by committing himself fully to a cost-of-living index-linked increase. (This index-linking promise remained a formally agreed government decision, but was not honoured by his Fianna Fáil successor, Síle de Valera, who "did not agree with it".)

In response to the chairman's sally that Teilifís na Gaeilge was going to cost money which RTÉ did not have, the minister said: "RTÉ should have set up Teilifís na Gaeilge on its own initiative, without waiting for my directive. Such a service is a deferred debt to the public." Then he let rip on our broadcasting philosophy. He pointed out that "we could not be the national broadcaster and a seedy version of the market", and proceeded to dissect the consumerist approach to public broadcasting. He even got in a nice dig at the prominent broadcasting personalities who patronise politicians but whose earnings are kept secret. In his opinion, RTÉ's defence of these personalities' secrecy clauses was "unconvincing" – which in ministerial speak means shabby and disingenuous.

He had a point.

These RTÉ-created personalities had over the years evolved into limited companies, businessmen and women subcontracted by RTÉ to provide "entertainment". But their employer, the RTÉ Authority, was as ignorant of their terms of business as the minister responsible for broadcasting. "Confidentiality" was a provision of their contracts which were personally supervised by the director general and paid for out of his own budget. There was some excuse for Gay Byrne to be prissy about his earnings. In middle-age he had lost most of his savings to a crooked accountant named Russell Murphy, who had the good sense to die in 1984 before he was found out. Byrne had to make up for lost ground.

By contrast, the limits of the RTÉ chief executive's own salary were strictly laid down and open to public inspection. Salaries of RTÉ producers and the fees of Authority members are all open to public scrutiny. We know exactly what the president and taoiseach are paid, but the very broadcasting personalities, who make a fine living from allegedly informing the public, shut up like clams when their earnings are mentioned. I have to admit a prejudice and say that I believe the programme-makers in RTÉ should be paid more than the "stars" and certainly more than their titular bosses. They are, after all, the ones who are responsible for the ultimate sounds and images which constitute the output of a broadcaster. They should be paid on a similar scale to jumbo jet pilots, having a greater impact on the lifelong sensibility, as distinct from the temporary physicality, of human beings. I exclude directors of quiz shows and soaps from this creative category. You may deduce that such a perspective is not popular in boardrooms.

In the increasingly warm boardroom, the minister spoke fluently and at length, never referring to notes. The mastery of his portfolio was impressive, and it was not simply because he had appointed me to the Authority that I felt like cheering his words.

Afterwards, Anne Tannahill said to me, "You must be a happy man now." I grinned. I felt I could have written parts of the minister's speech. I had noticed Joe Barry glancing sideways down the table at me while it was going

on. Maybe he thought I had prompted some of the minister's comments? Flattering, but obviously untrue. The only
thing that occurred to me was that my job should be easier after this.

When we had all seen the minister safely off the premises, I commented happily to Joe Barry, Bob Collins and
Farrel Corcoran, "Glorious words. How do we put them
into effect?" To which the future director general, Bob
Collins responded, "First they have to be decoded." I was
instantly deflated.

Although the minister had spoken unequivocally, especially about RTÉ's relationship with the market and consumerism, I realised that in the world of RTÉ there was no
such thing as "face value". Every exhortation was treated
as rhetoric. Every opinion was negotiable. Every proposal
was examined in the immutable context of the organisation's survival. Essentially what Bob Collins was saying
was: let the minister put his money where his mouth is.

Yes, we would get an increase in the licence fee, but this
would be wiped out by the looming burden of supplying
365 hours of programming annually to Teilifís na Gaeilge.
Despite even the promised increase and indexation of the
licence fee, there could be no question of diminishing the
intensity of RTÉ's commercial policy. It would be business
as usual.

The minister's stirring words made absolutely no impact
on RTÉ. There would be no "Father, forgive me for I have
sinned", no amendment of its life. Instead, in the *Sunday
Independent* on the following 4 February 1996, there was
an attack on the minister by DCU communications lecturer Colum Kenny.

It occurred to me that if the RTÉ Executive would not
listen to a purely philosophic critique of broadcasting from
a person who also possessed considerable political clout,
what chance had my ideas got? It was always made clear to
me that not everybody was a crank about commercials and
The Late Late Toy Show, the endless diet of sitcoms, soap

operas, prizes and glitter; that, in fact, that was what the punters wanted. Only cranks thought otherwise. Essentially then, sociologist/politician Michael D. Higgins was also no more than a crank. I steeled myself for further battles.

Even allowing for the possible geriatrification of my taste buds, I could not see how on every conceivable occasion the offer of, say, a free T-shirt made of recycled Kellogg's Corn Flakes to everyone in the audience was contributing more than a sick joke to the gaiety of the nation. Nor could I see how giving a free, show-long promotion to a Toyota car so that somebody could drive it away buckshee and total it on a stone wall in Ballyjamesduff made good economic sense, even if the vehicle was endorsed by a poet.

Such identical giveaways – posturing as quizzes – were the staple attraction of such as Pat Kenny and Gay Byrne. Allowing for their considerably different talents, both men and their producers approached TV in the same way: plenty of coloured lights and a freebie for everyone in the audience. But Byrne was an old greasepaint sniffer who understood performers and knew the showbiz game intimately; Kenny's talent existed in the completely different arena of hard current affairs, a talent that was lost in this frothy dimension. It could be seen as odd that two such disparately talented individuals and their presumably intelligent producers used the same shoddy techniques of audience maximisation.

There was really no incongruity: such a unified approach pleased advertisers and attracted audiences for their goods and services so that RTÉ could sell more ads and therefore maintain a staff of 1,400 permanent and 700 contracted souls. The real question was this: is the maintainance of protected employment in a sheltered environment the sole aim of a public broadcaster? This was what I meant when I had said to Professor Corcoran that I thought RTÉ was out of control.

To qualify that: the fact that two-thirds of RTÉ's income

came from advertising, i.e. big business, suggested to me that if there were any control, this was its source. If this, as has been illustrated by successive tribunals, is true of politics, it must be true of RTÉ. The entire staff of RTÉ are, whether they like it or not, in the pocket of big business. This is not to suggest that anybody in RTÉ is personally accepting backhanders. Certainly I never saw any evidence of sharp practice, although I do remember a period in the eighties when staff car boots were searched at the Montrose exits because technical equipment was disappearing wholesale from the station. There was also the cheque – for a disputed sum of between £1,700 and £5,000 – handed by Oliver Barry of Century Radio to Peter Branagan, head of RTÉ's engineering section in a pub called Mother Redcap's in Dublin; but I understand that this gift was intended solely for the purchase of drink by the RTÉ staff who so efficiently had set up Century's transmission network. Still, the fact that none of the recipients of free booze saw anything wrong with this generous gesture from a commercial rival seems to me to have been a significant development in the culture of the station.

Despite its protestations to the contrary, RTÉ must pipe the tunes of those who pay the most, that is to say, the commercial interests who want bland pap that will not disturb the trance of consumers. Certainly some tunes must necessarily be dictated by the people who authorise or pay the licence fee, but these are placatory offerings to appease vengeful minor gods. The real business is bread and circuses at the behest of the advertising pantheon. And this has always been RTÉ's balancing act: trying to keep both paymasters happy. The choice is easy. One lobby is a well-heeled and articulate coterie of global profiteers; the other is the disorganised and disparate million-odd who pay the licence fee which is their personal entertainment tax, and who are effectively disenfranchised.

Here I might mention the distinction between the two processes by which RTÉ sources its income. RTÉ has a department of commercial enterprise, fully staffed with its own employees, all charged with maximising commercial income. And they have been very successful; even the *RTÉ Guide* contributes a couple of million annually to RTÉ – which is what one would expect from a glossy tabloid. It also has an entire sales department devoted to serving the advertisers. On the other hand, RTÉ has to go cap in hand to its political masters to beg for its relative pittance of public money. Muiris Mac Conghail, one-time programme controller of RTÉ and now lecturer in the Dublin Institute of Technology, pointed out long after he left the coalface of broadcasting: "The Government had power over the licence fee and no other coherent policy on broadcasting. In other words, it had power without responsibility." Mac Conghail also wrote, in November 1995, to the RTÉ Authority an outraged comment on RTÉ's unimaginative response to the Green Paper on Broadcasting in which he commented: "Governments like to control or supervise broadcasting but rarely to pay for it. The history of Irish broadcasting is no exemption to this practice."

No wonder RTÉ's dependence on commercial income doubled since 1990. This was not entirely RTÉ's choice – a point forcibly made to me many times during my last four years behind the mast. My general rejoinder was that we were yielding too easily to both pressure points.

While RTÉ was trying to interpret and survive the pragmatic diktats which successive governments made up as they went along, it saw its salvation in the private sector and ran into its arms. It was a dangerous embrace, because the decisions of this lobby are even more ad hoc and, by definition, responsive to little but the profit motive. The pendulum had swung irretrievably far. Weak attempts by management to stick its finger in the dyke and curb the big business influence produced some bizarre effects. There is an apocryphal story about Gay Byrne wrapping a "free" car entirely in brown paper and thus thumbing his nose at the management who had tried to curb the grosser giveaway aspects of *The Late Late Show*. But Byrne was entitled, like any decent artist, to bite the hand that fed him. As he wrote in his 1989 autobiography: "I am not a staff member of RTÉ and never was. I am a self-employed contract person." The story of the gift-wrapped car could in theory be true; because Byrne also attracted substantial advertising revenue to the public broadcaster, he was almost a law unto himself.

The rhetoric about the man single-handedly changing Irish culture with his *Late Late Show* is a journalistic fantasy. He was simply an effective apparatchik of universal change which would have happened without him – the change from a conservative, money-in-the-mattress, live-within-your means society to a member of the global consumer economy.

From his embryonic days as a presenter of a radio programme sponsored by Urney's Chocolates, Gay has always known on which side his bread is buttered – if one works hard and keeps one's nose clean. He sniffs the wind impeccably. I know this because I come from precisely the same generation, class, culture, school and city and am only a little younger than the star. But just as two siblings can turn out quite differently, so have we. Gay's entire professional life has been devoted to welcoming the new and exclusive definition of the human being: the decent, ordinary, smiling and liberated supermarket customer as advertised on TV and radio. Gay has always hated poopers of this party. He has been a superior Hughie Green of Irish TV.

He has also been the most talented, successful and professional control freak I ever encountered or observed in show business. The night in the sixties when he savaged the late journalist John Feeney, who was attacking Archbishop John Charles McQuaid's questionable policy of "doing good by stealth" – although Gay interpreted the assault as a personal diatribe about J.C. McQuaid owning shares in Durex – was a revelation of the iron fist in the velvet glove. Byrne was a streetfighter. Ulick O'Connor used to say privately, with a vitriolic curl of his lips, "What do you expect from a squaddie's son?" And indeed, the suave presenter was light years ahead of Kevin Myers in fostering admiration for the Irish boys who fought and died for Empire. That is why he may not have been altogether upset if, as he claimed, management forbade him to shake Sinn Féiner Gerry Adams' hand on *The Late Late Show*. Frankly, I cannot imagine Byrne acceding to any such demand if it did not suit him.

He was ambivalent about the Section 31 censorship, although he has said in his autobiography that "overall" he was against it – at least in 1989 when his audience, the general public, were beginning to realise its stupidity.

Insofar as I can imagine it, the truth about Gay Byrne is that he has always been at base an actor and an artiste, and in my book that entitles him to some licence. However, when success goes to artists' heads they can exceed their competence and – like T.S. Eliot and W.B. Yeats – develop slightly fascist attitudes. It springs from a certain kind of intelligence and an impatience with the perceived stupidity of the human race.

I confess that while I was serving on the Authority I became irritated by Byrne's pontificating on radio about old ladies being mugged by thugs, politicians being a bunch of wasters, youngsters deserving the birch – the usual conservative and populist rhetoric. It was a time of media paranoia about the crime wave, about old people being murdered in their homes. It required a calm approach. Pandering to their fears and prejudices, Byrne told a half million listeners: "There is a wave of badness over the country. People are really scared and frightened and outraged and angry at the moment . . . the Garda Síochána are in disarray, the legal system is so bunged up. The whole system is so mad and insane and weighted in favour of the criminal and against the victim."

He conveniently overlooked the demography of the

population of Mountjoy gaol: as its governor, John Loner-
gan, has many times pointed out, its inmates were and are
almost exclusively drawn from the destroyed communities
of inner city Dublin.

It dawned on me that Gay Byrne was a spokesman for
RTÉ, of whose governing board I was a member. It could
be argued that he was representing my views. Perhaps,
being human, if I shared the same crowd-pleasing views, I
might have kept quiet. But I argued at one Authority meeting that I objected to him expressing reactionary views in
my name.

My point was poo-poohed by some members and dismissed out of hand by the Executive, whereupon I asked
for a ruling from RTÉ's legal advisors.

It resulted in a joint opinion from two barristers, who
upheld my opinion that the views of an RTÉ broadcasting
personality, expressed regularly and over a long period,
could be concluded by the public to be "condoned and
implicitly approved of by the Authority". I have no idea
how, or even if, this opinion was conveyed to Gay Byrne.
I would hate to have had the job of telling him. A couple
of years later when his approach in a radio interview on
the subject of racism was queried by Garret FitzGerald,
Director General Bob Collins defended Byrne's right to say
what he liked. The DG thus ignored his own legal advice,
i.e. that the public might identify Byrne's opinions with
those of RTÉ.

Again, in this topsy-turvy land, when Paddy O'Gorman,
an RTÉ personality (*Queuing for a Living*) wrote words
(February 1997) in his column in the then *Cork Examiner*
which were critical of Gay Byrne's lack of sympathy for the
underclass, he was immediately slapped down by his boss,
Kevin Healy. Criticising Byrne, our main money-spinner,
was tantamount to criticising RTÉ itself. To the Executive,
Gay Byrne and RTÉ were sycophantically synonymous.
Yet, according to a contemporary MRBI survey, at least
some of the public criticised Gay Byrne as patronising,

condescending and opinionated, and for, chameleon-like, adapting his tone to the status of the person he was interviewing. The sparkle was gone from Gay, and yet, as a senior manager in the station said to me, in forty years RTÉ had failed to develop any talent to replace him.

The strange thing was that in the course of my own battles about my right to speak in public, the DG and the Authority applied the reverse logic and maintained that the public would think I was speaking on behalf of the RTÉ Authority – despite my attacking certain RTÉ policies! Even when I prefaced my remarks by declaring the obvious: that what I had to say was only my personal opinion. I know this is confusing. Can you imagine how I felt?

As T.S. Eliot said, "Words slip, slide, perish, decay with imprecision." Predictably, when I appeared in a discussion about Teilifís na Gaeilge on the Derek Davis TV show, in May of 1996, and spoke sympathetically about RTÉ, nobody commented. Certainly nobody on the RTÉ Executive or Authority objected. It could have been my way to win friends and influence managers, but it was too soon for me to "go native".

Once upon a time RTÉ produced political commentators who were capable of treading the tightrope between government influence and freedom of speech. In the sixties, seventies and eighties, a couple of them into the nineties, people like Brian Farrell, John O'Donoghue, Paddy Gallagher, John Bowman, Olivia O'Leary, David Thornley and David Hanley were enabled to establish a *gravitas* and continuity that permitted them to interrogate politicians with authority, respect and acute awareness of how their position depended on the whim of government. Sometimes they faltered – as happened long ago (1970) in the moneylending tribunal – but on the whole they kept a straight face.

They were so good that RTÉ realised that in this route lay a limited freedom from Seán Lemass' "instrument of public policy" straitjacket. It was harder for politicians to attack a well-known and respected personality than the organisation itself. The disadvantage was that since the same TV people met the same politicians year after year, an intimacy developed which made it even less likely that the interviewers would boldly confront or even embarass their paymasters. Long before he achieved power, Michael D. Higgins, as sociologist, described this as the "cosy consensus". Thus the custom evolved whereby RTÉ employees could shape-shift from being objective public broadcasters to becoming functionaries of the Government Information Service or personal advisers to ministers. I think of Ted Nealon, Muiris Mac Conghail, Liam Hourican, Kathy Herbert, Shane Kenny, Michael Ronayne, Seán Duignan and the latest, Una Claffey. The relationship between RTÉ and government has, despite well-publicised burps, been seamless – rather like an unhappy marriage. It is strange that these RTÉ people on loan seemed never to be able to educate governments to the inherent social and educative value – as distinct from the manipulative possibilities – of public broadcasting, or if they did, how it never manifested itself in government policy.

On the other hand, in TV light entertainment a cosy consensus is essential. The feel-good factor and the "if you can fake sincerity you have it made" syndrome is always the aim. Thus developed the lighter entertainment personalities who acquired a protective veneer in the form of popular appeal: the Gay Byrnes, Pat Kennys, Mike Murphys, Ronan Collins, Joe Duffys, Marian Finucanes and Gerry Ryans.

National figures and private fortunes were made through this insight. Quite apart from some of these individuals' private fees from RTÉ, the national broadcaster's exposure of them on its airwaves gave them a national profile which could be encashed. It is likely that the RTÉ stipend was merely the bread and butter of a few. The real money came from opening supermarkets around the country – as, for instance, the Fermoy and Bunratty Co-op Superstores, whose opening Pat Kenny graced, and the cinema complex that Dave Fanning reportedly got £2,500 for opening. Gerry Ryan can command up to £3,000 for endorsing a product. Ryan was in the "stable of stars" run by Carol Associates, which marketed him as "adding a touch of class and prestige" to commercial events. This was the man who began his trek to stardom by publicly, on the Gay Byrne radio show, falsely claiming to have killed a sheep with a "rock in a sock" to survive. A popular Irish-language broadcaster once told me that even he could get £500 for opening a shop; in cash, he emphasised. But he was small fry. Their high public profiles make the big TV fish untouchable by government, which is good, but, and here is the rub, also by their employer, RTÉ. Thus smooth-talking beasts, their hour come round at last, slouched towards Studio One to be born.

Stalin denounced the cult of the personality. I hope it was for different reasons that I developed an abhorrence of the cult of the TV personality. It would take a different book to analyse the insecurity – both psychological and economic – that drives such people on. Perhaps they are just the public projection of the private inadequacies of Tollund men and women.

REGIONALISM

Tarmacadam the whole feckin' lot over.
Flann Ó Riain

Like many people of my age, I am given to wondering whether my life choices were wise, specifically in the matter of abandoning Dublin and RTÉ thirty years ago for the freedom and beauty of Conamara. Occasionally I am reassured. For instance:

> As a born and bred Dubliner, with a lifelong unsentimental but deep affection for the place, I have in the past couple of years come to thoroughly dislike this clogged, short-tempered, loud, greedy, mean-minded, overpriced kip of a city.

That comes from one of my favourite journalists, Gene Kerrigan. I did not have these reasons for leaving thirty years ago; in fact I can hardly remember their specifics. Certainly one of the oddest was that I actually wanted to emigrate again, to leave the limiting island of Ireland; but I had seen enough of other countries to know that their attractions also had disadvantages. Therefore, the next best thing was to become an *interior émigré* – so I actually *immigrated* to Conamara, which had a physical spaciousness that suited my temperament and by happy chance also had the vestiges of a linguistic bulwark against Coca-Coladom.

There must also have been a touch of the romantic Castroesque idea of retreating to the mountains and bogs and practising rapparee-like intellectual warfare on the Jackeen centre of paralysis, Dublin. The only result of that policy was that I was out of sight and out of mind; I could be safely ignored. Another instinct was to emulate the Joycean policy of silence, cunning and exile. But silence was a contradiction in terms for the gregarious likes of me; and since I was not clever enough to be cunning, exile has been my only real achievement.

When you live 170 miles from Dublin in the peace of Conamara where the only sounds that disturb are raucous magpies, the occasional car, the cat hissing at the puppy and the children running riot, there is considered, in these thrusting times, to be a certain unreality about life. This air of surrealism intensifies when the national broadcaster in Dublin tells you that the sun is melting the tarmacadam and you look out the window and see another Atlantic storm heading straight at you. Conversely, when RTÉ says that the country is drowning in thunderstorms, a section of your peat-based, drought-plagued garden may be quietly being eaten away by the smouldering remnants of last week's bonfire. It is rather like the old BBC weather forecasts where there was shown to be absolutely no weather in the twenty-six counties of Ireland; weather started at the border. Soon after my *Atlantean* film trilogy in 1984 drew attention to this meteorological marvel, the BBC relented and accepted that there might be some significance to the patch of island protecting Britain from the worst depredations of the Atlantic.

Although the traffic on the road between my house and Galway has dramatically increased within the past five years, it is still surreal to hear DART accents on the radio bemoaning road rage, gridlocked traffic and parking meters while you are watching a snipe zigzagging through the bog cotton or a heron hunching his shoulders in rapt contemplation of himself in the mirror of a pond.

In the dark before dawn from this haven of peace, almost every month for four long years I would either drive the thirty miles into Galway to catch the first train or continue on the long road to my old hometown, Strumpet City, for Authority meetings. Here, as RTÉ music and art facilitator as well as commercial voice-over, John Kelly, latterly wrote, was "tigerish Dublin, proudly licking its paws as the world's capital of banality, exploitation and media excess".

I was born in and spent half my life in Dublin. I know it better than most provincial migrants, can certainly navigate its streets with ease and know pubs where mobile phones are not all the rage. I have often been exposed to the Friday evening haemorrhage of young people at Heuston station who, armed with their mobiles, their Walkmans and their packs of Budweiser, are escaping for the weekend to their real lives in towns and cities outside the Pale.

But like a fox in the suburbs, what such distancing develops is, I claim, a sharper ear and eye for the lunatic developments of the capital and its denizens and how they infect other parts of the country. What it also develops is an irritation at the imbalance of regional development in this island.

I had a certain advantage over those assembled at the Authority table in Montrose. I could demonstrate, by virtue of my three-channel location in the West of Ireland (I refused to support Rupert Murdoch's satellite empire), that I was the only one who had watched and listened exclusively to RTÉ for the previous thirty years. My ignorance of the outputs of BBC, S4C, UTV, ITV, Channel 4 (apart from the fact that most of them had bought, shown or commissioned works of mine) was in fact an advantage. I could see and hear RTÉ on its own terms. I also knew that I was not alone.

More than twice the percentage of people (53 per cent) watched RTÉ 1 in Munster and Connacht/Ulster than in

Dublin (25 per cent). And there was substance behind this extraordinary statistic: two-thirds of RTÉ's licence fee income comes from outside Dublin. Nobody could ever persuade me that RTÉ programming represented or even vaguely reflected the interests of this loyal audience. We have the bizarre situation of a station tailoring its output to a minority in Dublin who deride it, and treating its loyal majority audience outside Dublin with what can only be described as contempt. RTÉ is essentially a Dublin local station.

Tom Widger, another Dubliner, could see this imbalance. In March 1999 in his radio column in *The Sunday Tribune*, he wrote, "RTÉ does not reflect what is going on in the entire country – when have you last heard from Leitrim, Roscommon, Donegal, Sligo, Kilkenny, Laois?" He referred scathingly to the same Dublin-based people turning up on programme interviews and panels, a phenomenon that was at last being discovered by a few other decent reviewers. The incestuousness of the RTÉ family of presenters and panellists has traditionally bordered on the genetically unsafe. When Brendan Balfe interviews Anne Doyle, Andy O'Mahony does Joe Mulholland, RTÉ newsreaders interview RTÉ journalists and the journalists interview each other, Marian Finucane does Fergal Keane, when the MacDowell brothers, Michael and Moore, play Tweedledum and Tweedledee on various programmes, Deirdre Purcell pops up everywhere, Olivia O'Leary *Calls the Tune* and has Peter Feeney on *Later with O'Leary*, Carrie Crowley interviews (retired) Joe Mulholland. When Philip Boucher-Hayes appears on *The View* and Charlie Bird does *The Living Word* on Lyric FM, when radio producers look into their own *Heartlands* every Tuesday for ten weeks, you sense that you are back in nineteenth-century Ireland where "incest flourished because the roads were bad".

As I write, there is a corporate advertisement for RTÉ appearing on its screens. It features the best and brightest presenters on the station, all appearing either grim, rueful or simply embarassed. The slogan is: "It's how we see ourselves." Quite.

The decentralisation of RTÉ was my next ambition. This was not a passing fancy.

As long ago as 1978, as an independent film-maker, I had stood in front of my own camera on the very administration building which now houses the RTÉ Authority and declaimed in roughly the following words:

> This complex houses the National Broadcasting Service which reaches into every nook and cranny of this island. Is it not odd that more than 85 per cent of the 2,000 personnel who heroically service this cultural imperialism are located here?

When I checked this statistic in the mid-nineties, I learned that an even greater percentage of RTÉ staff was now based in Dublin. Only 180 of the 2,200 staff now worked in the so-called regions. How could this be? Communications technology has surely meant that deployment of functions around the country is now easier than ever before. It was not as if RTÉ's output needed to be lugged on gargantuan, road-destroying trailers out to the farthest reaches of the land. All they needed were telephone lines, computers, satellite vans and energetic personnel. A studio in Ballyferriter could now function as perfectly as one in Dublin. So why did everything – hardware, staff, management, the RTÉ Authority – all have to be crammed into a tiny area of Donnybrook, to contribute to the motor congestion and soaring house prices of Dublin?

The tardy onset of teleworking – employees working from their homes – has illustrated one of the obstacles to decentralisation. Specialists in teleworking have pinpointed managers as the greatest opponents of this sensible trend. Managers feel insecure if they are not surrounded by their troops and sense a loss of control if their inferiors are not directly under their eyes and thumbs. This may be a contributory cause of RTÉ's refusal to decentralise its activities. It must be satisfying for the boss to look out of his or her plate glass window and know that a couple of thousand people are within barking distance.

At the Are We Forgetting Something? conference in Clare in 1998, Professor Joe Lee said that the centralisation of the media and the peer group pressure within helps to create the 80 per cent uniformity of outlook in the Dublin organs of public expression. He also pointed to the concentration of bureaucratic power around Kildare Street, Merrion Square, Ballsbridge, and of intellectual power within UCD, TCD and DCU. He is right. Ireland is the most centralised country in Europe.

And yet, the maligned civil service has at least begun to take timid decentralising steps. Four thousand civil servants have been moved out of Dublin since 1987. The Central Applications Office is in Athlone, the Motor Registration service is in Wexford, the Central Statistics Office is in Cork, the Revenue Commissioners have a section in Limerick, the Legal Aid Board is in Cahirciveen, Air Navigation Service is at Shannon and the army's finance department is in Galway. I pay my telephone bill to County Clare, my electricity bill to Limerick. Even if much of this dispersal is the result of cynical ministerial cultivation of their own constituencies, it is to be welcomed. In December 1999, the government bravely announced plans to move 10,000 officials out of Dublin. But twelve months later, like the grand old Duke of York, the government marched the 10,000 down again to a more pragmatic, dribs and drabs plan.

By contrast, RTÉ makes no apologies for almost all of its staff being located close to the heart of stockbroker Dublin.

A favoured excuse for this situation, at least in RTÉ, is that when "creative" people are bumping into one another every day in crowded cubicles, prefabs and the canteen, a kind of symbiosis occurs where brilliant insights are transferred from one creative worker to another. Strictly speaking, a symbiotic relationship is the vital partnership of primitive organisms such as the fungus and algae in lichens. This is an appropriate simile. In human partnerships such as exist in RTÉ, it can result in a sameness of outlook which reflects itself in an incestuous programme output. Besides, the "creatives" constitute less than one-fifth of the personnel.

RTÉ has news-gathering offices in eleven provincial towns and cities. It has studios in several, but no continuous programme-making output from any of them. Even *Nationwide*, the supposed provincial magazine-style programme, is as soft as blancmange and up until recently was collated in Dublin. However, in the summer of 1996, Jim Fahy, that indefatigable RTÉ newsman in Galway, tried to show his superiors what could be done. Using portable equipment, the boot of a car and a tiny but energetic crew, he spent that wet summer making a series of half-hour documentary news programmes at the rate of one per week. It was a colossal achievement. Was any attention paid to it? Did the powers-that-be award Fahy a medal and say, "Hey, this we can do"? Did they immediately install programme-makers in these half-used studios round the country? The short answer is no.

Instead of using modern lightweight technology to decentralise broadcasting, the programme-planners used it to further clutch power to their bosoms. When the *Nationwide* programme achieved a higher audience rating than *Six One News* in 1995, did they prick up their ears and say: "Good Lord, there are people who live real lives out there, north, south and west of Dublin – and not just in summer. They don't all get paralytic on *poitín* and they don't look as if they eat their young; they even watch TV. There must be a substantial audience there, too." No, the powers that be did not. They said, "How are we going to contain this phenomenon?" There were vague intimations about broadcasting *Nationwide* nightly. Six years later this had still not happened. As one RTÉ newsman put it to me: "Management have a stunning capacity for inaction."

On 3 November 2000, RTÉ tentatively dipped its toes into these unfamiliar waters by providing brief local opt-outs on one weekly edition of the *Nationwide* programme. Such a laggardly action on what had been obvious for years does not bode well for RTÉ's future flexibility, even with the advent of digital multichannel options.

At one heated Authority meeting in February 1997, I pointed out that we were proposing to spend less on regional development than on individual items in Montrose, listed vicariously as "colonnade conversion" or studio ventilators or office furniture or restaurant upgrading or even blinds replacement.

I discovered this imbalance by painstakingly trawling through the capital programme estimates for the following three years, a job I loathe and for which I am by nature totally unsuited. But by using a fine-toothed comb, I was able to track down anomalies such as the above. There was a relatively tiny allocation for regional development – £45,000 – possibly to mollify the likes of me. But after this good news, there was the admission that no concrete plans had been formulated to spend the pittance.

There was a certain amount of rhubarb used in the ensuing discussion. Eventually it was explained to me that these were just estimates. At the next discussion on the subject, a month later, the figures had been juggled. Terms like "studios" had been changed to "facilities". Items on pages 6 and 9 a month ago, say, were on page 10 this month; others were put under different headings. In the middle of a page, printed large, was the announcement: Pending Updated Regional Plan. The perhaps unintended consequence of this was to muddy the issue for amateurs like me and give the impression that the regional allocation had been increased.

Long before my second coming in RTÉ, I had realised that the profession of accountancy is the most creative of all and in broadcasting a more useful talent to managers than the services of the "creatives", the producer/directors. In RTÉ's case it came down to treating the whole organisation as one great complex ball of shape-shifting molecules, the movement of each element of which must be finely, but untraceably, manipulated to maintain the survival of the organism itself. This is an excellent survival tactic, rather like the dense black cloud a squid ejects when threatened. In private enterprise it is done to defraud the Revenue Commissioners. In public service it is done for the highest motives: to protect the inner nugget of virtue, public broadcasting. But the unwieldiness of it can lead to a certain amount of unaccountability, particularly in the undivulged fine detail. In one particular instance, Garret FitzGerald referred to the "intolerable sloppiness" of our television accounting.

For instance, in the middle of the fine tuning it was not noticed until too late – in 1996 – that in the previous seven years a transmitter engineer had ripped off RTÉ for £198,000 in "petty cash". The culprit's essential inspection duties had kept him happily moving around the countryside far from headquarters and with a chequebook at his disposal. His lapse may have further solidified prejudices against staff being allowed to stray too far from the mother house of Montrose. This was an enclosed order.

But the real reason the engineer had got away with it was that RTÉ's administration, like the Roman Catholic Church, was living in the past. Its procedures were Dickensian. If, for example, a cameraman required a "sub" to travel to a broadcast outside Dublin, he needed three signatures. If he/she asked for an advance to cover travel abroad, his application required five signatures. There was a "manager" for every five staff in this division, and much of the cross-checking was done manually, as if computers had never been invented. It was a classic case of too many chiefs and too few Indians. The form of budgeting approach which was appropriate when I first joined RTÉ in 1961 must, thirty-five years later, reinforce inefficiencies. In other words, the incongruities that a financial illiterate like me could point out were less the result of deception than of somebody trying to fit things in somewhere, anywhere, like a child desperately forcing non-fitting pieces of a jigsaw puzzle together.

Naturally the Executive would never admit things like this to outsiders such as members of the RTÉ Authority.

The pressures for clarity and accountability are increasing. In its own staff's major *Review of RTÉ's Structures and Operations, 1998*, it was recommended that all production facilities plus ancillary services be transferred to a business unit subsidiary which would have a separate account. Many people in the organisation favour this move – which was suggested as long ago as 1970 in the Doolan, Dowling, Quinn book, *Sit Down and Be Counted*. When a similar measure was also recommended fifteen years ago by the Stokes Kennedy Crowley report, nothing happened. By the way, the above staff review, which took six months to prepare, was rejected by the RTÉ trade union group. In one respect, I thought this was a pity as one of the review's recommendations was for a strong policy of regionalisation.

I was not holding my breath. In November 1995, Joe Barry had prematurely announced, on a visit to his home town, Cork, RTÉ's intention to transfer control of Network 2 presentation there. A committee was set up to examine the proposal, and this particular barrel of pork was quietly dropped, mainly because none of the Donnybrook workers was willing to exchange the delights of the RTÉ social club for the wilds of Leeside. I am sure their unions were not inactive on the matter either.

There are certain interiorised attitudes that must be excavated in order to understand why RTÉ has failed as a national, as distinct from a local, Dublin, broadcaster. In our first written briefing, the Authority was informed that "Outside Broadcast is an expensive resource as coverage of events outside Dublin also involves travel/subsistence payments for the entire crew." It was as if coverage of events inside Dublin were not also expensive. Mind you, when TG4 was starting up, cameras were installed in the Raidió na Gaeltachta studios in Gaoth Dobhair and Baile na nGall. It was a healthy portent, but they were never used and were removed not long afterwards.

Other than a penny-pinching one, there appears to be no philosophy underpinning the broadcasting distinction between Dublin and not-Dublin. For the cost of B & B and petrol, the boondocks are abandoned to their dark fate. But there is a certain widespread and deadening attitude among the formative elements in the capital of this country. Even the director of the Arts Council, Patricia Quinn, could say, in 1999, "I don't think in a population this size it makes sense to regionalise or devolve an arts council." When in January 2000, Minister for Education Michael Woods appointed a twenty-three-member action group on access to third-level education, it had only one member from outside Dublin. Oddly, Mr Woods comes from Wicklow.

What is built into this ancient mindset is that Dublin *is* the nation. Coverage outside Dublin is still considered exceptional by the "national" broadcaster. I say ancient because the transcendant importance of Dublin goes back a thousand years to when the Vikings turned it into a city and made it, appropriately, the centre for their slave-trading. It was continued by the Tudors in the institution of the Pale. But at least the Vikings and the British were as extremely active outside the Pale, in places like Waterfjord, Limerick and Wexfjord – even in west Cork, as Tom Barry's adventures indicated. So self-centred is this Dublin image of Dublin that ragtrade journalist Robert O'Byrne was shocked to find, in February 2001, that a London PR woman thought his newspaper, *The Irish Times*, was a regional UK newspaper. On mature reflection of the British High Street culture of the city in which he works, he admitted that the woman's misapprehension was justified.

Into this atmosphere in early 1996 came an Executive

proposal to spend £10 million on a new building in Donnybrook.

The unfortunate staff were living like rabbits in pre-fabricated warrens. Cars were being parked on the immaculate lawns. There were health risks. The proposed solution was to cover one of the few remaining areas of grass with an immense office and underground car park. And this while RTÉ was moaning that we must tighten our belts, that we were losing £150,000 per week, that the future was bleak. We were losing audience. Our broadcasting activities were in the red, and so on and so forth. I could hardly believe the preposterousness of the notion and said so.

It was bad enough to have recently wasted £3-4 million on a new studio at Montrose "to match and compete with the production look of cross-channel Light Entertainment", but it was going a bit far to spend another £10 million on an extra building at Montrose when a commitment to decentralise had been formally expressed in RTÉ's response to the Green Paper on Broadcasting. Would it not help the overcrowding if a few of the staff were decentralised?

One of the curious reasons given by Peter Branagan, director of engineering, to justify such expenditure was that if the bad times really rolled, we could sublet the monstrosity to a financial institution. In my opinion it was a disastrous step to take, would show RTÉ in an irresponsible light, and was simply a ponderously unimaginative solution to the very contradictions inherent in RTÉ's existence. It was a bit like Charlie Haughey spending millions on government buildings in the law-making environs of Leinster House while courthouses all over the country, where the laws were actually applied, were falling apart from dry rot. But in RTÉ the trade unionists and politicians on the Authority were all for keeping their constituency, the staff, warm and comfortable.

The other members saw nothing wrong with digging the over-centralised grave of RTÉ even deeper. Certainly

Garret FitzGerald, that master of timetables and detail, apart from some quibbling over minor calculations of floor space per person, had no objection in principle, and he tended to be leader of the pack in this gathering. He was used to living within easy access of the important buildings in this centralised state: Leinster House, the Central Bank, the state broadcasting service, three universities – to one of which he was soon to be elected chancellor – the biggest hospital in Ireland (St Vincent's) and, of course, Dublin Castle. On 1 March 1997, FitzGerald had written an *Irish Times* piece entitled "Tackling the Dead Hand of Irish Localism".

He expertly threaded his way through the rationalisations, the imperatives of equity, the dangers of precedents: the depressing litany used by the government and the civil service to avoid determined action on any front. It reminded me of the paralysis that besets a centipede when it is asked which foot it puts forward first. Essentially FitzGerald was making an apologia for government and civil service inaction on inner city Dublin deprivation by blaming the 87 per cent of rural deputies who, if any selective remedial action was taken, would demand similar help for their deprived areas. It did not seem to occur to him that a redistribution of the innate resources and wealth of Dublin city itself might go a long way towards sorting out the deprivations of Darndale and Summerhill. He seemed to have forgotten the impact one man, Tony Gregory, had in 1982 when he held the balance of seats to form a new government and horse-traded with Charlie Haughey to get some investment in the inner city – and succeeded beyond even his, Gregory's, expectations. FitzGerald was the rejected suitor in that little bit of wooing. In the summer of 2000 the two were still fighting in print over the details of the matter, with FitzGerald pathetically and irrelevantly claiming that he was not responsible for putting VAT on children's shoes. My sympathies in the dispute lie with the indefatigible Gregory.

In another (September 1998) article by FitzGerald in the same paper, the heading was "Rush to Regionalise Ill-conceived", which reminded me that he was an irredeemable man of the Pale.

So the new building went ahead – it is actually a pleasing architectural structure – and now stands as a monument to the no-surrender attitude of RTÉ and to the inevitable decline of its artificially maintained and over-centralised existence. Its final cost was £14 million. I wonder how soon the staff will nickname it Stormont.

It is almost funny to remember that seven of the candidates for the position of director general in succession to Joe Barry put their metaphorical hands on their hearts in their written submissions and swore that they were sincerely bound to pay homage to the regions. This may have been because the grapevine told them that yours truly, a member of the subcommittee to choose the new director general, was obsessed with regional development. They must have felt like schoolboys preparing for the Leaving Certificate. What are the politically correct answers to give, out of the innumerable possible answers? Indeed, one of them almost paraphrased what I had been advocating for eighteen months: "RTÉ must recognise that the best defence against international competition is to deepen its roots within its own community. The development of quality output from the regions must be a high priority."

A better analogy would be those politicians who try to anticipate what the voters want to hear. Civilisation seems not only to breed, but to reward, such ambitious courtiers. How sad for them that their protestations of faith fell on deaf ears when the said regional obsessive, this writer, was sacked – for reasons to be detailed in "The Rat Race" – from the interview panel for director general. They now had to persuade my substitute, Garret FitzGerald, that they were not really *that* devoted to the boondocks of the republic. Only one appears to have had the Jesuitical astuteness to successfully perform that acrobatic manoeuvre.

The objective reader may now reasonably demand: did I spend my four years endlessly fulminating about the system? Was I ever constructive? Did I make any practical proposals? The answer is: yes, equally endlessly. Mikhail Bakunin wrote in 1842, "The urge to destroy is also a creative urge." Not one of my suggestions appears in the official minutes of RTÉ. Indeed, once when I specifically asked that one of my carefully researched papers be read into the minutes, my request was refused.

Here is one of the many ignored suggestions I made to the Authority:

30.4.96

Dear Chairman

Further to recent references to a policy of regionalism I suggest discussion on the following practical lines:

Each of the existing RTÉ centres in Waterford, Cork, Limerick, Galway, Sligo, Athlone etc. be invested with a Programme Production Unit consisting of a Writer/Producer/Director, a Production Assistant, a Camera operator and a Sound operator – all initially on 1-year renewable contracts (one-year secondment in the case of existing staff who wish to relocate). These to be quite separate from, but working in loose comradeship with, existing news staff in these centres. Such versatile and energetic people to be headhunted outside and inside RTÉ.

Editing facilities in each centre to be upgraded, where necessary, to minimal on-line facilities. Minimal sound dubbing facilities also essential. I use the word minimal because this should be a lean operation. Fancy optical effects and dubbing techniques to be eschewed. If the subject and approach are good it won't need tarting up. If it is not there, no amount of ditto will help. Simplest of credits to be adopted. Each centre to be capable of producing a finished product, broadcast standard.

Nationwide to be extended to five days per week, at a dedicated time each day. Each broadcast to feature a

26'30" production on one subject. Free rein to be given to each production unit. No direct day-to-day editorial control either by Dir. of TV programmes or IPU [Independent Production Unit] in course of work. We're trying to liberate energy here. Ultimate control obviously to reside with Editor-in-chief.

Each of the seven centres would have to produce a half-hour of television every ten days. Advice in this respect might be sought from staff member Nuala Ní Dhomhnaill. Her experience of the logistics of producing, writing and directing (with only a cameraman and soundman) a ½ hour feature every week (*Súil Thart*) for years may help to energise tightknit production units. It doesn't mean a heavier burden but a more focussed direction for the energy and talent that exists within and without the station.

(Historical note: In the sixties Peter Kennerly and myself could each produce a documentary film – not video – every ten days. Some were award winners.)

Rationale: It is admitted that the RTÉ family is showing signs of jadedness. This may be due to programmatic inter-breeding, arguably due to excessive contiguity of practitioners. It is the downside of synergy. There's no point in bringing in from the four corners new (not necessarily young) blood if it is to be acculturated by the organisation to the degree of losing its fresh perspective. Wild flowers don't do well in suburban windows. Never pick one. Encourage it to bloom in the ecological environment to which it is accustomed or attracted.

Would J.B. Keane have written the same plays, or written as well, in Leeson St as in Listowel? I doubt it. By the way it took twenty years for Dublin to accept his unique contribution to the flavour of our theatre.

Brian Bourke, John Behan, Edward Delaney, Brian Friel, Tom Kilroy, Dermot Healy, Pat McCabe, Joe Comerford, John McGahern, Jane O'Leary, Vincent Browne (the real one, a sculptor), Tony O'Malley, Barrie Cooke, Camille Souter, Maria Simonds-Gooding, Hubert Butler, Desmond

Fennell, John Montague – an endless list of essayists, novelists, playwrights, poets, sculptor, composers have done their best work many miles from the "Centre".

And they are not working in isolated rustic garrets.

Believe me, it is their acquired rootedness in a local social reality that gives them the fulcrum to recreate and illuminate worlds which lie disregarded around us – until there is a triple murder or a Lotto winner.

The obvious query is: what have art and artists – not to mention serious thought – to do with the making of television?

If that question has to be asked and answered we are in more trouble than I thought.

Yours sincerely

I was assured by the director general in 1997 that my constant harangues were simply pushing an open door. At least they finally persuaded the Executive to set up a working party under the chairmanship of Pól Ó Gallchóir, then head of Raidió na Gaeltachta, to examine the possibilities of regional production. The working party reported back in April 1998, and I was pleased that their and my proposals were on similar lines. They said:

> RTÉ's services must be both National and Regional in texture . . . they must reflect and record the diversity of Irish life on a nationwide basis . . . All regional blackspots must be eliminated . . . RTÉ is perceived by many as being biased towards Dublin . . . RTÉ should enable programme makers based outside Dublin to originate material . . . it must decentralise its own production capacity . . . it should commission independent producers in the regions.

It was a profound critique of their own station by its employees:

> RTÉ's home-produced programmes reflect "a dash down the country" by Dublin-based programme makers. It is an absolute imperative that RTÉ sets about creating a culture

and structure which empowers people in every corner of Ireland to be part of the broadcasting process.

Strong words. And the reaction from the Executive? The report was damned with faint praise, the only substantial criticism being that the proposals were not properly costed. Three months later the proposals were still not costed by the legion of accountants in RTÉ. Their proposal for a director of regional affairs was binned. However, a commissioning editor for regional programmes was eventually appointed. Where was he to be based? Dublin.

The RTÉ Executive and Authority continued to ignore the explicit directive of the houses of the Oireachtas in a Broadcasting Amendment in 1976 which said, "it must ensure that *the* programmes [not *some* programmes] reflect the varied elements which make up the culture of the whole island of Ireland, and have special regard for the elements which distinguish that culture . . ."

The Executive knew that advertisers are not interested in programmes from the "sticks" – unless it is a "dash down the country" with *Questions and Answers*. The only part of this island that was endlessly and excruciatingly attended to was the North – which, strictly speaking, was part of the United Kingdom.

Redlich and the Authority worried about the professional standards of the "culchies", i.e. the programme-makers outside Dublin. That she was expressing a general attitude probably accounted in some considerable part for the fact that of fifty-six independent RTÉ commissions in 1996, forty-three went to Dublin, eight to the regions and five to Northern Ireland.

Des Geraghty thought that the existence of TnaG and RnaG should be enough to satisfy the same "culchies". As president of an over-centralised trade union in Liberty Hall and as an ex-member of the old Workers' Party which had ruthlessly effected "democratic centralism", Geraghty knew what he was talking about, knew the dangers of real decentralisation. He also knew his members in RTÉ would not like it either. That was the last I heard of Pól Ó Gallchóir's report. Geraghty's trade union (SIPTU) is also responsible for clutching to its Dublin bosom the so-called Irish film industry: incoming productions are dissuaded from going thirty miles beyond the Dublin production zone because they will incur punitive crew travelling expenses. To date the union also refuses to allow the setting up of similar "zones" outside Dublin.

Admittedly it is difficult for the formative elements, living in the cushioned atmosphere of Dublin, to have any interest in the situation west of Leixlip. A warm man cannot imagine how a cold man feels. When their eyes are not leapfrogging over the muddy fields towards New York and Washington, they are firmly focussed on London and Brussels. The majority population outside Dublin is keenly aware of this perspective. A neighbour of mine, commenting on RTÉ's coverage of a disastrous factory fire in Belmullet, County Mayo, which destroyed most of the town's employment capacity, said: "What are they up to in Montrose? They have live pictures from Kosovo. They can only manage a map of Mayo!"

Six years after I first began my campaign, there are a series of regional "opt-out" segments of *Nationwide* on Friday evenings. Technically this could have been done thirty years ago. Why did it take so long?

In January 2000 the Fianna Fáil/Progressive Democrat government wrong-footed everybody by holding the first meeting of the cabinet in the history of the republic outside Dublin, in Ballaghadereen, County Roscommon, and repeating the act some weeks later in Cork. This dramatic regional gesture had nothing to do with broadcasting and all to do with the panic caused by a woman named Dana (Rosemary Scallon) stealing the European Parliament seat for Connacht-Ulster from under all of their political noses.

Will RTÉ ever take the hint? I doubt it. In the latest national telephone directory, West of Ireland section, there is no telephone number given for RTÉ's headquarters in

Galway city. Instead it gives useful RTÉ numbers in Dublin. If at this stage I begin to sound hysterical on the subject of regional imbalance, it is because of the following straw. In July 2000, the *Sunday Business Post* reported that RTÉ had begun serious discussions, under the leadership of Ed Mulhall, director of News, about the need for a special Dublin correspondent!

It may seem strange to make an analogy between broadcasting and my other favourite spectator sport, rugby football, but here goes. When the Irish rugby team was humiliated by Argentina in the World Cup, and the following February, 2000, was squashed by England, the Dublin alickadoos realised the error of their ways. Twenty years after Munster beat the All-Blacks in Limerick, the IRFU bosses finally pocketed their pride, admitted that their century-long snobbery towards provincial rugby had been misguided and appealed to Munster for help. They dramatically replaced most of the Irish team with Munster players, and the Irish international team suddenly became a force to be reckoned with. Perhaps the entire RTÉ Executive should be temporarily replaced by the top brass of the Irish Rugby Football Union.

"Perhaps the real bumpkins", Liam Fay wrote (*The Sunday Times*, April 2001), "are not the country folk, but the television professionals who have yet to realise their viewers are no longer in the mood to be patronised by grinning game-show stooges."

THE RAT RACE

Habemus Papam.
The Vatican

From autumn 1996 to January 1997 the question on everybody's lips in RTÉ was: who will be the next director general?

The selection process was approached with a meticulousness worthy of the consistory of cardinals that chooses a pope. My lack of reverence for such processes should have made me turn down the chairman's invitation to be a member of the subcommittee to choose a candidate. Such foresight might have avoided the next fireworks on the Authority.

The invitation was obviously not based on my talent for objective judgement. There was simply a need for a member who would give the committee a semblance of political balance. Somebody with experience of programme-making could be a vague advantage, too. By a process of deduction, that person had to be me.

In the mess that was RTÉ, my preference for a person to run the place would have been an outsider of impeccable objectivity and total altruism, one whose least personal concern was money, but who possessed a certain amount of basic common sense. On balance, I would have favoured the good rather than the clever.

One night in November 1996, I said as much on Vincent Browne's radio programme. That is how the row started. Here are my notes of the event:

Thurs. Nov 7th '96

Return from Gael Media recording of *Síbín* for TnaG. Stimulated by liveliness, youth and enthusiasm of crew and performers. Two phone messages: one from director of corporate affairs advising that *Tonight with Vincent Browne* is to discuss new DG position and the chairman has said he wants nothing to do with it.

Second message from RTÉ inviting me to participate in the show.

I think of the dead hand of RTÉ. When a similar matter arose last year, I reserved my right to express my opinions in public whenever I thought it appropriate.

Was the chairman forbidding me to appear on the show? I think not. In such a case he knows I would likely appear. Has he communicated the same message to other members of the subcommittee or am I the only one?

Was he simply saying: "This will be of interest to the subcommittee. Listen to it."

Decide to ring the show anyway. They're on air in 16 seconds. I hang on.

Browne introduces me as a member of the Authority, asks me details about DG job prospects. I emphasise I am not speaking on behalf of Authority and claim to know little or nothing about candidates for DG job etc. (We have interviewed nobody yet).

But I did talk in comparative terms about the BBC and RTÉ and the immense difference in remuneration between the respective director generals, meaning that our selection committee would have to think of a better carrot than money. What I had in mind was this: just as the great John XXIII was able to open a window on the Roman Catholic organisation in the sixties and his successor John Paul II was able to rapidly close it, so the chief executive of any organisation can introduce a period of enlightenment or darkness. And as Brian Farrell once said about John XXIII, he was a disappointment to the cardinals because he fulfilled none of the needs of the beleaguered Church: he was neither brilliant nor diplomatic nor a theologian. To their great chagrin he was merely "holy". It was in these terms, I mused on air, that a chief executive of the major cultural organisation in this country must be measured.

I also dared to say on air, "Any fool can make a profit." I had in mind what the one-time director general of the BBC, Dublin-born Charles Curran, said in 1969: "Any fool can run a majority service with commercials but the problem is to run a comprehensive service." Curran, incidentally, also said that running advertisements "would mean the end of any increase in licence fees and would destroy the principle of public service broadcasting". He was prophetic.

I also said, according to the transcript of the show: "I am just one highly eccentric person in the middle of ten people, so I am just putting down what I personally, in my own tiny area, would like. It has nothing to do with what will ultimately happen."

At the end of the show the offending passage occurs:

> Browne: "What do you think of RTÉ's current affairs programmes?"
> Me: "In general, I am ashamed of RTÉ, by the way."
> Mary Leland (ex-member RTÉ Authority and long ago my production assistant): "That is the value of eccentricity."

I remember it as not a great interview, very waffly on my part, very much kicking to touch; nothing to get excited about. In fact, John Boland, a television critic who was on the same show, commented that my remarks were "very cagey, incredibly mild, almost status quo" and "not the sort of firebrand stuff normally expected from Bob Quinn". My notes show that there existed an opposite impression:

Friday evening: Chairman rings. Appalled. Says he has listened to tape of show over and over. (Why had he to listen to it repeatedly? Was my alleged misdemeanour not obvious, a cut and dried case?) I believe the chairman is trying to be as fair to me as possible. I can imagine the pressure put on him by management and particularly by internal candidates for DG position.

Eventually, he says, he was decided by my saying, "In general I am ashamed of RTÉ." He says that the process of selecting a new DG has been "damaged irreparably" and invites me to "consider my position". He elaborates by saying that prospective candidates who might have heard me would have severe worries about the confidentiality of their applications, CVs, etc., in the hands of such as me. The implication is that I would not respect their confidentiality. There is no evidence to support that [up to now!]. I ask does that mean resign, and he says, "Yes."

The chairman may conceivably have meant my position on the Authority, but I disingenuously interpreted it as an invitation to resign from the subcommittee. I immediately accepted his invitation to step down, but pointed out that such a step might cause more problems than it solved. As it happened, the *Sunday Independent* had a full page account of the matter. They never contacted me. But there were plenty of press comments from RTÉ management, none of them personally attributed. The *Sunday Business Post* printed the names of all the RTÉ candidates. Where did they get them? *The Irish Times* rang me to ask had I been sacked. I said, "Yes," and refused to comment further. They printed the story on the front page. I also refused a comment to both Raidió na Gaeltachta and the *Cork Examiner*.

By this time there had emerged, according to press reports, a shortlist for the grand prize, all drawn from the senior echelon of management. It seemed that nowhere in the real world outside was there any outstanding person interested in such a position. In fact there should have been a note to the advertisement: No Outsiders Need Apply. The experienced Tom Quinn, who, after all, was director of corporate affairs and should know, had warned us of this dimension. He said they rarely got "serious" applications from outside the station. The exception to this was obviously before Tom's time, in 1966, when Conor Cruise O'Brien applied for the job and was not even afforded an interview. Nowadays it seemed that no broadcasting outsider thought the headaches entailed in RTÉ were worth the money – about £80,000 p.a. (now over £100,000 with performance bonuses). Or perhaps the management consultants charging RTÉ £12,000 to find candidates and prepare a shortlist had not the budget to scour the highways and byways for saints?

As business columnist Sheila O'Flanagan has since remarked (*The Irish Times*, 13 October 2000):

> One of the difficulties of replacing a corporate senior executive is whether to recruit from within the company or to cast your net elsewhere. The problem with in-house promotions is that you don't necessarily get the best person for the job that way but you will, in all likelihood, get the most politically astute person.

In the RTÉ situation there was an atavistic attitude inherited from the organisation's origins in the civil service. There the top jobs were still unavailable to any but those who had entered the service immediately on leaving university and thus been properly acculturated. Similarly, in the last quarter century, no outsider has become director general of RTÉ; nor has any chief executive ever had any hands-on experience of programme producing or directing. Less than a third of the fourteen senior managers had such experience. The analogy may be made to a religious order, the election of whose superior is guided subtly by its own congregation – although their decision must ultimately be approved by the pope, in this case the taoiseach of the day.

"Why then do we go through this charade?" I had asked

before I was expunged from the process. "Why not just give Bob Collins the job and save money? He's the obvious candidate from inside." He was certainly the one I favoured.

But we had to go through the public motions.

In getting the chairman to do the distasteful job of dumping me from the subcommittee, the mandarins were testing the authority and nerve of the chairman – whom at that point I still felt deserved support. But it was easier for him to get rid of me than to confront the Executive. I believe he sacrificed me for the best of reasons – the same reason Emperor Constantine adopted Christianity as the official religion of Rome in AD 300 – for the sake of peace. The Executive won hands down. Betty Purcell later told me that although she thought my radio remarks were unwise, I should not have stepped down; the Executive had got its way and now there was nobody with programme experience on the panel. But what was done was done. I stepped aside, not before getting from the chairman my requested note that it was at his express request. All I could now do was try, not so subtly, to warn that decent man of the degree to which he was "going native". I requested him to authorise the RTÉ library to supply me with a number of anthropological and business studies with the following titles:

The Effects of Board versus Managerial Controls, by R.A. Johnson, R.E. Hoskisson and M.A. Hitt (1993).

Chairmen and Chief Executives, an Exploration of their Relationship, by R. Stewart (1991).

Managerial Domination of Boards of Directors . . ., by R. Molz (1988).

Inside/Outside Succession . . . the Pragmatics of Executive Replacement, by D.R. Dalton and I.F. Kesner (1983).

Succession . . . Internal Impediments to Outsider Selection, by A.A. Cannella and M. Lubatkin (1993).

Ambitious middle managers rushed to support their Executive and formally express outrage at my radio comments. The chairman of the RTÉ Managers' Association wrote to Professor Corcoran:

Now that the intitial disgust of the RTÉ Managers' Association at the comments . . . has subsided somewhat, I wish to register in the most forceful manner our abhorrence at the slur cast [etc., etc.] . . . Mr Quinn should make his shameful comments in lodge [*sic!*] . . . If he were a member of [our association] his resignation would by now be accepted.

In an address entitled "Surrendering Without a Struggle" to a Norwegian conference on architecture and design in August 1999, Michael D. Higgins said:

One of the scandals of applied economics is the unpreparedness of middle management for change. Minds that for decades have ceased to ask why they do what they do have doomed themselves to mere systems maintenance.

Betty Purcell reported to the Authority an unofficial straw poll of staff's reaction to my broadcast comments: 60 per cent were against me, but 40 per cent thought I was right to say what I did.

What interested me most about this flurry was that not one single person on the Executive, on the Authority, on the staff or anywhere inside or outside the station ever asked me to state what, precisely, I was ashamed of in RTÉ. It was as if everybody knew, but must not say.

Another detail: I had a call from Brigid Ruane of *The Late Late Show* inviting me to repeat my comments on the show. After twenty-eight years of doing what I hoped were various interesting things like making films and writing books, this was the one pretext they had ever discovered for inviting me on the show again. I refused. The invitation, however, was an insight into the opinion Gay Byrne and the staff had of RTÉ.

At the next meeting of the Authority, there was a heated session and more angry calls from a couple of members for me to resign. I quoted Jim FitzGerald, once head of Drama in RTÉ: never apologise, never explain and never resign. In a kind of toast to Jack Dowling, I said that resignation was one cheque I was not going to give the Authority to cash. I pointed out that since the so-called "irreparable damage" had been swiftly repaired by appointing Garret FitzGerald to fill my vacancy, comment would appear to be superfluous. However, out of courtesy to the slow learners on the Authority, I repeated my free speech defence and endured the consequent fulminations. If you can't do the time, don't do the crime. At lunch when I told Des Geraghty I was not a political animal, he grinned and said, "Don't be coddin' yourself. You know the first and most important principle of politics: never resign."

It was a recurrent point of friction. Did a member of the RTÉ Authority automatically lose his/her identity and freedom of expression as a citizen on assumption of this exalted role? In my case, should I take a vow of silence on the only subject in which I had some kind of specialisation, i.e. broadcasting? The chairman himself had said in July 1995 that he regarded the Authority as being the public trustees of RTÉ. Such noble sentiments were often expressed, but in practice, in my experience, were rapidly digested and emerged as flatulence.

Was our function on the Authority solely to protect the organisation, ensure the survival of RTÉ on the principle "my country right or wrong"? Or was it to protect the public ownership of broadcasting, if necessary from the organisation itself? The latter approach was the one I favoured, for the following long-held reason:

All organisations, public or private, have two basic functions: one is their manifest function – in RTÉ's case the stated role of development and survival of public broadcasting. The second is equally present and is called the latent function. This is fuelled by what I refer to as "dynamic conservatism", that memorable expression coined by Denis Donoghue in the late seventies when he delivered the BBC Reith Lectures. It refers to the phenomenon of using all available energy to preserve the status quo. It is an expression which I use on all possible occasions.

So what does RTÉ's latent function actually entail?

It is to maintain the employment of over 2,000 and, more than by implication, the salaries and status of its senior executives. In this interpretation, the business of public broadcasting, although manifest, is essentially a supportive function. This does not imply that this function is forgotten; not at all. Any organisation under siege will first seek self-preservation. Otherwise how can it perform the function which justifies its existence? In this matter RTÉ is like politics, where the aims of the practitioners may begin idealistically but in many cases become a pragmatic struggle to attain and retain power, money and status at all costs.

There is, as Garret FitzGerald once said to me, a vestigial sense of public service in politicians, but, being human, the ego is a considerable ingredient in the menu. Which combination of traits presumably was why he accepted the offer to replace me on the panel to choose a director general.

The chairman issued a statement to the staff which distanced the Authority from my sentiments. In essence, it reassured the staff that their managers had the full support of the Authority. What else could he say? Especially since his statement bore the hallmarks of Executive drafting.

So far, I realise, this may seem like a full frontal assault on RTÉ, a kind of sour grapes at not getting my way. All I am trying to illustrate is the truth of what Jack Dowling said to me over thirty years ago. It should be carved in stone over every office in the civilised world: "The nicest people do the most monstrous things in the nicest possible way."

The people in RTÉ are the friendliest, most intelligent group of people it has been my privilege to know over a period of forty years. I have hardly had a personal altercation with a single worker there. So what am I trying to say?

My point is that each of us is individually responsible, at least to the extent of our comprehension, for our part in the great scheme of things – if there is any such scheme.

This is not romanticism; it is necessary for the survival of our individual and collective humanity. Essentially it accepts that we are all trundling towards the scaffold, most of us in resigned and often resentful silence, fearful of our jobs, our mortgages, our superiors. But the quality of a society is proportionate to the number of people who feel free to say openly: "Hang on a second! Are we going in the right direction towards the scaffold?" It is easy to say with hindsight, as generations of journalists have discovered, that we were on the wrong path all the time. But the contemporary yelp from the middle of the crowd of "Stop the cart, I want to get off!" is usually dismissed as crankiness, querulousness, obstructionism, eccentricity, fundamentalism, nationalism or plain stupidity – take your pick.

The substance which must ultimately be attended to is the internal and external forces with which all of us actors have a love/hate relationship and within whose suffocating embrace we must strive to think and act independently. That we are invariably and ultimately unsuccessful (death takes care of that) is beside the point. As MacMurphy said in Ken Kesey's masterpiece, *One Flew Over the Cuckoo's Nest*, when, in the film version, he failed to lift an impossibly heavy fridge, "At least I tried."

Joe Barry's successor would have to be an exceptional person to handle the complexities of the director generalship of RTÉ. For instance, apart from the viper within its bosom – the commercial imperatives which its dual funding mandate involves – RTÉ is a good paradigm of the forces that have in recent times, consciously or inadvertently, effected for good or ill the destruction of Ireland as it was. Within that paradigm, many otherwise intelligent people slavishly and unquestioningly followed a so-called neo-liberal market agenda. There was a seemingly endless civil war in the North of Ireland where propaganda was 50 per cent of the struggle. The extraordinary institutional achievements of this young republic were seen as underpinning the Provo campaign in the North. Because this guerrilla campaign was fearfully regarded in the South as threatening the political status quo here – and especially its economy – there was no shortage of opportunists to collaborate in the destruction of those things imagined to be underpinning the nationalist struggle in the North.

At least the new DG would not have to also contend with the "Stickies" (a breakaway group from republicanism) which had a disproportionate influence on current affairs programmes in the eighties. Gerald Barry of RTÉ said as much on RTÉ in 1990. Their bundled targets included the Provos, the Catholic Church, the Irish language movement, Irish neutrality, especially everything rural, any aspiration to economic self-sufficiency, all echoes of the aspirations of 1916; in brief, nationalism in all its suspected forms.

But it is hard to kill a bad thing. On 14 January 1997 *Léargas* produced a fine programme on the IRA raid on Brookeborough RUC station which had taken place on New Year's Eve 1956. The TAM rating registered 13 per cent, the largest audience in years for an Irish language programme. The interest Irish people have in their country and its chequered history cannot be dismissed by namecalling.

The US is the most nationalistic country I have experienced. I have filmed its schoolchildren, hands on hearts, swearing allegiance to the flag first thing in the school morning. Its principal ally, Britain, invented and invokes jingoism when it is expedient – as in the Falklands in 1982. It is useful to consider the 1999 remarks in *The Sunday Times* of Mr Nicholas Tate, for ten years the chief adviser to the British government on the schools' curriculum:

> What we need therefore is for it to be intellectually respectable once again to signal that the *nation state* is a desirable focus for our loyalties. We need to believe that a sense of identity with the *nation*, however understated, indirect and *even ironical*, is essential for the future of democracy and for social cohesion. We need the ideal that

English, as well as British, identity is not an ethnic matter but involves a sense of community among all those who were born in this country, have chosen to live here and are committed to it as their long-term home. *This sense of identity has nothing to do with jingoism, racism or xeno-phobia* [all my italics].

What would the new director general's attitude be to the fact that in recent years Irish citizens had been encouraged to repress similar sentiments at home. It has appeared to be an essential step in our wooing investment from monoliths with whom we share a common language. In this context, what proposals would a new director general have for RTÉ to maintain the vestiges of a unique cultural entity? These are the hard questions I might have asked the candidates.

In such a morass, must one be either a fool or insanely ambitious to aspire to the job of director general of RTÉ? Is it why most sane people in RTÉ keep their heads down and try to do their jobs as efficiently as possible without being absorbed into an ambitious rat race, with its plea-sures and pitfalls? The trouble, as actress Lily Tomlin observed, with being in the rat race is that even if you win, you're still a rat.

Unfortunately for all my theorising, Bob Collins, who in January 1997 in the Burlington Hotel was introduced to us as the successful director general designate of RTÉ, was sane, certainly no fool and, in my experience, not a rat. It would take all his diplomatic skill, subtlety and clarity of mind to navigate through the quagmire.

It was probably asking too much to expect him to be "holy" as well.

A NEW BROOM

April is the cruellest month, breeding
Lilacs out of the dead land.
T.S. Eliot, *The Waste Land*

In early April 1997 in the Montrose Hotel in Dublin 4, there was a private farewell dinner for the outgoing director general, Joe Barry. The RTÉ Authority was assembled for its first exclusively informal gathering in nearly two years. People, I thought, might even let their hair down for once.

I sat beside Des Geraghty and opposite Garret FitzGerald. I mentioned to Des that in the present state of national affairs he must have his work cut out protecting the workers' interests. He said that his main problem was trying to give the union back to the workers. I think he was being ironic, but I can't be sure. I could never follow the subtleties of Des Geraghty's mind, nor indeed the intricacies of trade unionism in general, whose largest organisations have made £17 million in the last few years by investing their funds in essentially capitalist enterprises. When the closure of the Japanese Asahi factory in Mayo was referred to at an Authority meeting, Geraghty said the workers had approached the matter in a hopelessly naive manner, as if they were bargaining at a cattle fair. He objected to RTÉ programme presenters referring to public representatives collectively and disparagingly as "the politicians". He was right, in the sense that politicians are rarely distinguished as left/right, conservative, socialist, neo-liberal, nationalist, etc. The collective noun is handier – and sloppier. I also agreed with Geraghty when he once suggested that RTÉ paid less programmatic attention to the workers' normal perspective on society than it did to that of big business. Still, the Programme for Prosperity and Fairness seemed to have forced this radical man into becoming a member of the establishment, whether he was comfortable there or not. In the opinion (*The Irish Times*, 14 November 2001) of UCD sociologist Kieran Allen, "The aim and achievement of social partnership [the PPF] was to disarm the labour movement by co-opting its leadership."

Garret FitzGerald and I had an amiable conversation about archaeology. He said that a genetic survey showed that 95 per cent of Irish genes were unchanged since the stone age. I cannot be certain whether he mentioned this as a tribute to an innate national consistency or as a sly jab at our neolithic habits of thought. We then discussed his collection of train tickets and other memorabilia. He assured me that I could not possibly have travelled by tram in the early fifties from Rathgar to St Stephen's Green for a penny, nor been admitted to the Green Cinema for fourpence; the cinema, he assured me, must have been the Princess in Rathmines. He thus demolished one of my fondest boasts. The conversation moved to things of which this country might be proud. He said that successive Irish governments had a more humane legislative record than most others.

I agreed and remarked that Fr Des Wilson sang our praises on this and other matters in his book *An End to Silence*. Garret responded with what seemed to me a cavalier dismissal of the radical priest.

It was the wrong thing to say to me. I had met Fr Wilson years before in the context of religious programmes when he had said, approximately, "The poor might always be with us, but only because we are utterly selfish." It seemed to me an impeccable analysis of the situation.

We sat down to eat, and as the wine flowed I realised that I was talking even more than Garret FitzGerald, so much so that the ex-taoiseach impatiently blurted out, "Can nobody else get a word in edgewise?" I wondered was this a first for him. Our raised voices attracted glances from the polite end of the table. Without the restraining influence of the chairman, I fear I must have seemed like John Milton's "Belial, flowing with wine and insolence".

It came to a stage where I was telling Garret that I had happily released Cyril Cusack from a film shoot for a day in 1977. The actor wanted to travel to Dublin and vote against "the Heavy Gang" coalition government in which Garret was minister for foreign affairs. I said I regretted that I didn't have the time to do the same myself. So much had his government disgusted fair-minded people that anything, even Fianna Fáil and its ludicrous promises (which almost bankrupted the country), was preferable. In response to some snide remark about Cusack, I pointed out that he was a devout Catholic. "Ah yes," said Garret dismissively, "but he was a Fianna Fáil Catholic." He was not joking. Then neither, at that stage, was I.

It illustrated for me the coincidence of attitudes between aristocratic English Catholicism (i.e. the Duke of Norfolk school) and its Irish equivalent, Castle Catholicism; both can perform acrobatics in their membership of the Universal Church to justify their despite for traditional Irish Catholicism and its imagined peasant roots. It had no such roots. Our recent Jansenism was imported by the national bourgeoisie in the nineteenth century and imposed on the peasants. I liked FitzGerald but was careful of his politics. The only "region" of Ireland he seemed to be interested in was the North, and his obsessional *bêtes noires* were unambiguously Fianna Fáil, meaning Charles J. Haughey, and Sinn Féin. Obsessions, like love, can unbalance a person's judgement.

I got my final clue to Garret's attitudes in the Seán Ó Mordha documentary series on the history of the state, *Seven Ages,* in March 2000. Garret confirmed that he and his wife-to-be had canvassed for the "Commonwealth Party" – as Fine Gael was then unashamedly known – in the 1940s. He declared himself to be quite taken aback when in 1949 his own party leader, speaking in Canada, declared his intention of calling the Free State a republic. Garret felt that the declaration made possible rapprochement between North and South even more difficult. It took him, Garret said, a long time to get used to the idea of a "republic".

It struck me that while Haughey was once imprudent enough to call the North of Ireland "a failed entity", FitzGerald may have had the same opinion of the independent South. Thus perhaps did the Civil War live on in its older children.

The conversation also moved on.

Joe Barry had previously asked me to say a few words at his farewell party. So I did, I think gladly, perhaps even a bit fulsomely. Later, when he was given a big going-away party by the staff and asked me why I had not turned up, I realised it was the staff occasion he had in mind, not this private Authority occasion. I regretted the misunderstanding, realising that he properly paid more attention to the good opinion of the staff than to the opinion of the Authority.

The new director general, Bob Collins, assumed what he described to us as the poisoned chalice on 25 April 1997.

It was the culmination of a process which began seriously some years before when I, a total outsider, noticed that in his public appearances he had dispensed with his thick-lensed spectacles and replaced them with contact lenses. He had also acquired a new hairstyle and took to wearing decent suits. It was a sign that he was either in love or focussing his ambitions, or possibly both.

His appointment as director general was almost a foregone conclusion, and I welcomed it. As I earlier said, there were no overwhelming outside candidates. Collins had regularly revealed to the Authority the subtlety of his mind, his mastery of organisational affairs, his public-speaking ability. Above all, he had the greatest advantage any candidate can have: we had grown accustomed to his face. He had sat beside Joe Barry as assistant DG for our previous eighteen months. He also happened to speak perfect Irish which, although no guarantee of sanctity, might be useful in running the most powerful cultural organisation in the state. I had certainly a healthy and friendly respect for him, a view shared by the other members. We felt we were in the best available hands – albeit a safe pair of hands. Despite the subsequent occasional friction between us, I still believe that.

Bob Collins has an astute understanding of the politics of survival; on his appointment he created prestigious new positions in the firing line for his nearest unsuccessful rivals: Joe Mulholland as managing director of television and Liam Miller as director of broadcasting developments. The first job attracted all programming criticism (of 718 letters sent to the director of programmes' office in the previous December and January, 375 were complaints). Liam Miller's new job included future digital development, which also turned out to be a can of worms.

Although commanding an enviable fluency in Irish, it would be superficial to describe Collins as a Gaelic Revivalist. He is too complex a person to be put in such a jaded category. He is certainly a lover of the language but does not display the passion that can sometimes accompany such idealism. I cannot, for instance, imagine his joining a mob in the Mansion House to shout down members of the old Language Freedom Movement. He might smile knowingly and imply that there are many ways of skinning a cat. Indeed, if I were to be asked what is the strongest impression the man imparts, it would be: attention to detail combined with steely control – both self-control and control of every situation. He leaves nothing to chance. In October 1996 he was interviewed by Seosamh Ó Cuaig on *Ath-Mhaidin*, the RnaG current affairs programme, about the availability of the new Teilifís na Gaeilge. Ó Cuaig lives in Conamara, twenty miles west of the new station's location. He asked Collins several hard questions, including: "Will I be able to receive the signal?" (There was considerable apprehension, as I have detailed, about the signal's availability to the Irish-speaking communities.) Collins assured him that he would. But afterwards Ó Cuaig was quietly spoken to to by one of his immediate bosses and informed that one didn't interrogate the assistant director general of RTÉ as if he were any old Joe Soap.

I heard Bob Collins defending RTÉ on 14 January 2000 on *Liveline*, Joe Duffy's phone-in show. His appearance was the culmination of a fortnight-long charm offensive mounted by the public relations department to counter the reaction to their unfortunate Newgrange solstice and New Year's Eve millennium offerings. Collins' was a carefully controlled interview, meaning that all looney callers were filtered out so that the interview could be constructive. This is normal practice on "public access" programmes.

On this day the filter system worked well: every questioner who passed the preliminary phone test was measured, positive, reasonable and at heart supportive of the RTÉ endeavour. They were all decent middle-class punters; no aggressive callers allowed. Thus it was easy for Collins to field every critique with fluency, confidence and persuasiveness. It suddenly dawned on me why Collins was the perfect representative for RTÉ: well-meaning, civilised, intelligent, a safe pair of hands, measured tones, a master of his brief – and ultimately defensive. Exactly like much of RTÉ's output. No one could possibly be annoyed or find fault with his remarks. Also, I'm afraid, nobody could be enthused by them. And there was certainly nobody allowed on air to attack him or at least liven the interview up.

I heard that one of Lenin's favourite expressions was, "Trust is good; control is better." I fear I did not make his new job easier for Bob Collins. I decided to strike while the iron was hot.

At the very first meeting under his new stewardship in April 1997, I unilaterally declared that mine and his predecessor Joe Barry's truce on child-targeted commercials was ended. I prepared and circulated a paper reminding the new director general and the Authority of "Santa's Little Sweatshops" as they were called by Trócaire. I asked that my paper be read into the minutes. The chairman refused. I asked for a debate. The chairman said he would give it ten minutes. Betty Purcell frantically tried to avoid me getting the bum's rush by proposing we have a full debate at the next meeting. The trouble for Betty's diplomacy was that from meeting to meeting I did not know if I would resign in disgust or not, so I could not risk procrastination. It might be the last ten minutes I would have. It was better than nothing. I launched into the attack.

For every overfed child in the West, there is an undernourished child in Asia. I quoted Trócaire's litany of abuse of women and children in toy factories from India to Vietnam: how a worker lost an arm and was given £15 – and sacked; how 200 workers painting toys for McDonalds in Vietnam had been poisoned by the fumes; how Disney paid twelve cents an hour to Hawaiian workers sewing Pocahontas pyjamas; how in Bangkok only 800 of 4,000 workers were unionised; how a Chinese worker would have to work for three months to earn as much as some of us spend on toys for a single child at Christmas (£150); how we spent £60 million in Ireland alone on such toys; how 60 per cent of the toys and clothes we bought our children were produced in these conditions. I then outlined the TV marketing techniques used to persuade our children to pester us to buy these products and once again accused RTÉ of colluding with this whole sordid business. My prose was, as Lelia Doolan said long ago, muscular.

Bill Attley was incensed. He pointed out that the trade unions and Trócaire were actually cooperating to put diplomatic pressure on such manufacturers. I was aware of this delicate, reformist and, in my opinion, harmless approach. They were saying to consumers: continue buying the toys but make the manufacturers aware of your concerns. As if, once the purchase had been made, the manufacturers cared tuppence about the consumer's guilt feelings. It was like those who said many years ago that sanctions against South Africa's apartheid policy would not work. Trade unions which once refused to handle South African goods now seemed to me to be more concerned about their SIPTU members' jobs at Milton and Bailey, toymaker Hasbro's subsidiary in Waterford, than any human rights violations by its subcontractors thousands of miles away.

I reminded the Authority of RTÉ's treatment of Trócaire's campaign not five months before: how Trócaire had been given generous coverage in the print media for the scandal but that there was hardly a mention on Radio Teilifís Éireann. In fact the *Gerry Ryan Show* initially expressed interest but, having kept a Trócaire spokesperson waiting at the end of a phone for a week, the interview never happened. I had personally brought the Trócaire campaign to the attention of the new, young *Late Late Show* producer, Cillian Fennell, and asked would it be mentioned on the Toy Show. He said no. Word would appear to have come down from on high: steer clear of this awkward subject.

The unruffleable Bob Collins lost his cool at my use of the term "imaginative paedophilia". He said he found it "personally offensive". I should really have modified the term to "paedophilia of the imagination", which would have been more precise. Redlich echoed the DG and demanded that I withdraw my intemperately worded proposal. Equally intemperately I told her to go to hell.

The chairman hastily brought the discussion to a close.

There would be no further action by the RTÉ Authority on the children front.

It did not stop me becoming a total pain in the posterior. For the next five months I brought the subject up at every opportunity. It became a joke on the Authority. "I think I see a chink here," I would say, and they would know precisely what was coming. On one occasion Authority member Des Geraghty said that we underestimated the toughness and resilience of children; that he did not think TV commercials did kids a damn bit of harm. The same opinion was repeated by the chairman and his director general, Bob Collins, in my presence. At least they were consistent. A couple of other members were not so sure. Occasionally Pat Hume and Betty Purcell would bravely support my position. But we were outnumbered.

What always struck me as odd was that if child-targeted commercials were considered to be absolutely harmless, why had an organisation like RTÉ suddenly submitted to pressure from one person – myself – in 1995 and banished commercials from the pre-school hour of programmes as well as cutting out sponsorship from all childrens' programmes? In his previous role as assistant DG, Bob Collins had personally researched and written that compromise. And why, if there was no harm, did Garret FitzGerald and Anne Tannahill agree with mine and Betty Purcell's proposal that a moratorium should be maintained on childrens' toy advertisements for the Christmas period? Why now was the very possibility of "harm" denied? It seemed to me that what had happened was that most of the Authority members had become tired of my interventions and relied entirely on the chairman to signal to them whatever the Executive wanted. In less than two years, most of the members had realised the vague immensities in which they were involved, had followed the chairman's lead and gone native. Betty Purcell and myself were simply nuisances.

The new director general could now slap me down with a simple "No" whenever I tried to reopen the debate. I would grin ruefully and harden my resolve. I wrote to *Access*, the RTÉ staff bulletin, giving them a blow by blow account; it was cleverly editorialised to show the Authority in a good light. I addressed the Sligo Social Services unit, the Galway One World Centre, briefed several newspapers, and in general fulfilled the Executive's view of me as a loose cannon.

The final straw for me was on 3 November 1997 when an RTÉ news bulletin had a breathless report by Rachel English on the likelihood of Teletubbies being in short supply. It seemed to me that such a report would inevitably exacerbate the frenzy already stirred up by advertising. That our news service should unthinkingly become an actor in the activity was, I wrote to the chairman, intolerable.

Therefore, on Bob Collins' first Christmas on the job, my gift to him was to publicly suspend myself from the RTÉ Authority for the entire Christmas period.

While I was absent, on 5 December, Betty Purcell was at least able to produce an edition of her *Divided World* programme which featured a report on the above well-intentioned campaign, how trade unions and human rights organisations had launched another pre-Christmas campaign against Disney over the huge profits they were making in the West while paying low wages to workers in the sweatshops of the Third World. At least somebody was taking the matter seriously – and RTÉ and the trade unions were covering their backs. Soon after Betty Purcell's tenure on the Authority expired, in May 2000, her *Divided World* programme was, without discussion, dropped. This was not long after it had won a prestigious European Humanitarian Award.

In the meantime, the RTÉ Sales Department remained oblivious. Its relentless Christmas targeting of children continued.

CHILDREN OF THE TIGER

You've got to be taught before it's too late
Before you are six, or seven or eight
. . . you've got to be carefully taught.
Rodgers and Hammerstein, *South Pacific*

The following February, 1998, I decided to visit a part of the Third World – India. It was unimaginably far from the RTÉ boardroom.

At midnight I sat with my twenty-four-year-old son beside the tiny swimming pool of the Royal Heritage Hotel in Goa. We had been transported there via a squalid charter flight where we were packed in as tightly as sardines. But three weeks in India had relaxed us into the non-aggressive pace of the subcontinent. It was an uncomfortable place for a conscience, especially when in Bombay late at night we had nearly stepped on a naked infant on the pavement, strategically placed there by its supplicant mother. We were constantly reminded of the scale of poverty and deprivation and never came home with change in our pockets.

We were discussing our various impressions when sounds of revelry from within the kitchen made us turn. They prefaced a young Indian man being frogmarched, fully clothed, towards the pool. He was dumped in. The British tourist who had single-handedly executed the manoeuvre laughed triumphantly. The Indian surfaced, rubbing his eyes, smiling ruefully. Then another tourist of the same nationality appeared with a similarly smiling staff member, who was also thrown into the pool. The Indians did not resist. The tourists were slightly drunk. There was then a chase in and around the premises for a member of the staff who had so far eluded this celebration. He was finally captured and, also smiling, thrown into the pool. The tourists were young enough to be squaddies or football hooligans, the Indians their contemporaries. It was shocking for two Irishmen to observe the performance. No, we did not rush to the natives' defence. We were of too philosophic and non-interventionist a disposition. After all, the British Raj had invented modern India. The *lingua franca* was English. Perhaps it was some traditional rite of post-colonialism. Our minds were already overloaded with experiences from this extraordinary country. Nothing could surprise us. But we did idly wonder why on earth the Indians could smile at their fate? Was this the lasting heritage of Gandhi? Perhaps these young Indians, citizens of a thousand million strong country with a history that long predated Europe, were confident that this touristic imperialism would also pass?

When I came home, I was reminded of that incident as I read a book, *The Impact of Television Advertising on Children*, by two female Indian sociologists, Namita Unnikrishnan and Shailaja Bajpai. The two women had interviewed 730 children in Delhi between 1990 and 1995. Their findings analysed the sudden impact of TVs, video recorders, multichannel satellite TV and Doordarshan (the Indian public broadcaster) on a largely impoverished people. Slum families that have hardly the price of their next meal go into debt to purchase these dream gadgets. They detect and illegally hack into an electricity source and hang satellite dishes precariously on their roof – if they have one.

The researchers pointed out that television had suddenly become the fairy tale of this unfortunate underclass, that consumerism was the new religion of the day and that its most devout followers were children. The vision of the good life being drilled into viewers' minds by TV advertising in India was reported to be better internalised by children than by the older generation.

> In this context [the sociologists summarised], advertising *does* have an ideological function in that it seeks to create an environment conducive to a particular interest group – that of manufacturers and marketeers – by altering people's perception of themselves and of reality in order to be able to orient the large Indian market to their products.

I remembered the squalor of an endless shanty town in Bombay. I did not blame these people for grasping at wisps of another "reality". For the duration of endlesss soap operas, they could imagine being well-fed, well-dressed, beautiful, clean, secularised – and white. They could imaginatively dwell in marble halls, in a different kind of Nirvana. As I read this disturbing book in the safety of Conamara, I selfishly thought: at least we westerners are at the producing end of these fantasies; we are the arrow, not the target.

The following morning I was woken early by the screeching of a cartoon. My own youngest child sat within arm's length of the TV, already sharing the fantasy world of his impoverished Indian counterpart. I waited and noticed that he paid more avid attention to the commercials than he did to the programme. The only difference between him and Indian kids is that if he demands something his parents may be able to afford it. He has not yet learned to take me seriously when I insist that my children may watch, but not listen to, the commercials. The ears are our most sensitive organ of apperception. Over the past thirty years, my five other children have become familiar with my war cry: "Turn Down the Lies".

I, old fogey, have not yet submitted to the coercion that makes us all tentative in our opinions; I still maintain my ancient stance of resisting the commercialisation of television. As must be obvious by now, I have never entertained for one minute the neo-liberal apologia which I imagine goes as follows: TV is the great transcendent unifier and saviour of the human race and the much vilified commercial is its earthly agent. Peoples separated by distance, language, culture and levels of economics are all televisually absorbed in the same aspirations towards wealth, comfort and possessions. This inexorable process must lead to some, however debased, worldwide community of shared dreams. The religious and political tensions, as well as the cultural and linguistic barriers that have for millennia separated people, may at last be dissolved by ordinary and identical aspirations towards plenty. Balkanisation will be arrested and world peacekeepers will no longer have to enter the fray and bomb the warring tribes into peaceful coexistence. This has to be the stated agenda of all western entrepeneurs, capitalists, smoked-salmon socialists, limousine liberals, presidents, pop stars, poets, TV personalities and the rest of us who follow their example.

Subsequent to writing the above fantasy, I came across the following speech by a Mr Joe Cappo, senior vice-president of the advertising agency, Crain Communications, which he delivered to the annual convention of the International Advertising Association in 1999. He discussed the phenomenon of the global market in terms of the wealthiest class, the 10 per cent most affluent segment of population in almost every country in the world:

> The remarkable feature of these people is that they are so similar in their consumption patterns. They drive the same brand of cars; they wear the same designer clothes; drink the same brands of whiskey and beer; stay at the same hotels; vacation at the same resorts; shop at the same high-end retail establishments; use the same credit cards. This same kind of commonality of buying patterns and brand awareness is filtering down to the middle class, and will eventually affect the less affluent. Not that they will be able

to afford the luxurious brands of the upper classes but they will have their own brands to bring them together. It is not only advertising that is doing this. It is the continued growth of global brands. Yes, it will lead to greater understanding in the years to come if only because we are more alike than we have ever imagined.

Apart from being repelled by the prospect of such a ghastly world, I disagree with such a rationale, for reasons analogous to Noam Chomsky's dismissal of the internet as a harbinger of universal prosperity. Chomsky pointed out that the majority of this planet's citizens have never even used a telephone. Ultimately and sadly, I contemplate the imaginative life of my own children being as exploited and debased by the likes of Mr Cappo, as is that of their poor Indian equivalents. They are all engaged in intensive courses in consumerism.

In this scenario, the first flaw that might strike even a casual observer is that less than 20 per cent of human beings already consume more than 80 per cent of the planet's resources. If everybody on this planet finally achieves the same level of growth, prosperity and consumption, a simple calculation, capable of being understood by a five year old, shows that the realisation of the hypothetical aim of everybody – especially those teeming Indian slum-dwellers – achieving the western level of consumption must result in a chewing up and spitting out of 400 per cent of the planet's natural and fossil resources. Such a percentage may seem a perfect abstract aspiration to an economist who cannot see that it is at the same time a nonsense – and a perilous nonsense.

The ultimate logic of this agenda is that, having turned this tiny sphere of real estate floating in space into a rubbish dump, we may find another planet capable of sustaining human life. This is because we all sense that our species has gone too far, that the planet is already beginning to object to our depredations, that Lovelock's Gaia principle makes sense. And nobody is listened to when they shout stop; least of all eco-warriors, who are regarded simply as inconveniences to be locked up. Even my small household annually produces 126 bags of rubbish which mainly constitute just the packaging on our purchases. A couple of years ago, in an effort to bring this wastefulness home, on a live broadcast on TG4, I had the opportunity to shoulder on to the set one of these rubbish bags. The presenter initially thought I was pretending to be Santa Claus until I dumped the nauseous mess all over the studio floor. After an embarrassed moment, everybody decided I was joking, and we discussed the Third World in a civilised fashion. I bury the daily waste from my kitchen in the garden.

Unlike prophets of doom in the past, every thinking person on this planet now has evidence of our carelessness and feels helpless. We have intimations of its apparent unstoppability thanks to people like Richard Douthwaite in his *The Growth Illusion*. Even Garret FitzGerald (*The Irish Times*, 29 January 2000) is now becoming nervous about unlimited growth. He rightly says that expansion was necessary in the fifties and sixties – he was was on the government committee which reported on the subject in 1967. But not now. We have enough. "Those driving our national train now [Fianna Fáil, naturally] seem to want to run us into the buffers by continuing to maximise economic growth." The following November Garret was becoming more desperate: "Money is being wasted on generating more external investment than we can accommodate"; and "Our present growth rate is well beyond anything that we can handle comfortably. The overheating of our economy . . . [etc.]."

The trouble is that the horse has bolted, and all Garret's tears cannot close the stable door. The mindset that demands growth is greedy and is decreasingly restrained by political ideologies or optimum cut-off levels. It is not susceptible to logistical or statistical dampening. Our consumer culture is now so inextricably interlaced with our jobs, our cars, our mortgages, our international political and economic alignments that it has become a Faustian pact. The Irish are already helplessly paying the price with the epidemic of materialism that has so suddenly over-whelmed their green and pleasant island.

So where did it start, and how do we at least moderate this rough beast in the corner that is inciting us to consume ourselves, to become, as Gillies MacBain, organic farmer and philosopher, put it, mice sailing on a ship of cheese?

I am not oblivious to the much-trumpeted economic success of Ireland and am conscious of the fact that my generational perspective forces me to look at it suspicious-ly, and to be heartened when I hear there is a slowdown in our economic growth. The growth in employment was phenomenal in the past ten years. The once-quiet road out-side my home in Conamara is at times now like the Naas dual-carriageway at rush hour. There are large clues as to how we have achieved this extraordinary situation. It starts at a most fundamental level.

In the summer of 1998, out of the blue, my then three year old demanded a drink called Sunny Delight. We, his parents, had never heard of it. The drink was supplied. A month later he demanded "Sunny D".

"You mean 'Sunny Delight', don't you?" we asked.

"No," he said, "Sunny D. Thats what the man on the TV calls it."

I later learned that not more than 5 per cent of this liquid garbage made by Procter & Gamble is nutritional fruit juice. The rest is water, sugar and chemicals. It sells more than Coca-Cola in these islands. Recently I read that it can turn children's skin yellow.

The advertisement did not warn us of this. But then, when did anybody last see an ad for junk food that warned that monosodium glutamate can result in brain damage and obesity? Freedom of speech does not extend to the dissem-ination of such truths. *Adbusters Magazine*, published in Vancouver, is essential reading for anybody concerned with these questions. One of its cartoons illustrated the fact that you may loudly declare "Buy Vulgar's Coffee", but to shout "Boycott Vulgar's Coffee" is forbidden on the grounds that such a statement is "political". The major networks in the United States refuse to feature the *Adbuster* anti-commercials. In 1996 I urged the RTÉ chairman to take out a subscription to this magazine. Nothing was done. I later deposited one of my copies in the RTÉ library.

Everything starts with our children. We try to teach them and they ignore us. But we do something and they mimic us perfectly. We sit for hours in front of a blinking screen and they do the same. We discuss the plots and characters in sitcoms and our children can correct us. We hum those catchy tunes that go along with TV commercials and our children know them better than "Jingle Bells". We are now not so much *Homo sapiens* as Homer Simpsons. We are an American underclass.

But as well as watching our adult programmes, the kids have their own programmes which we certainly do not watch. So the children watch twice as much television as their parents, and here is the rub: parents have little or no idea what their children are watching. I recently asked a classroom of under-twelve children in Kiltiernan, County Galway, this specific question: "Do your parents watch your TV programmes with you?" There was a united and derisive chorus of "No!"

This suggests that busy parents have little or no grasp of what ideas, images, cultures, values, intimations or persuasions their little innocents are absorbing from television. Perhaps the exceptions to this are the unemployed and the "relatively" poor in Ireland whose TV licence fees are paid by the Department of Social Welfare. The welfare recipients may have some insight into the problem, but the views of such no-hopers are usually ignored in these thrusting, successful times.

The big secret that has emerged to rationalise this child exploitation is the following:

There Is No Such Thing As Childhood

According to a psychology lecturer on the staff of Exeter University, our concept of childhood is a fiction. The idea of innocent, guillible kids is a romantic Victorian ideal. This academic's name is Dr Brian Young and he often speaks at seminars organised by the advertising industry. The theory is that we really do not know the precise effects of advertising on children.

In September 1998 in London, a conference of marketeers was organised in Simpson's on the Strand. The title of the conference was "Marketing to Kids". Though Dr Young has claimed, with the usual academic modesty, that the subject needs much more research, he was scheduled to tell the assembly precisely how children at different ages understand marketing communications, what children want and why, the significance of peer pressure, having the right stuff and how to communicate at the age level of children.

Among the other speakers were representatives of Ogilvy & Mather UK, Rainbow Productions Ltd, Saatchi & Saatchi, Hill & Knowlton (Lifestyle Division), Siebert Head Ltd, Mattel UK, the Cartoon Network and Net Profit. These are all leaders in the field of child-targeted marketing.

Among the topics were: The future of kids' promotions; Developing an internal communications platform which delivers for kids, for clients; Analysing the impact characters have on the young consumer; Aiming for the ultimate child-orientated experience; Playground cred, playground speak, playground ownership; Catching the children's eye; The role packaging plays to attract a young customer; Creating brand awareness . . . in toy stores; Pester power – how young children are drawn to picking up products on display; Children . . . leave them wanting more . . . and so on and depressingly on. I immediately distributed copies of this schedule to each member of the RTÉ Authority. There was no reaction.

At the time of writing, Dr Brian Young is chair of the School Ethics Committee at the University of Exeter. His web page says that he is also part of a group that studies animal behaviour such as feeding and foraging in rodents and birds. He is well qualified to talk in behaviourist terms about children's responses to TV commercials.

I first heard Dr Young speaking at a seminar in the Dublin Institute of Technology. The chairman of the RTÉ Authority, Professor Corcoran, introduced his fellow academic, and it was interesting to me how little his views clashed with Dr Young's. Indeed, later the chairman wrote to me personally and with his usual unfailing courtesy to convey the same opinion: that we must not become over-concerned about the impact of child-targeted commercialism. At the seminar in question, Professor Corcoran opened his remarks by saying, "I am particularly frustrated by the lack of debate on issues concerning the media and children in this country." He cannot say that I did not try to open such debates on the RTÉ Authority.

The point is that it is convenient for an academic like Dr Brian Young to describe human concepts of childhood as naive, outdated and inappropriate in the modern world. In other words, that children are not innocent; they have a kind of native cunning; they know what they want; they are not easily fooled; they are really miniature adults at best, at worst small animals capable of being conditioned. Just as Des Geraghty implied.

It is extraordinary that in the twenty-first century the same justifications for the exploitation of children are those which were used by Victorians to turn infants into chimney sweeps and factory and mine workers. Further, if one applies this concept of childhood to the decades of shame in Ireland when children were mercilessly and sexually abused in institutions, one would be not far from understanding why precisely such scandals happened and were allowed to go on for so long. This concept of childhood is an abdication of the responsibility of all adults to protect the weak, the innocent, the vulnerable and the young under our care.

Child abuse of the sexual kind may still be going on in Ireland, for all we know. Other examples of the abuse of innocence in the form of social neglect are daily paraded through its courts. Certainly, the abuse known as child-targeted commercials went generally unquestioned for thirty years in Ireland. A 1992 Australian advertisers' report on the subject said, "a cyclical dynamic of media criticism of advertising relating to peak advertising periods such as Christmas was noted in Ireland; however, no interest in the issue has so far been signalled". Joe Mulholland, ex-managing director, RTÉ television, admitted to me in autumn 2000, that he had only just found out – after five years of my campaigning – how large a political issue the matter had become.

The parents of young children who experience the pressure resulting from this child-targeting were also ignored. This was proved in 1995 when RTÉ – again at my instigation – commissioned a "private" Lansdowne survey on the subject. Because it was a limited survey (a sample of just over 1,000 people), RTÉ did not publicise it but agreed that I might quote from the findings.

The significant flaw in the research was that everybody from fifteen year olds to adults were lumped together to say what they thought of child-targeted commercials. Single people and adults without children undoubtedly would give the matter even less thought than fifteen year olds. Despite this, 26 per cent of those questioned found the commercials "unacceptable". When those with children aged 6–10 years were asked, they almost unanimously favoured the discontinuation of such commercials. Many said they would be prepared to pay an extra £5 on their licence fee to facilitate such a ban. The main reason why advertising aimed at children was found unacceptable was that "children put pressure on parents to buy toys". Other reasons given were as follows: children are guillible. Ads give them unreal expectations. Ads have too much influence on children. Ads cause rows, are a form of blackmail, give children too many ideas, are particularly bad at Christmas, are too commercialised.

Apart from the nuisance the pressure of ads causes, the survey respondents indicated a view of childhood that is exactly the opposite to Dr Brian Young, as well as the practitioners of *laissez-faire* on the RTÉ Executive and Authority. So whom does one believe? The parents? Or the broadcasters who have a vested interest in the continuance of this source of income?

Parents of young children are the real experts. Parents of young children are forced by the imperatives of "pester power" to become painfully familiar with these commercial pressures.

To get back to Dr Brian Young. Writing in 1990 about the perceptions of this problem, he offered the following: "The particular relationship that seems to emerge is of the advertiser seen as seducer and the child as an innocent. Advertising in this context is more than just an insidious threat, it is a positive evil." He considered this perception to be naive.

The choice seems to me to be straightforward: for those who consider children to be as streetwise as adults and as needless of protection (like the street urchins of India), there is no problem. For those who believe in some kind of concept of innocence, child-targeted commercials are an evil.

And what can one say about parents who actually sell their children into the slave labour of participating in TV commercials? The practise of using children in advertising is now a cornerstone of international advertising. Children are routinely used because of the emotional appeal they lend and their potential for attracting adult attention. As the Indian researchers say: "Shown together with their parents and siblings, they reinforce the concept of the happy, well-knit nuclear family which is improving its status with the purchase of yet another satisfying product."

From our western perspective we might cynically observe, "India must by now be inured to the concept of child slave labour." But what excuse have we? Regarding the ethics of using children in advertising, people in the ad world see nothing amiss and disclaim responsibility by saying, "Well, if their parents don't mind, why should we?" And the parents do not mind because their own role models – entertainers, TV personalities, sportsmen and academics – are all happy to engage in this well-rewarded exploitation. Even their own national public broadcaster endorses the practice.

What dismayed me most during my period on the RTÉ Authority was the subjugation of such ethical concerns to the pragmatic business of the organisation's fiscal imperatives, particularly the protection of jobs.

It is my belief that the Lansdowne survey of 1995 was not carried out to find out what we should do, but rather to establish what we could get away with. What was got away with was a cosmetic abolition of commercials during the single hour between two and three o'clock in the afternoon. It did not satisfy me and I continued the battle for the next four years. Few paid any heed. It was a bloodless battle, usually fought with exquisite politeness, and nobody suffering more than glancing blows to the ego. But knowledge enters through pain, and I was prompted to explore further the context in which we were skirmishing.

A musical analogy occurs to me. Classical music resonates with a sense of melancholy. This is usually attributed to the pains of romantic love. It is more likely that the shocking rate of child mortality in earlier centuries moved Mozart, Schumann, Mahler and company to this overwhelming sense of sadness. The death of a child is infinitely more painful than the death of romance. Nobody gets over it. In our triumphant western age, the death of the concepts of innocence and childhood should be our emotional Achilles heel.

It is certainly mine.

An End to Innocence

The Grizzly Bear is huge and wild;
He has devoured the infant child.
The infant child is not aware
He has been eaten by the bear.
A.E. Housman, "Infant Innocence" (1938)

It is my impression that the intense love parents have for their children is focussed on their physical well-being, in the rudimentary instinct to feed and protect them from physical harm. This love often takes for granted those specific qualities which distinguish their offspring's nature from that of baboons and which deserve as intense a concern. I refer to children's imaginative life and their emotional vulnerability, their miraculous aptitude for language, music and dance, and their preoccupation with play.

I have also noticed that many adults switch off when children are discussed in these terms. I suspect that the average non-parent may at this moment be tempted to do so. But stay: we are *all* implicated. There is a specific class of adult who is more intensely interested in these childish things than the parents themselves.

Nancy Shalek, president of the Shalek Agency, talked freely to the *Los Angeles Times* about the phenomenon

> . . . of making people feel that without their product, you're a loser. Kids are very sensitive to that. If you tell them to

179

buy something, they are resistant. But if you tell them they'll
be a dork if they don't, you've got their attention. You open
up emotional vulnerabilities and it's very easy to do with
kids because they're the most emotionally vulnerable.

"If you own this child at an early age, you can own this
child for years to come," said Mike Searles, president of
Kids-R-Us.

Johann Wachs of Saatchi & Saatchi's Kid Connection
Unit agreed: "Marketeers are just waking up to the enormous possibility of kids-targeted products."

"We believe in getting them early and having them for
life," declared Wayne Chilicki, General Mills executive.

To these people, a child's mind is a cash cow.

However, the owner of McFarlane Toys, Todd McFarlane, was given an award by Ernst & Young for creating a
best-selling line of grotesque and violent *Spawn* toys and
comic books. McFarlane was asked if he would allow his
daughters access to his own toys and comic books. "Are
you kidding?" he said. "I'm still a dad after five o'clock."

I learned about these people from a group in Washington led by Ralph Nader, the consumer watchdog and US
presidential candidate in 2000. On 21 September 1999,
Nader sent a letter to key members of the US Congress. His
first sentence was this: "In 1980, the US Congress passed
a law to protect adults who prey on children."

After this eye-catching opening, he explained:

> You read that correctly. Public Law 96–252 prohibits the
> Federal Communications Commission (FCC) from enact-
> ing rules that would protect the nation's children from
> advertising that exploits their vulnerable and trusting
> natures. This law is corporate abuse incarnate. It should be
> the role of Congress to protect children, not those who
> prey upon them. We urge you to repeal it.

The present in Ireland usually equates to twenty years
ago in the US. Few in Irish broadcasting realise it, and fewer
will admit it. In 1997 the RTÉ chairman wrote to me:

There *is* a case to be made that heavy reliance on advertising leads to bland/insipid programming *in the American television and radio system* [my italics]. But I do not believe there is a "direct relationship" in the case of Ireland or Britain (which is not to say there isn't bland programming here).

In other words, we possess some, perhaps spiritual, quality that will save the Irish from the worst excesses of American commercial broadcasting, including the targeting of children. In fact, the Irish have been undiscriminating in these matters, have taken to commercialisation like beggars on horseback. I have long accepted that adults have to make their own discriminations and choices in the matter of the commercialisation of broadcasting, but I can never accept the implications of our slothful disposition towards children.

As Ralph Nader pointed out, after 1980, once the FCC had decided that this aspect of American TV should be deregulated, the televisual debauchery of children intensified. Its grounds were that there were now so many sources providing TV for children – cable, satellite, video cassettes – that the kids were bound to get educational programmes somewhere. This was emphasised by Ronald Reagan in 1984 with his stated belief that the market would regulate itself. The market did. Commercial TV immediately divested itself of all responsibility for providing intelligent programmes for children. Margaret Thatcher acted, as always in unison with Reagan, as if the British Annan Report of 1977, which had taken three years to prepare, had never existed.This report had recommended the removal of television commercials from within children's programming.

An American writer, Dale Kunkel, has suggested that we try to imagine an adult television schedule consisting exclusively of cartoons, situation comedies, action adventure films (and, of course, commercials). There would be protests at such a diet. Yet that is precisely the exclusive schedule offered to children – and not just in the US. Take the panorama of children's viewing on one day in late 1999 on RTÉ. From early morning to late afternoon there is the following succession of items: *Bananas in Pyjamas, The Rocky and Bullwinkle Story, The Fantastic Four, Pippi Longstocking, The Hunchback of Notre Dame, The Bears Who Saved Christmas, Cartoon Time, The Apple Dumpling Gang, Catdog, The Addams Family, Namu the Killer Whale, Rugrats, Pokemon, Rugrats* (again), *Sister, Sister, The Great Valley Adventure, The New Addams Family, The Simpsons.* I cannot identify many non-American items in that list.

That was not an exceptional day's viewing for children on Ireland's national public broadcaster. There were few serious dramatic programmes, less news and information shows, little to stimulate children's curiosity about the real world. In this context, it is worth reproducing a paragraph of a speech delivered by the future director general of RTÉ, Bob Collins, to a Dublin conference in 1996:

> The extent to which children's programming is used, not as an end in itself, not as a means of serving young audiences, but as a mechanism through which merchandising campaigns can be built for the sale of all manner of things, is a depressing and a depressingly common feature of contemporary broadcasting. For this reason it would be detrimental were children to depend more on external broadcasting than on indigenous broadcasting for their information, education and entertainment. Very well-funded, attractively packaged, day-long children's series are having an obvious impact, and the kinds of editorial decisions that are made in relation to material broadcast for children are dramatically different in satellite broadcasting from those operating in public-service broadcasting.

I should mention that the most entertaining and educational programme ever made for children, *Sesame Street,* is sometimes shown at 6 a.m. on RTÉ, while the sickly sweet mess of *Barney* (the purple dinosaur) is shown at the peak hour for pre-school children, 2 p.m. In 1972 I laughed with my first-born at Oscar the Grouch; in the year 2001 I squirm with my last-born at the embarassment of *Barney*. So, miraculously, do some children.

Up to a few years ago, the justification for providing a junk-food diet of TV for children was that it was more economic to purchase the above programmes than to provide intelligent home-made material. Nobody paid much attention, least of all the advertisers. Children's programmes in Ireland were not considered significant as a vehicle for advertising. The law of large numbers which guides adult schedules was inapplicable. So was the law of right people, which refers to viewers with the greatest potential buying power. But a sinister change has taken place. Advertisers have perceived that the adult market is saturated; persuasion now concentrates on holding market share, on rivalry between brands. However, the increase in children's pocket money, plus the rise of pester power, has opened up a green field and has now made the child market the most potentially lucrative target for television advertising.

Advertisers have realised that the guilt induced in parents by their latch-key children makes them bend over backwards to listen to their children's demands and opinions. The Celtic Tiger takes both working parents out of the home and in turn renders them less acquainted with what is happening to their children. A new form of guilt pervades the home. That is why the precocious child actor advocating a new "family" car is now considered to be more effective than the traditional tactic of draping a blonde bimbo over the bonnet. Hence also the consequence that the "streetwise" child has had to be fostered, with a concomitant diminution of the concept of childhood innocence.

To sum up: children are us, twenty, thirty, forty years hence. Television increasingly constitutes their referential system. It is more influential than formal schooling. Parents know this – perhaps only in a vague, inarticulated way because public discourse on the matter is oddly muted on Western airwaves. The optimistic signs are that Sweden and Norway ban advertising directed at children under twelve. Greece bans toy advertising. If in the middle of national school lessons in Ireland, Barbie Dolls or Pokemon were loudly advertised, there would be a public outcry. It is obtuse of us to pretend that such an analogy is inappropriate.

The Swedish consumer ombudsman, Axel Edling, has not given up. The following excerpts come from a speech made by him in November 1999 in London.

* The position in my country is that TV advertising should not be targeted at children. This ban has been in existence since 1991 and is now contained in the Radio and Television Act.
* According to the commercial community itself, advertising should be easily identified as such. This means that everybody in the target group should be able to distinguish easily an advertisement from other media content, and also understand the purpose of it. But children below a certain level of maturity cannot tell the difference between TV advertising and other TV programmes.
* If advertisers really took the business codes seriously they should not target TV advertising at small children. But a glance around the world reveals that this is just what they do.
* It provides the finance for programmes? If there are compelling reasons why TV advertising should not be targeted at young children it shouldn't do so, regardless of how the advertising income is spent.
* Commercial Freedom of Speech? There must be acknowledged the difference between the highly respected principle of freedom of expression in political, religious, scientific and artistic matters, and the right of a merchant to promote the sale of certain products.
* There is in fact plenty of room for advertising children's products quite legally on TV in Sweden. You are free to

> let the commercials speak – [but only] to parents, grand-
> parents or any other grown-up with a full understand-
> ing of what it is all about.

When I came across the full text of this speech, my age-ing bones rattled with joy. Mr Edling had expressed suc-cinctly what I had been trying to impress on the RTÉ Authority for several years. I immediately sent copies of the text of the speech to twenty randomly selected members of the houses of the Oireachtas. I got three reactions: Ruairi Quinn's secretary could not decode the document. Síle de Valera's secretary acknowledged receipt. Joe O'Toole, leader of the Irish National Teachers Organisation, sent word that he might circulate the speech to his members. Among the majority who did not acknowledge my letter, or the speech, was the minister for children, Mary Hanafin. The copies I sent to various key people in RTÉ, including the chairman-designate, Paddy Wright, were also not acknowledged. The only member of the Oireachtas who took the information and thoroughly pursued it was Brian O'Shea, Labour TD for Waterford, who proposed several amendments to the new Broadcasting Bill.

As I shall detail, the Swedish assumption of the presi-dency of the EU on 1 January 2001 gave reason for pause to many vested interests.

How long before our Oireachtas finds – as the US Con-gress found in 1990 in the context of children's television – that "children [in the United States] are lagging behind those in other countries in fundamental intellectual skills, including reading, writing, mathematics, science and geog-raphy"? Since Ireland has not yet reached this stage of con-cern, I wonder how long before its children achieve the 25–30 per cent obesity levels of American children? Severe obesity in this category has nearly doubled since 1960. The American surgeon general has stated, "We have the most sedentary generation of young people in American history."

In 1999 I proved to the RTÉ Authority that it was mak-ing at least £2 million *profit* on children's programmes and

was investing the cash in everything except children's programmes – despite European Broadcasting Union claims
that this commercial income was devoted to the making of
such programmes. For example, more than the extra £1
million income that RTÉ derived from toy advertising at
Christmas 1998 was spent on the packaging and presentation alone – by Bill O'Herlihy, Eamon Dunphy et al – of a
cross-channel soccer series, the transmission rights of
which had been bought for a third of that amount!

RTÉ's traditional defence of its children's advertising
policy is: "Others do it. If we don't take these commercials,
we shall lose the income to our competitors." To which I
can only respond that one expects a certain ethic from a
publicly, however stingily, financed organisation. Besides,
just because somebody else sticks their finger in the fire is
no reason for you to do it. The national public broadcaster is competing in the child-abuse market.

The paradox is that if RTÉ as an instrument of public
policy has been pushed into this mendacious activity, then
the successive governments who dictate the broadcaster's
fiscal policy are ultimately responsible for the child abuse
in question.

It is an extraordinary testament to RTÉ, to the people
who work there and the public who maintain them, that
having gone from years of monopoly smugness to the present years of panic, it still retains any vestige of identity as
a national broadcaster. But I believe that on this rock, that
of its collaboration with child-exploiters everywhere, it
will ultimately founder.

Aidan Burns, second in command of RTÉ's advertising
sales division in 1998, made the following personal fore-
cast in my presence: "In ten years time RTÉ will consist of
one TV channel and one radio channel." The rest, I gathered, would be under commercial control.

There could have been a certain amount of resigned antic-
ipation in this prognostication, because when Aidan Burns
retired that year, he very soon got a job as chief executive of

the Association of Advertisers in Ireland, whose board consisted of representatives of Erin Foods, the Bank of Ireland, Smithkline Beecham, Calor Teoranta and Lever Fabergé. The AAI is affiliated to the World Federation of Advertisers, whose own executive committee represents Unilever, Procter & Gamble, Pepsi-Cola, McDonalds, Mars Inc., Nestle and Philip Morris. It is a roll-call of some of the biggest multinationals in the world.

Early in 2000, knowing that people were becoming vaguely aware of the child-targeting problem, the World Federation of Advertisers commissioned GFK, a London research agency, to produce a glossy survey to counter this trend. The agency interviewed 300 parents in each European "market" and dressed up its findings in the manner desired by the WFA. They reported the apparently obvious: that family, school and friends exert the highest influence on children. TV advertising was presented as coming innocuously somewhere down the line.

The presentation shared the traditional disingenuousness of advertisers and broadcasters in claiming large numbers of viewers but downplaying their influence on these viewers, in this case children. It was the methodology of the survey that was, as always, suspect. This was a survey of perceptions, a singularly unscientific way to discover the truth of any event or situation – rather like asking people which way they are going to vote. Parents are understandably noted for presenting their children and themselves in the best possible light. We must insist that our little dears think we are infallible, and that school is not loathed. Even if the average parent suspected it, how could he or she admit that the attractive messages on the box in the corner exert a more formative influence on their darlings than they themselves do. But as they are increasingly finding out, it does.

There is a simple reason why most adults do not take this matter seriously. Apart from rarely watching children's TV, they conceive of TV commercials as harmless one-off messages. How could these lively, colourful, cheerful items affect their children or themselves adversely? Taken singly, they could not. But if repeated over and over as they are in a single viewing session, they become as pervasive and interiorised as the rote-learning of the ten-times table. The secret is not in the quality – banality in these techniques is a virtue – but in the frequency of the exhortations. The frequency with which the same TV commercials are repeatedly shown over a short intensive period of childrens' programming can be usefully described as brainwashing.

Nowadays only large multinationals can afford to pay for the necessary frequency of their commercial messages to children. As the children in Kiltiernan national school in Galway showed, parents are rarely present for this intensive selling. Therefore, partly through their lack of interest in kids' TV and partly through having to work, the important socialising context and reinforcement of identity which they normally supply is also absent. This leaves a large social space around children which advertisers fall over themselves trying to fill.

In April 1997 I suggested to the RTÉ Authority that at least we should show commercials in half-hour blocks, perhaps at teatime, as they did in some European countries. This would diminish their individual impact as well as the annoyance of programme interruptions. The new director general, Bob Collins, was quick and clever enough to point out that in Ireland we were statutorily prevented from showing more than a limited amount of advertising per hour. I did not get the impression that he would be energetically pushing for an adjustment in the legislation, because, as he said, such a block "would not hold audiences".

Part of my bog, a few yards east of the house, was once an evil-smelling swamp. I tried planting willows and reedmace there. Nothing grew. In March 1998 I got my neighbour, Tom Terry Mac Donncha, to attack it with his JCB.

For two days we enjoyed ourselves excavating the substance of the swamp – which was actually liquid, if stagnant, peat overlying the granite – and piling it up on one side. The result was a grand swimming and rafting pool for the local children from which in summer they emerge muddy but happy. The reward for me was a fine new bank of peat on which I had room to plant four alders, one each of maple, Scots pine and Japanese larch, several spruce and one hydrangea bush. If only, I thought as I worked, the swamp of commercial television and radio could be so easily redeemed for the fruitful enjoyment of children and adults.

Some years ago at the funeral of that great RTÉ broadcaster Paddy Gallagher, I met Gloria, his one-time wife. She greeted me with a big hello and the question, "Are you still baying at the moon?"

What could I say but "Yes!"

INDEPENDENTS

I see men as trees, walking.
Mark 8:24

Here is one of the things that fascinate me about living things.

If you get fifty baby trees from the same nursery – "whips" they are called – and plant them six feet apart in identical soil, subject to the same cold winds, warm sun and Conamara rain, they will all grow differently. Some will be robust, some straggly and frail. A few will die very young. I have spent the past seven years learning how trees parallel the uniqueness of human beings. Applying this principle to my other preoccupations of film, TV and radio, I have been encouraged to ask the question: why do the majority of films and TV programmes, imaginative products of unique individuals, increasingly tend towards a deadening conformity of style and content?

Since 1973 I have worked as an independent film and TV programme-maker. In the seventies and eighties I was relatively fortunate: RTÉ, the only limited outlet in Ireland for independent films, was familiar with my work and, with a few significant exceptions, had little hesitation in buying and showing it. The same applied to David Shaw-Smith, Éamon de Buitléir and Gerrit Van Gelderen. Other independents were not so lucky. People like Louis Marcus,

Colm Ó Laoire, Tom Hayes, Kieran Hickey and Jim Mulkerns survived on crumbs from the rich man's table – corporate promotions, tourist films for Bord Fáilte, rare government commissions and the like. The late, lamented Áine O'Connor described the atmosphere well in 1990 when she talked about the attitude of entrenched RTÉ employees towards independent programme-makers: "They are like settled people, looking out their plate-glass windows at the travellers."

In 1980 RTÉ invited us few independent film-makers to meet in Montrose and be briefed on the station's requirements. Stimulated by the international success of their self-financed and entirely home-produced *Strumpet City*, RTÉ's object was to familiarise us with the requirements of potential foreign purchasers of our work so that it could be also included in RTÉ's sales portfolio. I expected about twenty people to respond to their invitation, but a large studio was crammed with, it seemed, hundreds. Rory O'Farrell was there. An ex-RTÉ man and brilliant film editor who ran his own editing rooms, he had helped many an impoverished film-maker complete their project. He even gave James Morris – the man who invented TV3 – his start in Ireland. Rory, who was a close friend of Charlie McCreevy, knew the film and TV scene as intimately as he read politics. He turned to me. "Do you recognise anybody?" All I could do was shake my head. Where had all these people suddenly sprung from? The times they were a-changing. There seemed to be money in the air.

It was a phantom pregnancy. The optimism was dissipated by the debacle of *Year of the French*, which was, significantly, a co-production. RTÉ was feeling the pinch, coming under pressure from an Oireachtas Joint Committe on State Sponsored Bodies. A member of this committee, by the way, was a certain Liam Lawlor, whose expertise, as I have recently learned, extended also to land development. The result was that RTÉ cut back severely on its independent commissions. The trouble for independents was that

RTÉ was the only game in town; there was no other TV station in this state, and cinemas were run by a monopoly which wanted only commercial product.

When in 1993 Minister Michael D. Higgins announced a bonanza for independent film-makers – 20 per cent of the entire RTÉ programme budget – I thought nostalgically of my early experiences of non-budget film-making. The new independents thought they had died and gone to heaven.

Programmatically it was a just move, since independents had increasingly been providing much of RTÉ's quality output in the form of documentary films; I think particularly of the works of Donald Taylor-Black, Louis Marcus, Alan Gilsenan and Seán Ó Mordha and latterly of Pat Comer, Pat Collins, Steve Carson, Justin McCarthy. Many other, less talented, independents had also been contributing quite a lot of the imitative dross considered by RTÉ to be essential to a balanced schedule; as one newspaper put it, these were less engaged in programme production than programme reproduction. But in part, at least, certain independent contributions to RTÉ schedules tended, like the cavalry in World War I, to add a touch of class to what otherwise would be a vulgar brawl.

The degree of gloom with which RTÉ greeted Michael D's decision was counterpointed by the delight in the independent sector where, ironically, film-makers had largely been superseded by businessmen. You could not now make a film or TV programme unless you were a limited company, employed an accountant and wrote on headed notepaper with a thrusting logo. Film artists had become hired hands or, as Thaddeus O'Sullivan once described himself, journeymen directors. There was now a bonanza of millions to be lusted after by the businessmen in charge.

On the RTÉ Authority, I felt ambivalent about these developments because I believed that an exclusively industrial approach to film and television was the death of film as art or even as social commentary. I rarely gave an opinion on the subject. Perhaps that was why a spokesman for Film

Makers Ireland, James Hickey, was quoted in 1999 as saying that my presence on the RTÉ Authority was useless to independents; that I represented nobody but myself. It was a modest estimate equalled only by my own modesty in thinking I represented the public, rather than any sectional interest. I certainly did not feel I was there to represent commercial interests – who in the nineties were the main players in film and TV-making. Film Makers Ireland sensibly never made representations to me on its position, although a few of its members did so privately. I was encouraged to discreetly ask several FMI members – producers and directors – for their advice. It was strangely unanimous. They all vented their spleen in the direction of the programme controller. One ex-RTÉ writer, film director and humorist went so far as to jokingly say, "Shoot Liam Miller." To them, an RTÉ programme controller was responsible for all the evils of the national broadcaster. It seemed to me a totally simplistic approach; Miller was only the messenger. He was doing a difficult job to the best of his ability.

Into this atmosphere dropped Michael D. Higgins' bonanza. But in the mid-nineties there was a snag: 20 per cent of RTÉ's programme budget is 20 per cent of precisely what, demanded James Hickey and the FMI? This leading question took up a not inconsiderable amount of RTÉ Authority time.

There began a battle to ascertain precisely what was the TV programme budget of the national broadcaster. The RTÉ Executive agonised aloud to the RTÉ Authority, whose chairman in turn agonised to the minister: since 25 per cent of the station's total home-produced budget was spent on sport, did it include the soaring fees demanded by Rupert Murdoch and his ilk for sports rights? What were the implications for the increased cost of imported programmes which competition from TV3 had already driven up? At least the fallacy that competition lowers prices was exposed. Did the 20 per cent figure include the £5 million that RTÉ was forced to spend on programming for TG4?

RTÉ staff also realised that an extra job in the independent sector probably meant one less job in RTÉ. James Hickey threatened RTÉ with legal action to get it to divulge precisely how it accounted for its programme expenditure.

Meanwhile in 1997 the government changed. An uneasy truce seemed to be called when Micheal D's successor, Síle de Valera, temporarily fixed the independent allocation at £16 million, £4 million less than James Hickey was demanding. It was still nice lolly. RTÉ lobbied Minister de Valera to revoke the 1993 legislation and lighten the burden of what it saw as an excessive obligation to independent programme-makers. The minister ignored RTÉ's supplications. The long-delayed broadcasting legislation (not signed into law until March 2001) gave little comfort to RTÉ. It proposed a consumer index-linked, basic allocation of £20 million for independent production. Ominously, it did not propose index-linking for the broadcasting licence fee. RTÉ drew the short straw on both counts.

It seemed so long ago and faraway that RTÉ provided the single national television channel in Ireland, a time when independent programme-makers were almost non-existent. Shell-shocked would be a good description for those in RTÉ who were reared in that culture. In fact RTÉ is now regarded by the big guns as only a relatively small part of the Irish film and television industry. The businessmen now are absorbed by what must be called "movies". In the Omniplex in Galway, I recently saw a sample of the recent wave of "Irish" films. It was a camel, an animal designed by a committee: there were at least seven "film production/distribution" credits. Why RTÉ was included in these credits I can only imagine to be the result of the broadcaster buying for a pittance the right to transmit the film after it fails, as it must, at the box office in Ireland and in the US, for which it was primarily designed. RTÉ will certainly make little money on such feature film investments.

In the international feature film industry, Ireland is now a backlot of New York, Los Angeles and London, but there

is now less Anglicisation than Los Angelisation, as James
Montgomery, the late Irish film censor, once put it. There is
unspoiled scenery and extras, plus trained workers, mainly
employed in the non-creative grades. The state gives generous tax concessions – sometimes even throws in the army
as extras. The State Film Board helps out with development
and production funding. RTÉ will buy a tiny share in a film
if the product is middle of the road enough. For foreign film
producers and their local fronts, this is fairyland.

With Section 481 tax incentives in Ireland, it is easier to
make a film for $10 million than for $100,000. While Irish
suitmen and suitwomen say film is a business as well as an
art, they concentrate exclusively on the business end, the
only dimension with which they can at least simulate
familiarity. The major money and talent decisions are
taken elsewhere; so it is stretching things to call what is
happening an "Irish" film and television industry. Does
that matter?

Conventional wisdom says: not in the least. As Sheamus
Smith and John Boorman said many years ago, there is no
such thing as an Irish film. What visionaries! Now that Ireland has officially shed its fundamentalist religious beliefs,
its linguistic identity, its sense of personal and communal
responsibility, its ethical inhibitions, its political sovereignty, even its own currency, and soon its national broadcasting service – all those things that retarded it for so long –
the future glows with promise. Particularly the future of
"independent movie-making".

Ironically, though the recent Gadarene prosperity was
originally greased by grants of £8 billion from European
Community funds, most of the "movies" made in Ireland
are designed for America and Britain. Because, happily, the
Irish speak English. Most of these objects are actually
made-for-TV serials and one-offs, not "movies" at all.
Even the few vaguely home-made "Irish" feature films,
though well-made, in the main doff the cap to middle
America. But the work such films provide is well paid,

albeit sporadic, and the Irish are still considered to be "learning their trade" – over eighty years after Sydney Alcott came to Killarney with the Kalem Movie Company and over sixty years since Tom Cooper made *The Dawn* out of his garage in Killarney. What they are actually learning is the dark and convoluted economics of film-making, which leaves little space for developing an original vision.

There is a tiny activity entitled to be called "indigenous" movie-making, but it is irrelevant in the international context except insofar as making no-budget twenty-minute films on 35mm can serve as a training vehicle and portfolio for youngsters hoping to break into the "real" world, i.e. sell a script abroad, preferably Amerikay. Why RTÉ pays the remotest attention to such efforts results from a sense of public service rather than belief in their cinematic genius.

The only innovative film-making talent in Ireland is and always has been expressed in television documentary, the unglamorous and therefore ignored reality of Irish film-making. It is the field in which the Irish can actually excel, requiring as it does more intelligence, hard work and real film-making talent than hustling ability. It is unglamorous because it does not have stars. It is ignored by businessmen and businesswomen because it does not have the financial fat available to keep them in the manner to which they wish to become accustomed. It is not widely encouraged because it examines reality in a non-romantic way, and humankind still cannot bear too much reality. The situation reminds me of what Ernst Neizvestny, an anti-establishment Russian sculptor, cheekily responded when Khrushchev – who had told the artist his work was "dogshit" – asked him how he had survived oppression. The sculptor said: "There are certain bacteria – very small, soft ones – which can live in a super-saline solution that could dissolve the hoof of a rhinoceros. The artist is like that." Khrushchev laughed and allowed Neizvestny's exhibition to go ahead.

Fortunately some artistic bacteria still barely survive inside and outside RTÉ, but the toxic solutions are getting stronger.

It is in the occasional commissioning of documentary work that RTÉ and TG4 fulfil their proper role towards independent Irish film-making. Excellent documentaries attract large and appreciative audiences. TV3 shows little interest in such an important activity. Neither does the tabloid print media, nor "arts" programmes on Irish television or radio.

On the other hand, and perhaps inevitably, Irish movie-makers now see the United States as their only salvation. Some are straight about it: when I asked my good friend Martin Duffy, writer/director of *The Boy from Mercury*, why he was casting two international "stars" in his film, he responded, "Bob, I'm not making a film; I'm making a movie." When Martin was subsequently invited to direct a New York film and make his fortune there, I congratulated him on going to his spiritual home. He was not insulted; he knew what I meant. Fortunately he returned home from New York while his head was still the same size. I wish others who keep a foot (and a penthouse) in each place would do likewise, cut out the pretence of making "Irish" films and desist from the pretension of "telling our own stories".

This island has reverted to its ancient role as a trading post and money launderer. The natives are pacified; interesting people pass briefly through Dublin and enliven the social swill and gossip columns there. The Indian agents are cleaning up on ecstasy, booze, designer stuff and brown paper envelopes, but at least we are now as upfront, straight-talking, pragmatic and confident as our Hollywood cradle-rockers. And Irish movie-makers can still delude themselves that they are independent.

The subject would make a good documentary. It could be called, "Films are made by fools like me, but only God can make a tree." Perhaps RTÉ will commission it.

Soap

Wit's empire now shall know a woman's reign.
Sarah Egerton, "The Emulation" (1703)

I used to study the RTÉ output and wonder why there was such a dreary succession – at least half the output and most at peak-viewing time – of sitcoms, soap operas and sludge from the United States, Australia and the UK which few intelligent viewers could possibly endure for an entire evening. I am assuming that the average viewer is rational and intelligent. (The alternative is to become the old cartoon in the *New Yorker* which showed a naked man in a cardboard box declaiming, "People are no damn good."). Anybody – priest, politician or TV scheduler – who maintains such a stance is also in that cardboard box, but hanging on to the suit. If I, demonstrably not qualifying for membership of Mensa, can find certain forms of TV cheap, patronising or pathetic, there must statistically be a respectable number of equally revolted viewers – including, from my conversations, many of the production staff of RTÉ – who share that assessment. I do not know how the latter reconcile themselves to the situation. I am preserved from utter pessimism by the following thought: even if half a million people on this island are at some stage watching, say, *Coronation Street* or *EastEnders*, *Home and Away*, *Fair City*, *Winning Streak* or *Who Wants to Be a Millionaire?*, and many others are in their cradles, it still leaves perhaps even a million thoughtful people who are otherwise occupied – perhaps with some more intelligent or at least more social activity than the goggle-box. Perhaps even with good radio?

It is a consistent fact that a considerable amount of the RTÉ programme budget and almost 1,000 hours of its programming is spent on promoting the mainly commercial business that is "Sport". There is also the fact, as the personal assistant to the director general pointed out to the Authority in 1997, that between 40 per cent and 60 per cent of RTÉ's transmission during prime time hours was built around news and public affairs, "a factor which has inescapable implications for the potential to make programmes in other genres". It also had and has implications for the boredom threshold of audiences hearing for the fiftieth time that day that the "Northern Executive is on the brink" of some crisis or other. Also as a matter of fact, no other broadcaster competing for a mainstream audience has created such a programmatic reliance on public affairs coverage as has RTÉ.

Further, almost the entire RTÉ drama budget was and is spent on home-produced soap operas. A healthy departure was the courageous decision – approved by the Authority of which I was a member, ahem – in 1999 to invest £1 million in the Beckett canon of plays, which initially attracted "only" 89,000 viewers but about which RTÉ could for once hold its head high. But apart from news and public affairs, soap operas are still the main home-produced diet.

In April 1997 Michael Garvey, one-time programme controller of RTÉ, wrote an insightful paper for the Authority's consumption in which, in passing, he pointed out how far soap operas are from the concept of drama. We received occasional papers like this, sharp insights into what was going on. I honestly don't know why we were given them, because not a damn bit of effective attention was ever paid to them.

Essentially, Michael Garvey explained that the soap-opera genre "diminishes the power of the dramatic experience [because] the proponents are absorbed into the flow of life rather than being isolated in their crisis". Being a gentleman, Michael Garvey put it nicely: that a soap is not what for two-and-a-half thousand years has been regarded as drama. His clear implication was that RTÉ may spend all its drama allocation on soaps, it may give much-needed work to actors, it may boost the ratings, but it in no way can be described as a legitimate drama output. He might have added that thirty years ago RTÉ was able in a single year to produce *Insurrection!*, an eight-part drama series on the 1916 Rising; four plays for young viewers by Bryan MacMahon; productions of *The Plough and the Stars* and *The Midnight Court*; *The Real Charlotte*; *Dear Liar* (adaptation of Shaw's letters to Mrs Patrick Campbell); Beckett's *Beginning to End*; *The Long Winter*, a six-part historical drama; and four other one-off plays – as well as the two soaps, *The Riordans* and *Tolka Row*.

I would put it more strongly than Michael Garvey: I would say that soaps are the pap in which atomised and alienated souls – many of us – become addicted to a surrogate version of the social and community identity whose reality lies in smithereens about us. They also particularly appeal to the romantic, Mills and Boon side of us where ideally all tensions are resolved and tragedy avoided. Senior TV executives with secure tenure certainly look down on this crap, but they love the audience figures, and they can with a stroke of the pen postulate a respectable drama output. During the hours of transmission of such programmes, they can go out and have a ride on their bicycles in the quiet lanes of south County Dublin.

Of course there would be a majority of dissenting voices to the views of such as Garvey and myself. For one, when I returned from my first exile in the late fifties, I found my own father already hooked on *Coronation Street*, an addiction from which only death released him.

But the original concept of soap opera – on radio – was designed specifically for the female audience by Procter & Gamble to advertise their soap powder. In 1974 a sociology post-graduate in UCD, Barbara O'Connor, asserted women's predisposition towards "soaps" and men's antipathy towards them. She wrote the following about the female audience:

> These [soap-opera] characters are frequently the TV characters to whom they can best relate. This is partly due to the parallel between the rhythm of the serial in its use of "naturalistic" time (i.e. time in the serial parallels chronological time) and the rhythm of the everyday lives of the female audience, housewives in particular, who are at home during the day and structure their day around particular radio and TV programmes.

It was an observation that I would agree was true for its time. Unfortunately Ms O'Connor also quoted a Rutgers University feminist paper which argued that:

> Soap operas require a viewer who is competent in the codes of personal relations in the domestic sphere or, in other words, must have a particular form of cultural capital.

I deduced from this line of reasoning that males were adjudged to be incompetent in such delicate spheres, whether they had domestic responsibilities or not. It was a sexist assumption aimed at defending, right or wrong, female taste, but in the process attributing to soap operas a subtlety which they demonstrably do not possess; if they did, advertisers would not be interested.

Studying the TAM ratings for such soap operas reveals that those in the category called "housekeepers", i.e. women, are indeed their main audience. It is as true in the year 2001 as it was in 1974. Why does the habit persist in the twenty-first century? What is odd here is that the new economic imperatives have long disrupted the old pattern of stay-at-home women. The sisters are now represented as the getter-uppers and goers. Or is this also a media invention, applying only to a minority of educated, middle-class, single women? Yet even these appear to have retained their apparently genetic affection for soap opera. Women also statistically constitute the greatest audience for the other quiz-type pap that is shown at peak hours between 6 p.m. and 9 p.m. – when most advertising revenue is achieved. And here is where the light breaks through.

It makes sense: women normally do the household and other shopping. Apart from alcohol and car advertisements directed at inadequate males, most advertising is and always has been designed to console women. Inevitably, programmes are made and transmitted that will attract the greatest number of these designated consumers.

Ellen Kelleher, a TV advertising time buyer with McConnell's advertising agency, said (3 February 2000) that "the mammy is the engine that drives most fast-moving consumer goods markets". And the TV person with the most "mammy" appeal? Pat Kenny, she said.

But on the radio front, Graham Taylor, a director of the specialist media firm GT Media, commented (June 1996) that the likes of Pat Kenny delivered an ageing audience, i.e. housewives with grown-up children. "Our clients want housewives with [young] kids," he asserted.

Adult males are sidelined in this world. This may be why they loathe the TV persona of poor Pat Kenny, while respecting him on radio, just as they were held to be jealous of Gay Byrne, both on radio and TV.

It follows that if TV executives want to compete for more advertising, they will show more pap for women. They have caught on to their "real" audience – females, whom they approach as cynically as children, purely as consumers to be exploited. There is a circle of mediocrity, which spirals downwards so that it is hard to find anything sentiently engaging being transmitted on any television channel during peak viewing hours. Programmes for "pointyheads" (books and arts programmes) are either banished or pushed to the late hour fringes. Current affairs programmes are chopped and changed, renamed, rearranged, their transmission times shifted around, emasculated and transmitted so erratically that one gets tired trying to follow them through the labyrinthine schedules and gets lost in the chase. The scheduler's approach increasingly alternates between the frantic and the cynical.

To try to understand this development outside of, but parallel to, the commercial pressures, it is useful to remember a news reporting technique that emerged in RTÉ in the eighties. This was the growing habit of asking shattered victims of the latest atrocity in Northern Ireland, "How do you feel about it?" The object of this question was to stimulate an emotional response in the viewers. The human answer to the question should have been, "How do you think I feel, you idiot?" The imbecility of the interrogation produced only confusion. I date the peak of this phenomen back to 1987.

In September of that year an RTÉ training and refresher course for reporters and researchers was conducted by a staff TV programme editor with aspirations to be a media guru. He pontificated to them that "television is not about thought. Television is about emotion." He further urged that "television can feel – so it can console". Since there were females among the listeners, he cleverly stated: "Only men think that thought (facts) are more important than feelings (moral beliefs)." Allowing for the peculiar equation of "feelings" with "moral beliefs" (they were his parentheses), the lecturer used some smart sleight of words as well as quite insightful ideas adapted from the collected clichés of Marshall McLuhan. ("Radio is hot, TV is cool.") It was the use to which these harmless guesses were put that stimulated comment: i.e. his effort to try to convince journalists that their professional mantra – "Comment is free; facts are sacred" – was not only obsolete but ignorant. The lecturer urged the abandonment of any aspiration to objectivity or professionalism in reportage and essentially the taking of one side in a propaganda battle over the northern war. Some of the weaker minded clearly fell under the guru's spell and lapsed into a policy of dredging up consumer emotion in place of facts, viz. the "how do you feel" questions. It is surprising how many talented professionals capitulated to this second-hand American idea that news and current affairs must adopt the techniques of "drama". "Infotainment" became the buzzword; news became an extension of show business. It is significant that this indoctrination took place at the end of four years of a Fine Gael/Labour coalition whose main policy was keeping the northern civil strife, rather like foot and mouth disease today, out of the twenty-six counties. The aspiring media guru was Eoghan Harris, whose influence on RTÉ up to then should never be underestimated and who appears never to have forgiven the organisation for not carrying out his varying instructions to the letter. But such was the force of his rhetoric that it may have contributed to a confusion on the national airwaves that caused intelligent viewers and listeners to doubt the line that emerged from RTÉ in the context of Northern Ireland. Whether or not such an undermining of the national broadcaster's authority may ultimately have been the real dialectical intention, it seemed to me that such a convergence was a question only that talented man himself could answer.

In summary, the emotional and dramatic approach so characteristic of lucrative soap operas and so beloved of the targeted female viewers became a technique of news, current affairs and documentaries. Gradually it was almost impossible to find a hard documentary report unsullied by saccharine music. This once again demonstrates the convergence between the hitherto separate aspirations of commercial, propaganda and journalistic mentalities. Such a convergence always debases broadcasting.

Helen O'Reilly was entrusted in 1998 with the the post of TV programmes director in RTÉ until she sensibly escaped back to the BBC in 1999. In a defiant response to criticism in *Phoenix* magazine, she looked forward to "being *enervated* and entertained and to making programmes that do the same for UK licence payers". According to the dictionary, the word enervate means "to deprive of force or strength; to weaken, to render effeminate, wanting in spirit, strength or vigour". It must have been a Freudian slip; I have never known a TV programmes head publicly to display such frankness.

Television was long ago discovered by American advertisers to be at its best, i.e. to suit their needs, when it is "enervating". This island has long been a figment of the American imagination, and the vestiges of Irish imagination have equally been colonised by the cultural output of that large country. Our most significant cultural export in the last twenty years has been *Riverdance*, a Broadway concept danced by Irish colleens in miniskirts to the rhythms and melodies of Bulgaria and Turkey. Ask the composer, Bill Whelan, who has no pretensions about the "Irishness" of his wonderful musical invention. Taking imagination as a cultural artefact, there is hardly a prominent Irish poetic, academic, political or thespian figure in recent years who has not earned his or her reputation – and real income – by intelligently slotting themselves into the hospitable embrace of American institutions and their expectations. Indeed, as recent expressions from Tanaiste Mary Harney and Minister Síle de Valera have shown, our economic and cultural faith largely aspires to Bostonian orthodoxy. Broadcasting in Ireland has in recent years truly reflected this *Zeitgeist*.

At the retail level, we in Ireland may have capitulated to what can be called UKisation – Tesco, Marks and Spencer, Boots, Ann Summers sex shops in our main streets and our mean thoughts – but in our mercenary hearts we are American. At the shopkeeper level, we may have unwittingly reversed back into the UK, but it barely camouflages our ever-present cultural mid-Atlantic limbo. And that class of women which can afford to be serial shoppers seems perfectly happy with these developments. The attitude of advertisers to them is summed up in what advertising man David Ogilvy wrote as long ago as 1963: "The consumer isn't a moron; she is your wife."

When will the empowerment of women result in a rage at the exploitation of their hitherto harmless pleasure in shopping? Never, if one can judge by the effusion of another powerful female, our enterprising Minister Mary O'Rourke, who uses the word "deregulation" as if it were "abracadabra", a magic panacea for all our ills. If she were a gardener, she would know that a deregulated garden, left to itself, will encourage only weeds to flourish.

The deregulated multinational mogul took away our freedom "by making us think he is giving us the freedom of having what we want", to quote John Waters. It is odd that this aspect of patriarchy is rarely criticised by the ideological female in Ireland. Canadian Naomi Klein in her *No Logo* book has set a headline which is well worth following here.

Underneath the glossy surface, Ireland at present is sinking under the weight of paper money, instant hotels, stag-party vomit, self-disgust, 400 male and 100 female suicides per year, 6,000 abortions, homelessness among children and even among the young middle classes, the horrific abandonment of abused children, road artery thrombosis, silence from its artists, a clamour from its tabloid journalists and, last but not least, an illusory liberation of women. I can think of no better description of this situation than "a deregulated society".

LYRIC

Put another nickel in,
In the nickelodeon.
All I want is loving you
And music, music, music.
"Music, Music, Music", recorded by Teresa Brewer, 1950

In early 1997 broadcasting minister, Michael D. Higgins, issued his *nihil obstat* to RTÉ's proposal for a music and arts channel whose purpose essentially was to subsume and extend to twenty-four hours the serious music programmes broadcast after 7.30 p.m. on FM3.

Director General Bob Collins wanted the new channel to have the widest possible appeal and thus be amenable to sponsorship and advertising. How else would RTÉ pay for it? I was reluctantly amenable to sponsorship but dead set against spot ads. I objected on the grounds that all of our other channels, apart from RnaG, were already sufficiently polluted. If we accepted the principle of a linguistic sanctuary from consumerism, should there not also be a sanctuary for threatened musical species? But the director general was as single-minded as usual. He campaigned personally and by letter with department officials to get them to see things his way. Minister Higgins had stayed silent on the matter, although having stipulated there should be no ads on the FM3 overnight retransmission of music supplied by the EBU service, it was clear where his inclination lay. However, in June 1997 the government changed and a new minister, Síle de Valera, took over. The Executive's worries that she, being a music lover, might also object to spot ads on the new service were ultimately unfounded. When Bob Collins said in March 1998 that the new channel would carry spot ads, my objections were brushed aside. Finally, Redlich and FitzGerald were for advertising, and the matter was clinched. In fact, by October 1998 there still had been no ministerial approval for the move, but by opening night the following May it was a done deal.

Lyric FM was to be the full-time successor to FM3, which had been a kind of maiden aunt fulfilling RTÉ's obligations to decent music in Ireland after 7.30 in the evenings.

FM3 shared wavelengths with RnaG and was frequently booted off the air when that station needed it for special occasions like the annual *sean-nós* competition at Oireachtas na Gaeilge. I have entertained fantasies of drunken classical music aesthetes falling asleep during FM3 and waking up to Sarah Grealish singing *"Amhráin Mhuinse"* and exclaiming, "Good Lord, how extraordinarily contemporary!"

But this poor-cousin arrangement was not completely satisfactory for sober lovers of contemporary and classical music. FM3 was a bit stuffy but satisfying, an evening oasis for refugees from the relative trivia of daytime radio and night-time television. Like RnaG, it ran no commercials. Once having travelled across Ireland by car to an Authority meeting and tried to find some tolerable daytime radio, I finally settled on RnaG as the least offensive choice. The rest, local and national, were similar in raucousness to the small-town radio stations I had heard driving across America thirty years ago. I mentioned this experience to the director general, who ruefully said that he was often tempted to do the same.

It occurred to me that if we could not personally stand this lowest common denominator of broadcasting, why were we imposing it on the general citizenry? Were we like those Ph.D.'s in anthropology who would like primitive peoples to have the benefits of civilisation but to continue making mud pies?

Lord Reith, first director general of the BBC, has in recent consumer times been much derided for imposing a diet of cultural elitism on audiences, i.e. giving audiences not what they wanted but what he thought would serve them best. This outraged many populists. By contrast, very few people actually demand commercially dense tabloid broadcasting, and a majority object to it. But such a diet is imposed on the public. Why is there not an equal amount of derision directed at this imposition? Are broadcasters totally compromised? Is the audience struck dumb?

But commercial-free FM3 in the evening was for people like me, a minority of 25,000 listeners (Lyric now boasts 100,000 listeners). We could tolerate plummy voices because they knew their music. We could even endure the smooth transatlantic tones that introduced the Texaco-sponsored live transmissions of Metropolitan Opera matinees. RTÉ has an honourable record in relation to classical music. Without the national broadcaster – there having traditionally been no formal music policy in this state – the Irish in general would never have been exposed to the classics or the music of contemporary composers. FM3 was no longer quite so good about the latter, but it would say that you can't please everybody all the time.

I heard my first Radio Éireann Symphony concert in the Phoenix Hall in Dublin in the fifties. Entry was free to these twice weekly recordings for radio. The more elaborate concerts were held in spring and autumn in the Gaiety Theatre. It cost money to get in there, although the wooden seats in the "gods" at half-a-crown were good value. Aged fourteen, I fell asleep at my first *Messiah* performed by Our Lady's Choral Society and the Radio Éireann

Symphony Orchestra in the Capitol Theatre, Dublin. I was the guest of a Carmelite Father whose designs on me were pure and confined to developing potential priest material. The only fruit of this pious ambition was that thereafter I would look forward to the *Messiah* annually in the National Boxing Stadium, the country not yet boasting a national concert hall. Without RTÉ it is unlikely I would have developed my musical taste further than Tennessee Ernie Ford and my father's love of Italian opera and Victorian ballads.

But of recent times RTÉ has adopted the UK consumer approach to decent music, a kind of *Last Night at the Proms* – but every day. The RTÉ sponsorship of the piano player from the *Late Late Show* and his December 1999 version of Handel's *Messiah*, which I found abominable, was a good illustration of how RTÉ has been tempted by the trendy approach.

When the RTÉ Authority was originally informed by its Executive of the imminence of the twenty-four-hour arts and music radio channel, I was delighted. When the lightweight name, Lyric FM, was imposed on us, I was a bit concerned. Even the director general, Bob Collins, had mild reservations about the name and agreed that the Authority might have been consulted. But when I heard that the new service would try to attract spot advertising, my heart sank. I knew that meant a diminution of seriousness. At lunch, following an Authority meeting during which FM3 and Lyric FM were discussed and where I had spoken in terms of dumbing-down, Bob Collins hissed at me, "S. N. O. B." I was taken aback by this good-humoured jibe because I love Fats Waller and Robert Johnson, Mississippi John Hurt and the Beatles, Freddie Mercury and Kate Bush as much as Bach, Mahler, Elgar, Ligeti and Penderescki. And when I remembered that in 1993 the future director general of RTÉ had publicly defended the Eurovision Song Contest as art, I did not feel too badly about the slight. I answered him spiritedly: "I will fight you on the beaches."

Nevertheless, the RTÉ Executive hired Chris Vesey, former head of programming with Classic FM in Britain, to teach the paddies how to make classical music pay. The RTÉ Authority was also not consulted on such a philosophically important appointment.

I want to mention that my affection for "classical" music is not unqualified. I have a theory that the nineteenth century development of the huge symphony orchestra, divided into ranks of uniformly dressed players, paralleled the rise of the huge armies of that period. The symphony orchestra is essentially militaristic. The uniformity, hierarchical structure, synchronised movements and egotistical generals were analogous to the increased size and overpowering volume of the new size of symphony orchestra. Delicate sonata form for piano or harpsichord was adapted by orchestration into massive and intimidating symphonic form. The form was hardly altered (nor often was the musical significance), but the size of the instrument and the concomitant decibel level thundered out one message: listen and tremble. The psychology of this is not musically unique: many a three-chord guitarist has felt his emanations to be greatly improved by attaching 1,000-watt amplifiers to his instrument. Goebbels also advocated telling a fib so large that it would have to be believed.

I am dangerously near to suggesting that a marshall's baton is metaphorically interchangeable with a conductor's baton, but, to undermine this analogy, even I can point out a significant difference: the fact that the individual weapons used by members of the orchestra have barely altered in a hundred years. The question arises: how has such an outmoded army survived?

The invocation on occasions of pomp and power of this agreeable but antique form of music-making and the extraordinary persistence of its acceptibility may not be coincidental. Musical taste is not usually a distinguishing feature of the powerful, which means government leaders and captains of industry, the great and the good. So why do formative elements approve the existence of such an expensive archaeological survival? Why are these people to be found in large numbers at concerts of centuries-old music? Free tickets cannot be the main inducement. In my opinion the symphony concert is a state status symbol. Is such an occasion not also a way of saying to the man in the street: you may have your tin whistles but we have the howitzers? Might is right. It is no coincidence that some of the greatest symphony orchestras have been developed by the empires of the Third Reich, Britannia, the USSR and the US.

Such large-scale music is an affirmation by association of the greatness of its sponsors. This was why in 1995, on one of its few social outings, the Authority was treated by the Executive to the best seats in the National Concert Hall for a concert by Shaun Davy and Liam Ó Floinn.

There is another aspect: classical orchestral music is labour intensive and highly unionised, which is why innovative modern music – which may only require a single instrument, even a synthesiser – is regarded as a slightly backstreet or blackleg activity. Further, the musical army is trotted out so often that there is little time or space for audiences to be exposed to, or develop a taste for, equally serious but more intimate developments in music, such as modern chamber music. In order to achieve notice, many adventurous composers – certainly this is true in Ireland – must first write in classical mode and score their music for the standing army of conventional instruments; they must make an act of faith in the past before they are taken seriously in the present. Few major commissions find their way to one-man bands.

Individual orchestral players realise this. Perhaps their propensity for spending their spare time playing chamber music in private is a means of retaining sanity?

The above speculation is not unrelated to the reasons RTÉ retains a symphony orchestra on its payroll. It can regularly be trotted out to flatter its masters, as in part fulfilling its public service brief and therefore as justification for the licence fee. If there were not such a *raison d'être*, I have no doubt the National Symphony Orchestra would be summarily dispensed with.

I am not alone in this perspective. Richard Boothby is a member of Fretwork, a British consort of violin players. On a recent tour of Ireland he said (*The Irish Times*, 6 June 2001): "Orchestral music is really finished. . . The death of the orchestra is imminent and we're living through its death throes." Through a similar melancholic prejudice, I listen to Lyric FM.

I understand that when the new service was first mooted, Bob Collins and Minister Higgins pressed hard for its location outside Dublin. Other RTÉ staff and services might have to be dislodged from the capital with a JCB, but this new service could form a precedent. I cheered that decision, which must have been a tough one to enforce on the Dublin musical scene.

But we serious music lovers were still in serious trouble. We were now being targeted as a potential market, being shunted into a twenty-four-hour gourmet siding. Despite Yehudi Menuhin's saying that music is the only unpunished passion, our passion for music was our undoing. RTÉ's rampant panic to make money from every source possible caused it to fix beady eyes on those it regarded as elitists and highbrows, those inhabiting the advertisers' magic A, B and C categories. In reality we were simply a cross-section of people with an ear for music other than Bono and U2, and a low tolerance of yap and pop broadcasting. RTÉ saw a niche to make more money and decided to expose us to their commercial masters. If RTÉ's granny was a radio service, they would in these straitened times be forced sell her piecemeal, in commercial bits.

In preparation for Lyric FM, the existing serious music service, FM3, had first to be softened up and dumbed down. FM3, the only begetter of Lyric FM, began the process of catering for those whose taste is stretched by Andrew Lloyd Webber. (An English composer, Harrison

Birtwistle, when asked why he hated Lloyd Weber, said, "It saves time.") Voices in love with themselves from the pop radio 2FM were imported. Gilbert and Sullivan began to percolate through the schedules; there was a pleasant series on this light music delivered to us by the ex-head of RTÉ music, Cathal McCabe, who, like myself, once was a pub pianist and loved Rodgers, Hammerstein and Sigmund Romberg. As if they sensed a wind of change, hitherto staid FM3 presenters began to sound hysterically good-humoured. It did not save them from the scaffold. Marian Dwan, she of the soft voice and exquisite music, who for years soothed us late at night and early in the morning, was unfortunately among the first to disappear, although in her case she herself left to pursue other studies.

In its advertisement for producers, the new radio channel demanded "a high level of motivation and skill" in developing, among other things, "finance and sponsorship". The result was Lyric FM, of whose final form, management, title and location the RTÉ Authority was informed in late 1998. The Authority had very little input into the venture, other than rubber-stamping the decisions. At least Lyric was put into the hands of a distinguished radio producer, Seamus Crimmins.

The public launch in Limerick on 1 May 1999 featured a day-long lucky dip of personalities and popular classics. The live concert broadcast that night from the University of Limerick was a success, despite the National Symphony Orchestra playing pot-boilers. But a local diva proved that intelligent choice of material and superb technique can convincingly postpone the deterioration of a wonderful voice. Afterwards in the hotel bar I congratulated the chairman and the director general on now having three commercial radio channels at their disposal: Radio 1, 2FM and Lyric FM. The director general said, "Lyric FM will never pay for itself." But at least, the three of us agreed, there would be something else besides sport to listen to on Saturday and Sunday afternoons.

Soon after the station began broadcasting, it became clear that the midday playlist of pop classics ("lollipops") and one or two auto-erotic 2FM voices on the station were specifically designed to attract advertising, to make it accessible to the same crass spot ads that echo and resound through the airwaves of corporate RTÉ and mock the sincerity of the people who take programming and music seriously. The temporary reappearance of Henry Kelly confirmed that. He said that he was happy in Lyric FM because the buzz was like Classic FM in Britain seven years before. Now Henry Kelly is gone, replaced by Des Keogh, who knows his music, and Lyric FM is rapidly assuming its rightful place as an occasional jewel in RTÉ's crown and soother of the nation's outraged musical sensibilities.

I have a deep interest in music, but my taste has always been limited to what is good rather than what is in the charts. Many years ago the singer Bono got his secretary to ask me to meet him after my *Atlantean* films showed the connection between Ireland and North Africa. My children heard me mentioning the name and went into hysterics. This was odd because I had hardly heard of the performer and was certainly not familiar with his work. I went out and bought a cassette but could make neither head nor tail of the lyrics. All I could hear was a disco beat. It transpired that Bono thought my theories might explain his own extraordinary vocal talents and had even passed the word on to Bob Dylan – with whose music at least I was familiar. That is the gist of what I learned during a long monologue from the young man in the Great Southern Hotel in Galway. His young wife was very nice. I learned that her name was Ali, and she later did good work with Chernobyl children, as did her husband in his publicising the gross indebtedness of poor nations. I have still not taken to his music, but at least my children got his autograph.

My continuing ignorance about such pop musical icons may be excused on more than the grounds of advancing age. My favourite vocal performer of all time has been

Dietrich Fischer-Dieskau and my favourite music is Schumann *lieder*. A close second comes John Lennon and then Conamara *sean-nós* singing. What chance would Bono have in that league? Fortunately, so far, he has stayed away from Lyric FM.

At the time of writing, daytime Lyric FM, despite its mainly refreshing qualities, must pay lip service to the commercial continuum from 2FM – including at least one, fortunately temporary, importation of Gerry Ryan – to Radio 1. Not often, but often enough to be irritating, there are voices conducting love affairs with their own timbre and sonority, talking about "updates" and "playlists" and "top twenties", proclaiming the virtue of some classical piece as also having been filleted for a TV commercial. There is a computerised playlist appropriate to the time of day compiled by those in the know, the military strategists, from which the corporals take their limited pick: the "Flower Song" from *Carmen*, Beethoven's *"Für Elise"*, Schubert's *"Die Forelle"*, Handel's "Water Music", Liszt's Hungarian Dance No. 2, the *"Casta Diva"* aria, Sibelius' *Finlandia* – all the usual suspects are wheeled out repetitively. Youngsters who do not know their Albéniz from their Elgar tend to go for pieces familiar to them from commercial exploitations and possibly from childhood music lessons. The result is, at certain daylight hours, a plethora of Pavarotti, Callas, the Three Tenors (and the Irish version, the Three Fivers), when one can at least grin ruefully at a presenter who makes Delibes sound like "jellybaby". There is, despite its honourable intentions, a danger that Lyric could bring serious music into disrepute by providing a limited menu of this rich resource. On each of the hundred nights leading up to 31 December 1999, music critic Michael Dervan played music in the "classical" tradition of the previous hundred years on Lyric FM. The musical range, diversity and invention which he revealed suggested a bottomless well from which Lyric FM could drink indefinitely. I fear the channel still feels it necessary to only sip at this well, like a child forced to take its castor oil. But I must be patient; in the beginning long symphonies and sonatas were irritatingly filleted for the single most attractive movements. This has since been compensated for by *The Full Score*, which defiantly plays entire pieces. Lyric FM is coming along nicely, and as beggars cannot be choosers, it is still one of RTÉ's lights in the tunnel.

So, credit where credit is due: despite the advertisers – or rather when they are not interested – the service in the early morning and most of the evening has rapidly become the only half-sanctuary from the everyday frenzy of selling. People like Lawlor, Herriot, Heffernan, Coburn, Nic Gearailt, Burnett, Curtis, Thurston and several others keep the flag of good music broadcasting flying. Admittedly some voices are reminiscent of Patrick Begley, who in the fifties was sacked from his announcing job in Radio Éireann because of what was imagined to be his Oxbridge accent. But at least the owners of some Lyric FM voices, those which are clearly refugees from the UK and the US, also know their music. And there is a courageous effort to introduce listeners to contemporary music. This even happens, but very accidentally, on one evening programme, *The Green Room*, which plays music from the "movies", in which I have a certain interest.

By film music is not at all meant *The Sound of Music*. By virtue of its subordinate relationship to the image, a film score does not have to try so hard to be accessible, in the concert sense, to a general audience. In fact the reverse is true: the best achieved film music is entirely abstract, non-programmatic, is more likely to experiment with divergent musical ideas, to be intentionally "dissonant", to defy popular taste and convention, to use chords and orchestrations that would be quite at home in the work of Berg, Stravinsky, Weill, Berkeley, Cage. As composer Frank Corcoran so elegantly put it in the first edition of the *Journal of Music in Ireland*: "Every film or television score parades subcutaneous tonal sophistication. We don't notice it."

Film music can cheekily do what would bankrupt the National Concert Hall (which Michael Dervan has accurately described as "a middlebrow musical heaven") if it relied exclusively on it. Film is potentially the most effective popular introduction to serious contemporary musical form. However, insofar as the film scores featured on Lyric FM are those which in the main oscillate between plagiarised classics, Hollywood musicals and the saccharine of such as Michael Nyman, I have the unfortunate impression that the producers and presenter of *The Green Room* would not be terribly impressed by what Frank Corcoran has to say.

To pursue the critical line: unless one has an unlimited appetite for lollipops like "The Poet and Peasant Overture", *"Nessun Dorma"*, one piece each by Barber and Albinoni, Beethoven's Ninth Symphony (the one where they sing, dy'e know) and Dvořák's *New World Symphony*, there is no unblemished public broadcasting refuge during the winter daylight hours now for people who like to relax and listen to music and words other than bland pop, "lifestyle" programmes and Hyde Park Corner talk radio. Perhaps I ask for too much. Perhaps having experienced such untarnished channels in the UK, France and Canada, I have been spoiled for taste. I hope Lyric FM does not panic too much and that the people in it who know music and adhere to their vision will continue bravely on.

I suppose, like any (ex-) public broadcaster, my prejudices are by now quite clear. And what are the sources of my prejudices?

Childhood was shared between Radio Éireann, the BBC Home Service and Radio Luxembourg. I moved easily between *Living with Lynch* and *The Billy Cotton Band Show*; between *Din Joe* and *The Goon Show*; between *Much Binding in the Marsh* and *The Kennedys of Castleross*; between Max Jaffa and Charles Lynch;

between the Walton's sponsored programme with Leo Maguire and Pete Murray's *Top Twenty from Luxembourg*; between *Making and Mending* on RÉ to *Dick Barton, Special Agent* on the BBC; between "Greensleeves" introducing the *Sunday Night Play* on Radio Éireann and Albert Sandler with the Palm Court Orchestra on BBC. In retrospect, the breadth of listening available then was extraordinary. The field of broadcasting may have been relatively tiny, but it was near to a balanced ecology.

I still listen to the Home Service successor, BBC Radio 4. It is a mixed pleasure for me to listen to unhurried voices given time to express ideas and concepts so pithily and unemphatically that I wonder why their articulate equivalent is so rarely heard on mainstream RTÉ. I refuse to believe there is not a proportionate number of thoughtful and articulate people on this gabby island. Perhaps it is that we have made such a virtue of informality that we expect to be interrupted if we try to express or even grapple with concepts other than the latest newspaper headline or political crisis. The soundbite rules. We increasingly constitute a kind of tabloid culture, and our broadcasting service reflects this. That is why Lyric FM constitutes an occasional oasis. True, there are a few other oases of considered thought to be found in the spectrum of mainstream RTÉ; they are in some of the programmes presented by the likes of Andy O'Mahony, Tim Lehane, Olivia O'Leary, Theo Dorgan, Norita Ní Chartúir and Seosamh Ó Cuaig (RnaG) and especially John Quinn. Rarely are they to be found on RTÉ's TV output and certainly not at peak hours. Therefore, I repeat, since beggars cannot be choosers, hooray for Lyric FM.

Do such assessments make people like me – as the director general of RTÉ implied – intellectual snobs, after all?

I wonder what will happen to the mindscape of Ireland when the same criterion of value is applied to educational institutions other then RTÉ? Perhaps it is already happening on this progressive island.

IMAGE IS EVERYTHING

*What the public wants is the image of passion, not
passion itself.*
Roland Barthes, *Mythologies* (1957)

When an anti-cyclone settles over Conamara in
late December, it makes Christmas and the New
Year bearable. Moroccan-blue skies, pierced in
the morning by white jet trails; two swans wheezing their
way through the still air to their nearby winter quarters;
the clear canopy of stars at night: they reassure me that not
all is lost. The Greeks called these the halcyon days, and I
revel in them. Then one morning the Beanna Beola, their
foothills swaddled in cotton wool clouds, appear to be lev-
itating, and I realise my imagination is running away with
me.

Long, long ago when the late singer and *bon viveur* Seán
Ó Conaire of Rosmuc saw well-groomed RTÉ executives
embarking on a boat at Ros a Bhíl to go to the Aran
Islands, he – a very natty dresser himself, nicknamed 007
– remarked, "I was thinking, if there was an accident, all
of them would go down to the bottom of the sea in their
good suits – with money in their pockets."

Money talks. Clothes maketh the man. Image replaces
substance. Ireland has long entered the age of the spin doctor, the flashy logo and the computer-generated soft sell.

The product is secondary to the brand, which entirely depends on a secular kind of religious belief.

When the RTÉ annual report is published, it must reflect the glossy, modern image which is essential to a multimillion pound media industry – or so the director of corporate affairs intimated to me in 1996. This report also must feature the individual photographs of those pillars of society who constitute the Authority which allegedly runs RTÉ. The trouble when I arrived was that I was not alone on the Authority in being disturbed by the glossiness and palpable expense of the publication. A couple of us resolved that the next year's report would be more modest, reflecting the austerity with which the national broadcaster was confronted.

When it came to having photographs taken for the following year's report, I refused to participate in the colour process, saying that if my picture were to appear, it must be in ascetic black and white to reflect the stark choices facing RTÉ. Nobody was impolite enough to mention that black and white might also represent the filter through which I seemed to view this whole business.

I supplied the director of corporate affairs with a black and white snap, taken by myself, holding the camera at arm's length. It presented a problem for the (outside) designer of the annual glossy brochure, but he overcame it very well. He balanced my stark image with a similar black and white of Maureen Rennicks, who had meantime resigned. We looked like images from an obituary card.

I sent a message through the secretariat to the designer of the annual report, complimenting him on his solution. He never got it. I sent a note directly to Des Gaffney, the staff photographer, saying my refusal to let him photograph me was no reflection on his competence. I got no reply there, either. I was forced to wonder if anybody was listening or was I simply in the position of James Thurber who wrote of himself, "Easy to rouse, he's hard to quiet and people usually just go away."

In my third year I capitulated to colour. Half in earnest,

I had tried to do a deal on the side with Tom Quinn: if he would release minutes of previous Authority meetings, I would submit to his colour photographers. He laughed at me. But to show I was not entirely a maverick, I consented to colour. I conceded that small defeat in the hope of achieving greater victories. The hope was unrealised.

Ever since, the RTÉ annual report continues to be a glossy compendium of self-congratulation which fools nobody. The Authority and its chief officers look confident and well-fed.

Sometimes, as I listened to the civilised discourse in the boardoom, I tried to imagine the undercurrents, the agendas, what each was thinking while we waited to interrupt each other. FitzGerald could urge programmatic changes in News and Current Affairs, investment in imaginative ideas; Purcell could point out that staff forced on to a treadmill had hardly time to bless themselves, never mind reflect on new ideas; Tannahill could urge focussed discussion on programmes. We talked about the individual trees while the wood itself was under threat. Polite exchanges on how precisely to avoid an iceberg seem to me pointless when we have already struck it and the ship is sinking. Attley could mention the anti-public service ethos of the government. I could go on about the overweening influence of big business. The Executive listened calmly to our waffle; its priority was the survival of the organisation, no matter what the cost.

In 1972 I wrote a fantasy novel about TV in which a paranoid director general imagines that the Silent Majority assembles daily and silently on the lawn below his window to stare up at him in silent rebuke. In growing panic he calls on a staff lavatory cleaner named Uriah to reassure him that he is not going mad. Uriah seizes his opportunity, reassures the DG and achieves such indispensability that he becomes privy to all the secrets on the third floor. Among these activities is a national telly bingo game, the profits from which are creamed off by everybody from the taoiseach to the director general. Because publishers are, in the main, sensible people, such nonsense was never published.

The reality in 1997, halfway through the Authority's term of office, was comparatively banal: one member in yellow tie and zoot suit, another with crumpled clothes and machine-gun delivery that few could follow, a third with his sinuses, myself ever disgruntled. The chairman's hair was already whitening, and the director general maintained a sparrow-like alertness to peripheral dangers. We were so polite, so courteous, so restrained, and ultimately so ineffectual. I recognise this as a rude little boy's perspective – perhaps the same perspective that saw the Emperor had no clothes? I also recognise that such a perilous vision is easily sensed by so-called rational minds and renders one's opinions open to automatic dismissal. In general I felt we we were analogous to sociologist Peter Berger's description: "Men build their cultures, huddling together, nervously loquacious at the edge of an abyss."

The abyss was the realpolitik of broadcasting in a consumer age. Some members at that table realised that with the legacy of Reaganism and Thatcherism, the rise of Murdoch and Black, with the destruction of the only monster – the USSR – that had kept these other monsters in check, the job in hand was to preserve the organisation's status quo on the assumption that it alone was the vessel of virtue, the guardian of the public broadcasting ethos. Certainly, the chairman believed that. He told me so. It followed that there must be maintained as much as possible of its present structure, its hierarchy, moral authority and the jobs of most of its staff.

I tended to believe that all these things were doomed, and that the task in hand was solely a matter of salvaging some small decencies from the inevitable shipwreck, so that when the present temporary, if worldwide, tidal wave of unbridled greed ebbed, there might be something to build on again. Mine is called a *catastrophs ansicht* in German. It was a time for recovering and nourishing abandoned roots, for shedding bad habits and for using RTÉ's considerable influence to set ethical examples. God knows, in the last decade of the millennium, the country never needed such things so badly. But in a looming shipwreck there is little of the heroism, much of the cost-cutting and plenty of the opportunism displayed on the *Titanic*. It is the sad case of every man for himself, his constituency and his pet hobbyhorses and hates. Or perhaps it is I who am being utterly naive; that it was always like this but that I never realised it. Over lunch one day I asked Conor Sexton of RTÉ Commercial Enterprises why the powers that be, implying ourselves, seemed to be paralysed into inaction by the problems consequent on rampant consumerism. He answered pithily, "There are too many lobbies."

There was another spectre looming over the good ship RTÉ. The concept of "broad"casting was nearly obsolete. Narrow-casting was the future, according to the farsighted. This meant a fragmenting of the audience, a dreadful prospect for a broadcaster two-thirds of whose income was derived from having universal access to Irish consumers. In other words, RTÉ's national semi-monopoly of advertising directed at three million consumers was being splintered and shattered into a multitude of local markets which might be of little interest to Adidas, Kellogg's, Hasbro, Nike or Persil. Put another way, the "Balkanisation" of every community or interest group, the dread of all totalitarians, was imminent. The advent of digital broadcasting would expedite this. To me it was wonderful news. It meant that each community might develop its own service and self-image. To RTÉ it spelled doom. Unless, of course, over the years it had developed a foothold in local communities, had fostered a loyalty in them, had developed a pattern of local access to the national airwaves. It had not. It was Radio Teilifís Dublin to the culchies. It could expect little mercy.

Like a rabbit trapped in oncoming headlights, RTÉ was paralysed. All it could think of was a series of cosmetic and increasingly desperate holding actions of which the principal one was to dumb down and entice youngsters away from UTV, Nickelodeon and BBC 1. It must be admitted that it did this very well with the aid of a bright man from the UK called Andrew Burns, who was appointed in autumn 1997 and given an inflated salary (rumoured to be £60,000), a relatively enormous budget (estimated at £1 million) and the title head of scheduling and packaging – sorry, planning.

This was the result of a review group which reported in September 1996 to Liam Miller, director of programmes. It focussed on the sharp decline in the Network 2 audience of young people, i.e. those between sixteen and thirty-nine. In July 1997 Joe Mulholland, the managing director of television, reported to us that the channel had little identity or distinctiveness due to a lack of home-produced programmes and also a lack of policy. His solution in the autumn was to hire Andrew Burns. The ex-UK Gold man's basic ploy was to package Network 2's goodies in a smother of music that had more hormones than harmonies, making it a capital offence, it seemed, to allow talking heads for more than the obligatory two seconds of a pop video. He gave graphic designers their heads with computer animations, allowed the decibel level of ambient sound be increased, allowed sound-bites to be substituted for coherent discussion and did not discourage programme participants from using the words "bollox", "Jasus" and "shite" as often as possible. One of the last straws was when he and his patron, Joe Mulholland, permitted the replacement of professional meteorologists with pretty young things, male and female. An outraged public soon reversed this ploy. Inexorably, new young presenters were fostered: clever and pretty young people who had spent hours practising the polished tones and demeanours of Gay Byrne and Pat Kenny – but never Joe Duffy. As Fergal Costello, ex-RTÉ trade unionist and cameraman, said to me: the youngsters had developed all the accoutrement of the successful broadcaster except one tiny thing – any idea or personality of their own. But with their "youthful" appearance and simulated enthusiasm, they filled the advertisers' shopping lists. And as with many media-adopted personae, they could talk faster than the speed of a bullshit-detector.

By default, the Authority approved these changes. I amused myself by imagining all of us sitting there like grotesque figures from a Francis Bacon painting. It was diverting, albeit not aesthetically pleasing. The panorama of paunches, red elbows, scrawny necks, thinning hair, sagging breasts, ancient dugs, drooping genitalia, unhealthily pale skin, all of us doomed to die soon, conjured up such a pathetic image that it could not in charity be entertained for long. And we were trying to appeal to a "yoof" audience.

The disease spread. On radio, the displacement of a great broadcaster like Andy O'Mahony from the *Sunday Show* by a "yoof" called Ryan Tubridy was a classic example of this new philosophy (although Andy has publicly expressed delight at his removal to gentler pastures and Tubridy, like another "voice" called Philip Boucher-Hayes, is completely *au fait* with the latest journalistic fashions).

In truth, the UK man, Andrew Burns, simply intensified a trend that already existed in RTÉ.

My own interest in films was supposed to be catered for on RTÉ 1 by a disc jockey – the best, I'm told – named Dave Fanning, who also did commercials for a car and a bank and professed himself in the *RTÉ Guide* (28 March 1997) to be "more interested in Tom Cruise's arse than in Fellini's *ouevre*. I am, I really am." At least this was balanced by the fine current affairs interviewer, Richard Crowley, describing that actor in the same publication as "an annoying little shite".

Fanning was the choice of now-departed Director of Programmes David Blake-Knox when the latter decided to put on a programme about the cinema. Fanning, the presenter, made it clear to successive producers Anita Notaro and Peter McEvoy that he was not interested in foreign or arthouse stuff and only Irish if they had Oscar potential.

As is now traditional in RTÉ, the presenter leads the show and the producer makes the best of it. No popcorn, no Fanning; no Fanning, no *Movie Show*. McEvoy was reluctant to do the programme on this basis, but then there might be no programme on cinema, and McEvoy was a cinema lover. Blake-Knox seems to have selected Fanning exclusively on the basis that he was a 2FM voice, i.e. a disc jockey, who had built up street-cred among the young audience which RTÉ needed. Put simply, Blake-Knox's duty was to deliver teeny-boppers to the advertisers. If there was to be a programme on cinema, Fanning must be the presenter. So, *The Movie Show* went ahead as a consumer guide to the latest Hollywood trivia. In Notaro's and McEvoy's hands it was not altogether bad. The latter was able to insert the occasional slice of intelligence into it, including an interview with William Friedkin (*The Exorcist*). And even though Friedkin was cut down to two minutes, at least his face was shown. I eventually found myself avoiding all but the opening credits on *The Movie Show* – they cued me to switch off – because I could not bear to witness what I considered to be a dumbing down of the art of cinema. When, at the desire of Fanning and with Andrew Burns' approval (but against producer McEvoy's advice), the show's slot was changed to Wednesday and was extended by ten minutes, it died a death. It lost much of its audience and RTÉ lost the film distributors' goodwill. In late 2000 the head of scheduling who had approved the change, Andrew Burns, departed, as previously had *The Movie Show*, neither deeply mourned

On Network 2 there was an Aero chocolate-sponsored season of films. Another enthusiast named Brian Reddin dented my enjoyment of some of the excellent films shown with bloomers like referring to Ingmar Bergman's best-known actor as "Max von Sindow" and actually putting people off Bergman's old masterpiece, *The Seventh Seal*, by warning them that it was pretty heavy going. Among other naiveties, he identified the director of *Darling* as John "Slysinger". At least he was later pushed beyond midnight to avoid offending the discerning who were in bed with our cocoa.

The RTÉ Authority was never asked for its advice about such mundane details; it was presented with decisions. It was considered prudent to have our heads kept above all this, in wreaths of general policy-making smoke. Decisions about the organisation's core activity, making programmes, were made somewhere down there beneath us.

Thus was RTÉ reinventing itself in 1997; Network 2, the second channel, was revamped and relaunched. And the tactic has succeeded well: now, few over forty and still not brain-dead can endure it – with eccentric and vulgarian exceptions like me who once enjoyed *Don't Feed the Gondolas* (a cog from *Have I Got News For You*) when Sean Moncrieff was in charge. There was also the wonderful turkey Dustin, who appealed to the iconoclast in me. But my age group is not categorised as big spenders.

Here are the supporting figures.

Bob Towler, head of research of the British Independent TV Commission, produced the following at a television conference on 29 March 1995 in London: the age group that watches most TV is over 65. They watch 5.07 hours daily. The 55–64 age group watches 4.12 hours daily. Therefore, people over 55 watch an average of 4.39 hours daily. By contrast, the 16–34 year olds watch only 3.07 hours daily.

So why do all television services – both public service and commercial – now exclusively target their peak-hour programmes at the younger group of viewers? Need I spell it out? The 16–34 year-olds have more disposable income. The advertisers call the shots. Programmes that might appeal to the "mature" – and most loyal – viewers and licence payers are pushed to late night "when they are old and grey and full of sleep, and nodding by the fire and dreaming of the soft look their eyes had once". These figures applied to all television in Britain in 1995 and, I would suggest, still apply to the Republic of Ireland. In 1996, the then RTÉ director of sales, Colm Molloy, was frank about it: advertisers are not interested in viewers over fifty, he wrote. Seventy per cent of RTÉ's advertising revenue came from advertising directed at the 15–35 age group. Grey power has made no impact in Irish tellyland yet – so we can be ignored; let us continue watching RTÉ 1 where we constitute, worryingly, a large proportion of the viewers. Worrying, because we are also mature enough to resist advertisers' blandishments.

Did these developments mean that the first television channel, RTÉ 1, became a bastion of intellect, taste and good broadcasting? It did not. Although most programmes of substance became confined to this channel, many of them were banished to the later, non-peak viewing hours after ten or eleven o'clock. It was pointed out to me recently by a despairing RTÉ executive that there were two categoric exceptions to this rule: religion and the Irish language, i.e. *Léargas* and *Would You Believe*? (which happened to be two of the finest RTÉ programmes and which I tried to make a point of watching). How strange that such limited audience-grabbers should be exempt from the general rule of dumbing-down. Even I cannot speculate on such reasoning, unless the Knights of Columbanus are even more influential than I think, or that the old *Gaeilgeoir* lobby still has a kick in it. Who says that the aspirations of the Irish people have been forgotten! Although I spent two years as producer of religious programmes in the sixties and have a passing interest in Irish language programmes, I still find this positive discrimination intriguing – and, I must grudgingly confess, encouraging.

But there was a problem. An internal RTÉ survey in 1996 showed that the 15–35 age group of Irish viewers disliked Irish language programmes so much that, of seventeen categories, this was the second on the list of those programmes which they would definitely exclude from any channel. And what came first in the "most-dispensable" list? Believe it or not, sport. A big question which was not asked was: why then is 25 per cent of RTÉ's TV production budget spent on sport?

I can suggest an even more important question: why do TV executives rely on such nonsensical attitude surveys? Is it because they cannot think for themselves or because such surveys, selectively interpreted, give them a rationalisation for doing what they already have decided? Or perhaps a little of both. In the context of sport, the home-grown financial wizard Dermot Desmond put his finger on it in an interview: "A lot of it is being dictated by TV advertising. *It is fundamental* [my italics]."

In broadcasting now it is not the producers and directors, not the writers and artists, not even the programme controllers who are in charge. The person who controls and arranges the one sacred text, the schedule, is high priest. All must bow down before him. In turn he must prostrate himself before the one true god, the advertiser. This startling new wisdom in Ireland was actually commonplace forty years ago – RTÉ TV was just being launched – in the US when Ed Murrow, America's premier broadcaster, was "remaindered" because of commercial pressures on television.

Murrow's involvement in CBS (Columbia Broadcasting System – one of the three major networks) dated from *See It Now* in 1951, through *CBS Reports, Person to Person* and *Small World*, in which the insights and utter integrity of his reports caused regular explosions in conservative circles. The main reason broadcasters in Europe might remember him was his 1954 programme about the witch-hunter, Senator Joe McCarthy. With Ed Murrow's forensic help, the communist-baiting senator was shown among other things to be a liar who had used factual distortion to destroy the careers of thousands of talented Americans. Murrow also had a sense of humour. In 1959 he gave Brendan Behan his head on *Small World* in a live transatlantic broadcast. The show was hilarious, particularly as a tipsy Behan defined Americans as "like a broken bicycle saddle – they give you a pain in the arse".

In general though, Ed Murrow's reports were solid, researched documents. They were a major contribution to the idea of America as the land of free speech. Unfortunately, his programmes were completely dependent on commercial sponsorship. When CBS was rocked by revelations of corruption on the *$64,000 Question* quiz show (the answers were supplied to a contestant with the right social profile), Murrow gave a speech in Chicago in 1958 in which he said:

> I can find nothing in the Bill of Rights or the Communications Act which says that [networks or individual stations] must increase their net profits each year lest the Republic collapse. No body politic is healthy until it begins to itch . . . I would like television to produce some itching pills rather than this endless outpouring of tranquilizers.

As always, he was biting the hand that ultimately fed him. Sponsors, including the late Pan American Airways, shied away from association with such a straight talker – on screen and off screen – and the CBS executives panicked. Fred Friendly, Murrow's longtime collaborator and producer, said that the executives simply became tired of fielding the flak that his and Murrow's programmes generated. Not so gradually, the Murrow approach was reduced and then vanished from American television.

The irony, as Friendly pointed out, was that if *See It Now* had continued, it might have exposed the fraud that was the *$64,000 Question* and saved American TV from losing for ever the respect of its viewers. There must be a moral for RTÉ there somewhere.

This is, for once, a chapter with a happy ending. In December 2000, after three years of resentments piling up and months of tensions and accusations, the RTÉ staff revolted against the Andrew Burns approach. He was forced to resign. The revolt was led successfully by none other than Dustin the Turkey from the children's advertising vehicle, *Den 2*.

THE APPEAL OF COUGHLAN

Confound their politics
Frustrate their knavish tricks.
"God Save the King"

The final saga began for me during an Authority meeting in April 1998. It was a long and painful episode and signalled the end of my days as a gadfly.

A message was passed down the table to the director general that a Mr Anthony Coughlan had won a case against RTÉ and the Broadcasting Complaints Commission in the High Court. I had never met Mr Coughlan although I had seen his name mentioned in connection with a complaint against RTÉ which had been dismissed by the Broadcasting Complaints Commission. It was something to do with a referendum. He had appealed the decision to the High Court. Now he had won.

At this announcement, a distinct pall settled over the boardroom table. I noticed the grimaces and began to pay attention. Coughlan seemed to be personally known to everybody except me. He was clearly a subject of anathema to most of these political movers and shakers having, as he later wrote, locked swords with FitzGerald, Geraghty and Attley over Ireland's involvement with the European Union. I knew nothing of that. And the present bone of contention being party political broadcasts, which to me

are the most abysmal form of television, I paid little attention. The fact that someone's complaint against RTÉ had
been upheld caused me to think: "So what! You win some,
you lose some."

My curiosity was only aroused when the director general muttered dark things about the implications of the High
Court decision for programming in general. That is my
bailiwick. So I inquired politely what it was all about. Bob
Collins patiently explained that the matter arose from
interpretations of Section 18 of the Broadcasting Act,
which I then went home and reread.

It seemed simple enough. RTÉ had a duty to be fair and
impartial, but it could also, if it chose, transmit uncontested party political broadcasts (which are by definition neither fair nor impartial). But RTÉ has transmitted these
broadcasts without question since Noah was a child.

So what was the problem? Well – and here I take a deep
breath – apparently in the divorce referendum of 1995 all
the main political parties were in favour of a Yes vote. Not
only did the government spend a fortune advocating a Yes
vote, RTÉ granted the political parties a total of forty minutes of uncontested broadcasts. Those saying No were
allowed only ten minutes. Even I, whose divorce was
enabled by the Yes vote, thought that a bit one-sided. The
fact that RTÉ was acknowledged to be fairly impartial in its
general coverage of the issue was considered to be irrelevant.

After that 1995 divorce referendum, MEP Patricia
McKenna proved in the Supreme Court that the government had been utterly unconstitutional in its spending of
taxpayers' money to support the Yes side. (McKenna was,
herself, in favour of divorce being made available, but a
principle is a principle. She bravely risked alienating her
own supporters in that case.)

Now the High Court had confirmed Anthony Coughlan's claim that RTÉ was unfair in allowing politicians on
one side of the debate a right to uncontested broadcasts in
referenda, and not giving an equal number of uncontested

broadcasts to those on the other side. The basis of the High Court decision seemed to be the previous Supreme Court decision. This, the McKenna judgement, had said that public money could not be used in a biased way by governments to support one side or another in a referendum. The implication was that free party political broadcasts came under the same umbrella of subsidy. However, a senior counsel had advised RTÉ that this had no implications for its general election coverage. So what was the problem? Uncontested party broadcasts could go ahead on these occasions until the politicians were blue in the face and the audience had died of stupefaction.

Even describing these matters causes me to go into *siesta* mode. The words referendum, party political, general election, High Court, Supreme Court normally trip a switch in my head that says: sleep.

But like everyone else I had often and idly wondered why political parties were allowed to bore the population with their extended – albeit less entertaining – commercials for themselves and the egos of their leaders. It seemed a rather heavier price than usual to pay for democracy, the broadcasts themselves seeming to be devised to score points off each other, rather than to inform citizens of policies. Both of the two main political parties also lied through their teeth and made outrageous promises, never to be kept.

The High Court judge (Carney) who had awarded Coughlan his victory incontrovertibly said, "RTÉ's starting point in relation to the allocation of such [uncontested] broadcasts is and always has been the political parties."

If the Carney judgement, about which we were now worrying, made it possible to drop these broadcasts altogether, I was all for it.

Anyway, at that April meeting the director general said RTÉ would have to examine the judgement and decide whether or not to appeal. RTÉ, as far as I am concerned –

and based on the legislation that set us up – *is* the RTÉ Authority. I could relax. We were in good hands. We could await further briefing and decide.

It was spring on my bog, and each day I happily traipsed around the six acres urging an assortment of alders, birch, poplar and others to burst forth in buds and leaves. A line of daffodils and irises had already shot up and were on the way out. Various willows, from *cinerea* to *fragilis* to *pubescens*, had obliged with catkins resembling caterpillars. I conducted another census of the trees I had planted in the previous four years: the majority were still surviving. This achievement gave me more satisfaction than any film or TV programme I had ever made. It was certainly more worthwhile than any real or imagined achievement of mine on the RTÉ Authority.

In the middle of my rusticating, I had a phone call from the director general. He was ringing around the Authority members to check that we agreed to suspend party political broadcasts during the forthcoming Good Friday and Amsterdam referenda. It was because of the uncertainty caused by Coughlan's victory in the High Court, he said. I told him I was delighted to agree.

It was hard to tear myself away from my bog for the next May meeting of the Authority. However, some instinct told me I should pay attention to the matter of Coughlan, particularly because the Executive had not deemed it important enough to be included on the agenda for the meeting. However, under that capacious umbrella called Any Other Business, the director general brought us up to date. He had consulted senior counsel who advised that this was an issue for the *Authority* and who promised to prepare a shorter paper before the final decision to appeal. The DG warned that there was a statutory time within which we had to appeal. He also said that, from "informal contacts", he had learned there was "political unhappiness" at the judgement. I did not care for the sound of this. Even though the DG later reassured us that such contacts had absolutely no impact on *his* decision to appeal, I began to feel a niggling concern.

It occurred to me that RTÉ did not need politicians to demand these broadcasts as a right. The attitude was interiorised. One does not have to get a directive in such matters. Powerful people do not have to spell out things. We have not yet emerged from our "nod nod, wink wink" culture. But I never spelt out my concern in these drastic terms. Perhaps I should have, and so lanced the boil at an early stage. Instead I suggested to the Authority that our action was a bit like crushing a fly with a sledgehammer. Why couldn't we let Coughlan have his small victory? It had shown that the small man could actually do something in this system. We would look petty if we did not accept the defeat gracefully. It is significant that, at that meeting, almost all of my colleagues on the RTÉ Authority shared my unease.

On 19 June 1998, I was pushed into taking a greater interest. A group calling itself the National Platform issued a press release, a copy of which was sent to me by a campaigning journalist, Nollaig Ó Gadhra. The press release named me, as well as the other Authority members, as having personally authorised an appeal against the Coughlan judgement. This was not true. I had no idea an appeal had been lodged and had certainly not personally authorised it. It took this press release to make me realise that I had a personal responsibility in the matter. Strangely, a week later the subject was still not considered by the Executive to be important enough to be featured on the June agenda. I had to raise the matter and ask whether in fact an appeal had been lodged. The DG said it had – nine days before, on 17 June – that is, nearly two months after the High Court decision and the precise statutory twenty-one days after the perfection of that decision. When I expressed surprise and mentioned that I thought we were to be further consulted, Bob Collins pointed out that he understood that the Authority members had authorised him to proceed with the appeal without further reference to them, and this was what he had done. This was news to me and I said so. It reinforced my general impression that RTÉ policy was formulated by its managers and that we, the Authority, were simply a rubber stamp – what Tim O'Connor, head of Sport, has referred to as "the historical lack of influence the Authority has had on RTÉ" (*The Sunday Tribune*, 2000). I do not like being taken for granted. It was clear from their remarks that the other members of the Authority were equally doubtful about the wisdom of our going down this road without examining the question more thoroughly. I went home and thought hard.

Perhaps we had after all given the RTÉ Executive a blank cheque? I looked up the minutes of April and confirmed that they only said "that RTÉ would have to examine the judgement, decide whether to lodge an appeal". I still retained the perhaps vainglorious illusion that the Authority *is* RTÉ – certainly in matters as important as the Constitution of Ireland.

At 5.40 p.m. on 27 June, I adopted my role as a public trustee of the national broadcaster. I rang Professor Corcoran and mentioned my misgivings. I repeated them in a long letter to him a few days later.

I wanted to know:

1. Whether or not we had actually given the Executive a blank cheque in April to go ahead without further consulting us.
2. Whether this was necessitated by time constraints.
3. Why, if the DG had personally rung each of us to agree to eliminating uncontested broadcasts during the latest referendum, he had not thought it necessary to check with us in this, much more significant, matter.
4. Who were the "informal contacts" whom the DG said had expressed "political unhappiness" at the Coughlan victory.

Over the phone the professor reassured me and said an interesting thing: RTÉ's appeal was not just to challenge

Coughlan's victory – with which he and most people in the station would not argue! The appeal was to clarify the implications for normal broadcasting. He promised that there would be a paper detailing the issue for the Authority at the next meeting. And true to his word, there was.

I also asked for a copy of RTÉ's senior counsel's advice plus a copy of the High Court judgement that had said Coughlan was right.

At the meeting on 24 July the director general answered all my points fairly and frankly. He even, amazingly, clarified who his "informal contacts" were: those whom he usually and ironically referred to as "our political masters", the Department of Arts, Heritage, Gaeltacht and the Islands, the Department of the Taoiseach, and Taoiseach Bertie Ahern himself. His frankness should have reassured us, but on me it had the opposite effect. (It is typical of my amateurishness in such matters that I did not notice until the saga ended that the DG also had had an informal conversation with Taoiseach Bertie Ahern in which the matter of indexation of the licence fee was discussed.)

Everybody on the Authority was now on the alert. They had by now read senior counsel's advice and most were as worried as I was about proceeding with the appeal. The DG was himself now so concerned that he suggested we might contribute to Coughlan's costs if he should lose. FitzGerald said this would make us look absurd and that we had perhaps acted unwisely in not initially seeking more information. The chairman admitted that, yes, there had been a certain ambiguity about the manner in which the decision to appeal had been arrived at, but he supported the DG's interpretation. I asked if we could confine our appeal to the aspect we thought was most worrying, i.e. its alleged implications for general broadcasting. FitzGerald said that we could not approach an appeal in *à lá carte* fashion. It had to be a full appeal, full stop.

I must now jump forward two years to the year 2000 to, albeit retrospectively, validate my concerns.

Early in November 2000, RTÉ's finance director, Gerry O'Brien, was questioned by the Flood Tribunal about quite another matter, the relationship between RTÉ and Ray Burke, the minister involved with Century Radio in 1989. Because it clearly illustrates the extraordinary influence which government has over RTÉ, it is worth transcribing parts of the newspaper report of his responses.

Station executives did not dispute Minister Burke's demand for RTÉ to reduce its fees, said Mr O'Brien, because "at the end of the day the minister has the trump card. RTÉ is that sort of organisation: if the minister wants something down, the minister gets something down. Our policy was to accommodate what was being put forward."

Asked by Mr Justice Flood if anybody from RTÉ actually asked what the minister wanted, Mr O'Brien said, "No one bit that bullet." As a state-sponsored body, RTÉ felt obliged to get the price down. It was always willing to "accommodate" public policy (of which, you may recall, Seán Lemass said RTÉ was an instrument). Asked by Mr Justice Flood if anybody argued the issue with the minister, the witness replied that RTÉ was "the sort of organisation that doesn't do that". He pointed out that RTÉ was a semi-state organisation, answerable to the political system: "the last thing we want to do is make enemies in that quarter". Political sanction was required for an increase in the licence fee and for other changes. RTÉ wanted to keep "an even diplomatic keel" in such areas of policy. The only other option would be "to go to war".

Now back to the present and the matter of Coughlan: my intuition told me that it was not just RTÉ that wanted to snatch Coughlan's victory from him. It was the body politic, too. That was too much for me. At the meeting of July 1998, I proposed withdrawing the appeal. This was still an option to save RTÉ getting egg all over its face. When I realised that the other members were as concerned as I was, my proposal seemed reasonable.

But I had not quite won yet. We kicked to touch. A

decision was made to defer the matter until September. Meanwhile, we would receive the full text of counsel's opinions and additional legal advice. That would keep us going during the August holidays. It certainly kept me reading for days and weeks on end when I should have been out tending my trees and battling the August growth of grass and brambles.

What was I doing, a complete layman trying to follow the contorted arguments of barristers and the complexities of High Court rulings – on top of the machiavellian nature of the RTÉ corporate mind? But I found myself enjoying it. I like reading and listening to experts in any field. I admire scholars, too, those who delve deeply and thoroughly into every aspect of their subject. Under my rowan trees, which were laden down with crimson berries, I studied the documents. Covered in insect repellant, I sat beside the boghole which we call a lake and covered reams of paper in notes, then tried to summarise them; failed; read everything again and again until I could see a pattern. When the heat oppressed me, I escaped indoors. I tried to follow the logic of each point, then looked for contradictions. When my brain overheated, I could wander out again to study the distant blue line of the Beanna Beola hills or lapse into vacancy in a study of the huge cumulus clouds over Cuan na Loinge.

One part of our legal advice concerning the 1995 divorce referendum disturbed me most. It claimed that fairness to all interests might require more coverage to one side of the debate than the other. How? In what circumstances? Answer: "When all responsible public or ascertainable private opinion is in favour . . . with only the flat earth lobby against." Who were these responsible people, I asked myself? Well, for one, *The Irish Times*, which had said after the ballot on divorce, "The referendum went as most people hoped it would." The actual result of that referendum showed that the people were almost evenly divided, the Yes vote just shaving it – probably thanks to the large financial government intervention. So who were "most people"?

It suggested to me an attitude that referenda are considered superfluous by "responsible" people, who already know what the result should be. And they will ensure that, if possible, the people will be guided by them. Thus the government spent taxpayers' money promoting a Yes vote in the divorce referendum. The Supreme Court said they were wrong. RTÉ gave too many uncontested broadcasts to the Yes side, and the High Court said they were wrong. "Responsible" opinion had been shown to be misguided. So, with RTÉ's much-vaunted independence of mind, why on earth were we appealing the latter judgement? Was it once again urban sophistry versus rural idiocy?

I again ploughed through the Carney judgement in the High Court which favoured Coughlan. I could not fault the judge's logic. He even said that his judgement should be confined to referenda, thus ring-fencing it from normal current affairs broadcasting. This protected RTÉ, I thought. I read again his references to the opinions of the Supreme Court judges who found in favour of McKenna in 1995, and I agreed more and more with the judges and less and less with our own legal advice.

I thought of the scholars I enjoy reading. The best of them excavate cleanly and leave others to interpret their findings. But some scholars start with a hypothesis and marshal evidence to support it. What occurred to me then was what I should have known from the start: legal advice has little to do with truth; it merely tells you what you want to know – that you have a chance of winning. It then marshals any arguments it can find that might be used in your favour, in this case RTÉ's. I thought their arguments were unconvincing.

The Supreme Court in 1995 expressed the following principles in relation to referendum matters in general. Justice Hamilton said, "Neither the Constitution nor the law for the time being in force in relation to the constitution gives to the

Government any role in the submission of the [referendum] proposal for the decision of the people." He also said that in this context the people should be free from "unauthorised interference by any of the organs of the State".

Organs of the state? I remembered, as always, Seán Lemass' definitive statement in 1966:

> RTÉ was set up by legislation as an instrument of public policy and as such is responsible to the Government. The Government have overall responsibility for its conduct and especially the obligation to ensure that its programmes do not offend against the public interest, or conflict with national policy as defined in legislation. To this extent *the Government rejected the view that RTÉ should be*, either generally or in regard to its current affairs programmes and news programmes, *completely independent of Government supervision.* [my italics]

This diktat caused a furore among programme-makers in 1966 and had been regularly sniped at, nose-thumbed, defied and challenged by broadcasters with varying degrees of subtlety and prudence, but the concept has never been erased from their minds. It always lurks in the depths like Jaws, waiting for what might be appropriately called "crunch-points". It is as ever present as the advertisers' economic influence on RTÉ's output.

The Coughlan appeal was one such friction point.

Justice Denham said in 1995 that Article 40, Section 1 of the Constitution "requires the organs of government in the execution of their powers to have due regard to the right of equality . . . it is irrelevant what view the Government takes." She also said, "To fund one side of a campaign in a referendum so as to enable media coverage and communications to promote a specific outcome is to treat unequally those who believe the contrary, whether they be a majority or a minority."

Ah, ha, I thought. Broadcasting costs money. If RTÉ gives unconcontested broadcasts to political parties, it is in a sense funding the protagonists. This had never been questioned before. Here was a tradition that nobody had queried in fifty years; further, that in allocating these broadcasts in proportion to the strength of political parties, RTÉ was favouring the powerful to the disadvantage of the weak. This was standard practice in general elections – which were actually not in question here – but, in regard to referenda it was unconstitutional because politicians and government had no legal, formal or any other role in a constitutional referendum once it was before the people.

RTÉ's attitude seeped right down to the workers at the coalface. In June 1999, Ming (Luke Flanagan), an independent candidate in the Connacht/Ulster European election, had to be restrained from storming into the Galway RTÉ studio during a live radio broadcast which featured only representatives of the majority political parties. The RTÉ producer of *News at One* told the *Connacht Tribune* that barring the candidate was justified on the grounds of "having to make hard editorial decisions based on representing political parties", as well as candidates' "previous voting patterns".

What I was learning was that a referendum is a way for citizens to legislate directly rather than leaving it to politicians. It is direct democracy and an important alternative to the usual party political dogfighting. The government is specifically excluded from influencing its outcome. Hooray for referenda.

Justice O'Flaherty had said, in relation to the the 1995 referendum, "The Public Purse must not be expended to espouse a point of view." Justice Blayney had said that the Executive (i.e. the government) "had thrown its weight behind those who support it [the Yes vote]".

The more I read, the more I wondered why on earth RTÉ was putting itself through this humiliating exercise. The Coughlan victory actually made life easier for RTÉ, in that it would not have to agonise about the allocation of party political broadcasts during referenda. It could just drop them. (This was confirmed by its own legal advice.) And it did, in the referendum that occurred in the middle of our deliberations. As already mentioned, the DG personally rang each of us to get our agreement to that decision. But in the more serious matter of Coughlan, which had constitutional implications, he did not ring us to ensure that his impression was correct and that we were in agreement with lodging RTÉ's appeal. By the way, RTÉ's coverage of these, the Amsterdam/Good Friday Agreement referenda in 1998, was the most entertaining and informative I have ever seen. The station for once actually did go out into the highways and byways. Significantly, without the influence of RTÉ's uncontested political broadcasts, 38 per cent of the people voted No to Amsterdam. This, I was told, alarmed the government as well as the political parties, who were in favour of the Amsterdam Agreement.

My impression at this point, right or wrong, was that as a class politicians had reached their lowest point in public esteem. For instance, Deputy Desmond O'Malley in January 2000 admitted on RTÉ radio that he feared that the Dáil as the people's representative body had lost much of its authority and power to, among others, the trade unions, IBEC (Irish Business and Employers Confederation) and Brussels. Indeed, the following month, his perception was confirmed by Des Geraghty on the same station. Speaking as president of SIPTU, he was reported as saying "We [the trade unions] create the framework within which government can and can't move." O'Malley did not mention the possibility that the number of leading politicians proved to have been in the pockets of big business might have had something to do with this diminution of respect for the Dáil. He also did not mention a more serious dimension to the undermining of the democratic process. As Jerry Mander, the adopted name of a former advertising executive in the United States and now implacable enemy of commercial TV, puts it:

Existing outside the boundaries of the country, the multi-national companies, in concert with banks, are capable of the economic domination of entire nations. Governments slip slowly into a new role subordinate to and supportive of them.

This seems to me to be manifestly true of Ireland.

I deduce that, though they themselves have submitted to this subjugation, our public representatives are justifiably smarting under the diminution of power. Their last assets are their seats. A powerful way of retaining these is through their access to the national broadcast media. Their principal contact (one-way) with the general public is the media, particularly radio and TV. The print media are relatively independent of them, but the national broadcaster, by virtue of political control of its purse strings, is largely at the government's mercy. RTÉ can make no major financial or technical decision without the approval of the relevant minister. I had four years' evidence of this. But even RTÉ's limited independence of mind was resented by government. The station was always drip-fed.

During this critical period of 1998, RTÉ was looking for a major role in Ireland's digital future in return for the excellent transmission infrastructure it had laboriously built up and maintained over forty years. It also needed indexation of the licence fee. It was lobbying to amend the 1993 legislation which had forced it to give 20 per cent of its programme budget to independent programme-makers. It needed a friendly government approach to these matters. But the station had few allies in the new political culture of treating everything as a disposable asset. And still it had to show some goodwill to the government.

If RTÉ is an instrument of public policy and the body politic legislates for this policy, then RTÉ must at least minimally conform to government wishes. Hence, when informal contacts suggest a political unhappiness with a situation – particularly a threat to politicians' unfettered and free access to the airwaves – it must be inevitable that there will be certain, perhaps inarticulated, pressures on RTÉ to act in the interests of its paymasters. The political establishment certainly could not be seen to challenge Coughlan directly. My perhaps naive deduction was that that was the reason why the attorney general, on behalf of the government, "associated" himself with RTÉ's appeal against the Coughlan judgement.

Joe Mulholland was a senior executive in RTÉ before his own "abolition" in March 2000. I learned very late in the game that, when asked privately by the Coughlan side why on earth RTÉ was appealing the High Court decision, Mulholland is alleged to have responded: "If I had my way, we wouldn't. But there are pressures . . ."

Without knowing this at the time but convinced of the accuracy of my assessment, I now resolved to fight tooth and nail to get RTÉ to withdraw its appeal. RTÉ would surely lose and would only confirm people's impression that it was simply doing the government's dirty work. My only concern was the good name of public broadcasting.

The legal advisers were rehearsing arguments that RTÉ might use if it actually proceeded with the appeal to the Supreme Court, but my reading convinced me that the court would never accept the undemocratic nature of these arguments.

One of them was this: Section 18 of the Broadcasting Act was traditionally interpreted as permitting a situation where, when RTÉ adjudges that a greater body of public opinion has emerged on one side of a referendum question, it might have the discretion to afford that side of the debate a proportionately larger coverage – as in general elections – in terms of uncontested broadcasts.

The question was: as adjudged by whom? By RTÉ? By the government? By right-thinking newspaper editorials? By its own staff? By the usual suspects whom it monotonously invites to participate in debates? By opinion polls? And if it so adjudges, is it not actually pre-empting the necessity of a referendum? Why have a referendum at all if certain key people, like de Valera of old, can look into their hearts and decide which side of the argument should win? I realised it was precisely because of these assumptions that the McKenna case had been fought and won in 1995 and why the Coughlan case had been fought and won in the High Court in 1998.

RTÉ's own legal advice perceived a major snag to the 1998 judgement: the High Court had emphasised the principle of equality. The legal advice described this as leaving RTÉ in "a straitjacket of equality". I thought: how can equality be a straitjacket except for those who do not believe in it? Equality is the cornerstone of democracy.

The principal concern seemed to be that the "fairness equals equality" principle could be extended in such a manner as to have unwanted repercussions for RTÉ. Like what?

I could only imagine it meaning that RTÉ would have to stop relying on tried and trusted members of the chattering classes to fill their news and current affairs schedules, that it would be forced to get out among the people and reflect the views, however disreputable and irresponsible, however unbalanced and subjective, of the populace as citizens, rather than spokespersons for vested interests. It might – horror of horrors – even mean treating, for instance, Sinn Féin as a serious political party with views as valid as any other party, instead of as the IRA by another name. As I had observed, this latter attitude, institutionalised after nearly twenty years of Section 31 censorship, was difficult to exclude from the broadcasting consciousness.

Equality meant, for instance, that if ninety-nine people and politicians were believed to favour a consititutional proposal to, say, reintroduce hanging, and only one diehard said no, the latter had to be afforded the same broadcasting time. But that is what a constitution is for: to protect minorities, no matter how small. History proved Copernicus and Galileo right. To a lazy mind, such a prospect could be viewed as what Lord Denning in another context described as "an appalling vista". To me as a broadcaster, it meant the liberation of a self-imposed broadcasting strait-jacket and freedom from the paternalistic and politically correct control of the so-called "responsible" people referred to above.

On 21 July 1998 I wrote another letter to Professor Corcoran outlining my concerns about the substance of the appeal in the light of my reading and expressing misgivings about the manner in which our appeal had been lodged. I again formally proposed that we withdraw it.

The bombshell exploded at our September meeting. I came prepared for battle and had the ground taken from under me by a pre-emptive strike. The Executive seemed to be past masters at this.

Bob Collins announced that having got further advice, which seemed to safeguard RTÉ, and having taken note of Authority members' worries expressed in July, he now proposed to withdraw the appeal currently lodged with the Supreme Court! (In fact, the director general had previously privately written a memo to the legal department in which he personally advocated altering RTÉ's traditional position and offering an equal number of broadcasts to both sides in referenda. Unfortunately, this memo was not released to us until twelve months later. Besides, I pondered, as Dean Acheson once said, "A memo is written not to inform the reader but to protect the writer.")

I refrained from cheering what I considered to be a courageous action by the DG.

The reason was, he stated, that as in all other legal matters, he was empowered to take such steps as were necessary to protect RTÉ's organisational and editorial interests in the future. I was never given the terms of his contract to read, but this suggested that he did not have to consult the Authority on any legal matter. The statement did not allow that he might fully consult and be guided by the Authority – which constituted the entity known as RTÉ – on a constitutional matter, which was precisely what was in question. On a superficial reading, the implication was that he had been, therefore, quite entitled to lodge the appeal originally without fully briefing the Authority.

But it did not matter now. The appeal was being withdrawn. I was not going to pursue such a niggling point. I did feel a little silly at having wasted all that time trying to enter the minds of senior counsels and High Court and Supreme Court judges, but I was very relieved that we were doing what looked to have been obvious to me from the start.

My relief, as they say, was short-lived.

Far from agreeing with the DG's step-down, Garret FitzGerald now was concerned that the Coughlan judgment would open the door to "fascists" and "lunatics" having equal access to the airwaves. I had no doubt that he had Sinn Féin in mind. Bill Attley also had developed the opinion that the Coughlan judgment would turn RTÉ into "an arm of government", an opinion that struck me, in this context, as superfluous. Two of the Authority heavyweights favoured continuing with the appeal. The third, Des Geraghty, sat on the fence.

My heart sank down to my boots as I heard the DG repeating his proposal to withdraw, but adding that he was still personally in favour of maintaining the appeal. The chairman then lost my last vestiges of support for him by saying he was also for continuing the appeal. Anne Haslam and Pat Hume gave no opinion either way.

What was going on here? I was flabbergasted. I said the Authority was acting like a headless chicken. How could a chief executive function with such an indecisive bunch as us? That courageous woman Betty Purcell once more made her own mind up and opposed the appeal. She had talked to her broadcasting colleagues, and they did not believe that the Coughlan judgement would make their jobs more difficult. I believe she and I shared the one object: to stop RTÉ from being exposed to public odium, to further accusations that RTÉ was a pawn of government. That left her and me once more out on a limb of opposition.

I could not understand what had happened.

If the big guns on the Authority were concerned in July, the subsequent documentation which they and I had received must have convinced them that we should withdraw the appeal. That is, if they read it as carefully as I had, and I was sure they had. And now the DG had presented a further legal reassurance that withdrawing the appeal would not damage RTÉ. So what was going on? Was it all a foregone conclusion? Had minds been made up long ago? Was all our debate just waffle?

Bill Attley suggested that we discuss the matter again the following month. I disliked this constant postponement of decision and knew that the more time we allowed the appeal to stand, the more reluctance there would be to withdraw it. I again proposed withdrawing the appeal, upping the ante by saying that if we did not, then I would publicly announce my opposition to our decision. I even demanded a vote on it, pointing out that, although legislation stated that "*Every* decision of the Authority *shall* be decided by formal vote," in three years we had never done so. Des Geraghty enlightened me as to the nature of consensus: that it was accepted as a legal voting procedure. I bowed to his experience. Purcell, that experienced campaigner, knew this fight could not be won immediately and, hoping to fight another day, suggested postponing the vote. So the matter was kicked to touch again.

At least, I thought, it's not final; the show is not over until the fat lady sings. In this, it transpired, I was once again utterly naive.

I went back to the drawing board for another month, renewing my studies. It was now autumn; there was a chill in the air in Conamara. The caterpillars had wrought havoc on the leaves of one species of my neglected alder (*Alnus cordata*) trees, and aphids were still munching away at the others (*Alnus glutinosa*). With the presentiment of doom suggested by falling leaves, I acted as devil's advocate to myself, searching desperately for some solid justification for continuing the appeal, trying to understand if and where I was wrong and if they, wiser heads, were right. I remained convinced that RTÉ was wrong and prepared a detailed rebuttal of its legal advice.

Come October and battle was resumed. One Friday two solemn-faced lawyers were brought in to convince Betty Purcell and myself, the two doubting Thomases on the Authority, that it was all right to go ahead with the appeal. I took them on, quoted chapter and verse, identified disparities between their original advice and their present opinons, and asked for answers to four specific questions. It was useless. Minds had been made up. Garret FitzGerald was not even present for all of the argumentation. He did not return after lunch, simply left word that he strongly felt the appeal should continue.

The worst part was when the lawyers left the room so that the remaining Authority members could finally resolve the problem. I made a last attempt to persuade the Authority to withdraw. I had marshalled and carefully written out all of my arguments, showing in detail how we must lose the appeal.

I was once more cut off at the pass, this time by the guillotine. The chairman would not allow me to continue – said we had talked enough and the time now was for a decision. It was the only time in three years that I saw him acting ruthlessly, so I knew the die was cast. Bill Attley accused me of getting professional legal advice on the side. In a way it was a compliment to my tedious hours and days of study. But, galloping along on my high horse, I demanded that he withdraw the remark. Being a gentleman, Bill withdrew it.

Everybody except myself and Purcell fell into line. Attley pointed out that we could hardly withdraw now that the attorney general and the Broadcasting Complaints Commission had joined with us in the appeal. It was then I realised how effective the delaying tactics had been. Even Des Geraghty, who up to this point had hedged his bets, saw this as a way out and said that was the only reason he was now agreeing to the appeal. Later, in private, I'm afraid I called Geraghty a turncoat. He took it in his usual good-humoured way.

My final gesture was to inform the members that I must now carry out my promise of going public. The meeting ended, and I left the boardroom feeling more angry and depressed than in the entire previous three years. But it was a great education in the realities of politics, where principle is always subservient to pragmatism.

At home in Conamara I licked my wounds, began to plant cuttings from my willow trees, probing for a little depth in the scrapings of the blanket bog. I should really resign from the RTÉ Authority. Such a move would no doubt be welcomed by some, but I could not give them the satisfaction. If I had to go, it should not be done quietly. There was also the fact that the RTÉ appeal against Coughlan was listed for mention in the Supreme Court within a few weeks. I would try one more desperate measure.

I sat down and wrote again to Professor Corcoran, stating plainly what at that stage I had come to believe. I set out my own opinions:

1. That the Executive was not entitled to make a legal decision on a constitutional matter without fully consulting and briefing the RTÉ Authority.

2. That the Executive had taken its decision in consultation with government and the major political parties. (The word "consult" means "take into consideration.")

3. That the decision to appeal was not communicated immediately to the Authority, nor was its explicit permission given before the appeal was lodged.

I suggested that the Executive had exceeded its powers in this matter. However, it should be pointed out that this view was stoutly denied by the chairman on behalf of the Executive.

Finally and outrageously, I proposed to send a copy of this letter to the National Platform (which I had learned was Anthony Coughlan's group), whose personal naming and shaming had originally woken me up. I even asked the chairman if there was anything in my statutory role that would prevent my so doing. This must have caused anguish in the dovecotes, because on 4 November 1998, I was faxed a five-page rocket in reply.

The chairman – and whoever had researched this letter – expressed himself in terms of shock and dismay. He absolutely denied and rejected all my suggestions and warned that if I passed my letter to a third party the Executive might sue me for defamation. It would also be in breach of my duty to the RTÉ Authority and its guidelines.

But he had fudged a couple of points – actually using the words "ambiguity" and "assumed" in relation to certain key points – which confirmed that my interpretation of events could be equally valid. He also did not clarify my statutory responsibilities, which are much larger than any private arrangements among the members of the RTÉ Authority and its Executive. I wrote back, pointing this out and explaining the sense in which I had used the word "consult". To back this up, I listed every minuted mention of RTÉ's political contacts over the previous four years, showing how normal such consultation was. I knew this would drive them up the wall, particularly since Supreme Court Justice Denham had so clearly said, in the matter of referenda, "It is irrelevant what view the Government takes."

I made a final appeal to the chairman to cut the Gordian knot and even at this late stage to withdraw the appeal. Knowing very well this would not happen, I put all all my notes and correspondence in a brown envelope and sent them off to the relevant minister, who happened to be Síle de Valera, and asked her to rule on my statutory responsibilities in the matter.

It was then, as they say in Conamara, *"a tháing an crú ar an tairne"*. To put it in English, crudely of course, that was when the shit really hit the fan.

TRIAL AND PUNISHMENT

The only safe course for the defeated is to expect no safety.
Virgil, *The Aeneid*, Book 2

What sparked the final row was a blow-by-blow account of the most recent RTÉ Authority meeting on the subject. It was printed in *Phoenix* magazine in November 1998.

I was impressed by the detail. Although its attribution of overt political argumentation to Attley, Geraghty and FitzGerald seemed to me to be over the top, *Phoenix* even had the voting accurate: six for, two against appealing the Coughlan judgement.

Leaks were always part and parcel of the RTÉ infrastructure. A room with twelve people and their huge organisational backup outside resembles nothing more than a leaky tub. Leaks were inevitable. Sometimes they were strategic, from senior staff; some were occasionally suspected to come from the Authority members themselves. I once naively rang *Phoenix* magazine and asked who their mole was in a particular instance, but was very properly denied the information. All the newspapers benefited from these leaks. Once there had been a blow-by-blow account of an Authority ding-dong about sporting matters in which Bill Attley figured prominently. The leak was so detailed and so biased towards Attley's point of view that he was clearly being set up by somebody antipathetic to him. Everybody suspected somebody. Sometimes I felt we were working in a hall of mirrors resembling Smiley's Circus. All except me pronounced themselves "disgusted" with *Phoenix*. Even Purcell used the word, which surprised me. Remote from the centres of gossip, I had found the magazine to be one of the few places where I could get even a sniff of what actually was going on in the country – even in RTÉ!

Certain people assumed that I was hand in glove with *Phoenix* in this latest revelation. I can state categorically that I had nothing to do with it. Chairman Corcoran had written a response to a previous, more significant leak, denying that the RTÉ Authority's approval of their appeal was retrospective. In my opinion his letter was ill-advised, but I had made no comment.

Very reluctantly – but perhaps a little grandiosely, feeling the kind of dread that Thomas Moore must have experienced – I carried out my earlier promise to the RTÉ Authority. I went public.

This took the form of a letter to *The Irish Times*:

> Sir,
> May I, through your columns, assure those interested in the matter that I applaud Mr Coughlan's action as a citizen in the tradition of Crotty and McKenna and was pleased with the success of his High Court Action.
>
> Since June I have been trying to persuade the RTÉ Authority to withdraw this appeal, but ultimately have failed.
>
> As this is the latest and most serious of my dissensions from RTÉ policy, I must now consider the usefulness of remaining on the RTÉ Authority.

I then sat back and waited for the sky to fall.

I had now committed two unpardonable sins. I had privately, according to the RTÉ Executive, defamed them, and publicly I had dissented from the RTÉ Authority. Of seven members of the public who took sufficient interest in the matter to comment to me on my actions, six thought I should stay and fight. The seventh, a private citizen, but whom I also believe was an ex-middle manager of RTÉ, replied to me in *The Irish Times*, asking me in so many words to please shut up.

My trial and sentencing by the RTÉ Authority took place on 27 November 1998 in the luxury of the St Helen's Hotel in Booterstown. This building was once owned by the Christian Brothers and was magnificently preserved. Nothing but the best for the RTÉ Authority. It is now part of the Scandinavian Radisson chain of hotels, and if, as I have already noted in these pages, you ring for a reservation, a voice in California services your request.

Carmel O'Reilly was waiting outside to welcome me and make sure I did not lose my way. She personally guided me to the courtroom, sorry, boardroom.

I knew I was on a hiding to nothing. But I had no intention of absenting myself in felicity – as the two trade union leaders had done earlier in the year when their own members in RTÉ pulled the rug from under the Authority's breakfast television plans. Attley and Geraghty simply stayed away from the ensuing Authority meeting. Why could I not develop their savvy? People like me never do, unfortunately.

For two hours I endured a succession of verbal attacks, accusations of irresponsibility, angry abuse from the Authority members. I told them I had given plenty of warning about my letter to the newspapers. I was even accused of being responsible for the leak to *Phoenix*, which was untrue. The Executive or chairman might have interjected the fact that every single action of mine in the past on the RTÉ Authority had been well signalled to them and always out in the open. But everybody wanted their pound of flesh, which suggested to me that there was a slight tinge of guilt about the appeal. I mostly rolled with the punches. The appeal was a *fait accompli*, and really I had not much else to say on the matter; I was actually compliant, for the most part, with their damage-limitation proposals. At one stage I left the room for a smoke so that they could fulminate in peace, only to be pursued by the chairman appealing to me to come back to take more. It was, as they say, heavy. I tried to explain that by consulation I meant "taking into consideration". In making that point I was never alleging that Bob Collins was deceitful.

I had few friends there. Even Betty Purcell said I should not have written the letter to the newspapers, although she did venture that in general I was entitled to publish my views. Des Geraghty "resented everything" I had done. Garret FitzGerald was the most restrained, only saying that my "supposition was untenable". It struck me that his restraint may have been due to his experience in politics: after a row and its conclusion, there is no point crowing over your opponent. He did suggest that he and Des Geraghty had been libelled by *Phoenix*. I suggested they sue. They have not, so far as I know. Bob Collins said my allegations about "consulting" politicians and government were "untruthful".

Des Geraghty laid down the rubrics of damage limitation: the appeal must be protected; the Executive must be protected; Authority members must be protected; the future of the organisation must be protected.

There was a shocked silence when I said I had carried out my stated intention of sending all correspondence to Minister de Valera. The chairman and the DG looked despairingly at each other; they then said they must consider how the return of these documents from the department could be organised.

The majority of members at that St Helen's meeting did not spell out the obvious solution, which was that I should fall on my sword. Only one had the opaqueness to do that. I had a sudden revelation: the worst thing possible for RTÉ at the moment would be for me to resign. It would make them look even worse. Perhaps Garret realised that first: it

was better to have me fulminating inside the tent than uri-
nating on it from without. I actually had a minor card left
if I wanted it – which I did not. At moments like this one
can sometimes achieve a kind of disinterest. Nevertheless,
all kinds of suggestions were made as to how this wild man
could be gagged. Max Weber wrote that the triumph of the
bureaucratic mind is to turn all problems of politics into
problems of administration.

That section of the business came to an uneasy end. We
broke for lunch. I sat between Liam Miller and the new
director of sales, a calm woman named Geraldine O'Leary
– appropriately, ex-Saatchi & Saatchi. As we went back
into the fray, Joe Mulholland, sitting with the head of
News, Ed Mulhall, called after me, "Are you still with us,
Bob?" Clearly, the staff knew exactly what was going on
inside the boardroom. So much for confidentiality. I
wagged a hand at them, indicating the dodginess of my
position.

The final crunch came when I objected to Bob Collins'
attribution of "untruthful" to me. Now I may be naive,
stubborn, unbiddable, incapable of accepting the subtler
modes of realpolitik, but I had tried hard to be above
board in my dealings. I was certainly not a liar. I said I
would next attend an Authority meeting when the DG
withdrew this allegation. After much mediation by the
chairman in the following weeks, the director general did
so, but begrudgingly, in a No Surrender sort of way, as
recorded in the minutes of their January meeting. As we
shared the same ideal of public broadcasting, I regretted
the difference between myself and Collins, whom I
admired, and the difficulties of whose position I did not
underestimate. However, I realised such a conflict was
inevitable. I had nothing to lose but a vague concept of
integrity; he had his organisational authority as well as his
career to protect. In that same year, 1998, Collins had been
elected honorary president of the television section of the
European Broadcasting Union. In September 2000 he was

reported as being a candidate for the full-time post of secretary to the entire EBU. His contract as director general of RTÉ runs until 2004. Was he being prescient about the receding future of RTÉ? It would be mean to suggest he was already arranging his own future, that the captain was ensuring his lifebelt was ready before abandoning the doomed tanker. The likelihood is that, as a dyed-in-the-wool public broadcaster, he saw the more powerful EBU as being a better protector of his ideals – and perhaps ultimately of RTÉ.

Although I had so far received no reply from Minister de Valera, shortly after that November meeting and, possibly as a result of whichever behind-the-scenes action the Executive and chairman took, she very promptly got rid of these documentary hot potatoes. She then wrote to me saying that she had no function in the matter and that she had not retained copies. I replied that, since her office had appointed me, to refuse to make a ruling on my statutory position was an abdication of her responsibilities.

But that is politics.

END OF THE AFFAIR

In my beginning is my end.
T.S. Eliot, *Four Quartets* (1940)

In spring 1999 I was now a *persona* pretty much *non grata* with the RTÉ Executive and with most of my colleagues on the Authority.

I had lost the Coughlan battle, my regionalism proposals had been effectively ignored, as were my trenchant criticisms of child-targeted commercials. All but a couple of my fellow members must have considered me to be at best a fool, at worst a traitor. It was with great reluctance that I dragged myself to a few more Authority meetings.

Life went on.

My friend, actor Donal McCann, was dying from cancer and I was trying to finish a documentary on him. This was produced by Tom Collins, that Scarlet Pimpernel from Derry, ironically in collaboration with RTÉ, which shows what a small country this is. I would call to McCann after every monthly meeting to sip tea and discuss old times and the job in hand, trying to encourage him that he could still conquer the disease. His calmness and humour in the face of the unknown put my petty concerns in perspective. We laughed over what he had said twenty years before in relation to RTÉ's ability to make films: "They're still wondering if the snaps will come out." I joked that he was just being bitchy because a fine ex-RTÉ cameraman, Peter Dorney, had years before beaten Donal for the part of Hamlet in a school production. I had entitled one of my photographic exhibitions, appropriately "The Snaps Came Out". We went back a long way, McCann and I. He died in July 1999.

At least, if only to give myself an interest in the lacklustre RTÉ proceedings, I could resume my sniping at child-targeted commercials. At the February meeting I raised the matter and was told by the director general that he did not intend to open this debate again. He knew, as victor, that he could peremptorily slap down any suggestion I might make and that I would get little support from the others. However, brave Purcell asked for another discussion on the subject, and it was agreed to have one in May. Another report would be prepared.

Meanwhile, Joe Mulholland, the managing director of TV, was under a shadow. The only thing he and myself had in common was that in the course of our producer duties many years before we each had the early initiative to ignore the rules and "hijack" a film crew. Mulholland's professional problems stemmed originally from a spend of £1.2 million on the studio presentation of the English Premier League. Mulholland and Tim O'Connor, head of Sports, had expertly snaffled the series from TV3. Unfortunately, their success was overshadowed by the spend on the series' studio presentation. The Authority was informed by the Executive, in trenchant and unambiguous terms, that this was intolerable. As Bill Attley whispered to me, "It looks like a kick in the arse for Joe."

The result was that when the European Champions League was up for auction Mulholland and O'Connor were inhibited in their bidding by the Executive-prompted Authority censure, and the series went to TV3. Attley, deeply involved in soccer, was completely incensed by this loss and made his feelings graphically clear. His remarks were leaked verbatim to a newspaper; by whom, nobody knows. The fact was that the two managers could not win; but while Tim O'Connor was considered indispensable, Joe Mulholland was singled out for his first yellow card. His second card was awarded for the outcry caused by trying to retire the Met Éireann forecasters and introduce shining new amateurs. Then there was his role as managing director, Television, at whose desk the buck stopped when RTÉ's New Year Millennium programming covered itself in a substance which was the opposite of glory. Perhaps the final card was red as a result of the flight of a second programme controller, Helen O'Reilly, a mere twelve months after her predecessor, David Blake-Knox.

I was not in the least surprised when, in March 2000, I read that Joe Mulholland's early "retirement" from RTÉ had been announced after a meeting of the RTÉ Authority. He had twice been a contender for the position of director general, the last time in competition with Bob Collins, with whom his relationship was understandably delicate. Mulholland's thirty-year service to RTÉ was finished, but, professional as ever, he stayed on to be midwife at the birth of one of RTÉ's better co-production achievements, the filming of all Beckett's plays.

As I care not a whit for the business of soccer, my programme-maker's viewpoint is this: I consider Mulholland's major mistake was to retain *The Late Late Show* under the aegis of Pat Kenny on the strange grounds that RTÉ needed to retain the title of the show or TV3 would rob that, too. This decision overlooked the fact that *The Late Late* inhered solely in the personality of Gay Byrne. No pretender, as has been proved, could possibly succeed him without tripping. Besides, when I asked a group of RTÉ producers in 1997 whether or not they thought Kenny "worked" on television, they all shook their heads sadly.

On the last of the very few occasions I have ever spoken to Joe Mulholland, I suggested that he would be better equipped to write this book than me. He said, "No. It's too close to the bone."

I continued researching the commercial exploitation of children. Because we had swallowed completely the American economic and broadcasting model, it would be interesting to find out what the future held for us. Ralph Nader's Commercial Alert organisation in Washington was still generous with the information it collects in its watchdog role.

I learned that my old favourite, *Sesame Street*, had succumbed to its commercial wooers. At the end of the programme, instead of the time-honoured announcement that an episode has been brought to you "by the letter Z and the number 2", it is now brought to you by Zithromax, an antibiotic promoted by the giant pharmaceutical company Pfizer.

Sesame Street has for thirty years been put out by PBS, America's public television service. Now its sponsors are encroaching greedily and more obviously on to its sacred space. Healthex (Zoboomafoo) markets its "playclothes for life's little lessons" on the show. Juicy Juice is "100% juice for 100% kids". An animated Ronald McDonald announces that he is "happy" to support children's television and makes sure a Happy Meal box with the familiar McDonald's golden arches is imprinted on the kids' consciousness. Kellogg's Frosted Flakes are identified with the exhortation "Thinking and creating are more than good; they're great!"

Such developments could not happen without the cosmetic imprimatur of tame academic specialists in child pychology and psychiatry. The complicity on the part of these professionals in the enormous advertising and marketing onslaught on children has reached epidemic proportions in the US and must constitute the largest single psychological project ever undertaken. Sixty concerned members of the American Psychological Association have actually written in these terms to their association's president, Dr Richard Suinn, and requested him to curb their own members' activities in this field:

> The sale of psychological expertise to advertisers to manipulate children for monetary gain goes without comment, let alone sanction. The profession does very little to protect innocent children from the psychological cajoling and assaults that it itself helps to create.

The sixty members urged their president to issue a public statement denouncing the use of psychological techniques to assist corporate marketing and advertising to children.

Once upon a time in America, children were viewed as vulnerable beings to be nurtured. Now they are viewed as an economic resource to be exploited. But Ireland, I have speculated, is invariably twenty years behind the US in everything. Such an approach to children could hardly be entertained in family-centred, cherish-all-the-children-equally Ireland, could it? The answer is Yes. It has already happened and the national broadcaster is a willing collaborator.

On 12 October 2000 in Dublin, a national marketing conference was organised by *Business and Finance* magazine. The opening theme was "Marketing to Children". Martin McEvoy, chairman of the organising committee, introduced it:

> Children are spending megabucks – so are we faced with a straightforward marketing challenge? We contrast the US and European experience and chart a way forward for dealing with what may become a more regulated environment.

The cost of participating in the day-long conference was £250, which confined attendance to marketeers with large expense accounts. Even I was amazed to read that the conference chairman who graced the proceedings was Geraldine O'Leary, director of sales in RTÉ.

The key speaker was Brian Ellis, an ex-employee of Hasbro, the toy manufacturing giant famed for its exploitation of Asian workers and whose subsidiary, Milton and Bailey, is located in Waterford. From his professional presentation it became clear that Ellis was outlining a semi-military campaign to overcome European resistance to the further Americanisation of child-marketing techniques. In impressive detail he listed the pockets of potential "resistance": in Belgium, UK, The Netherlands, France, Italy, Greece, Norway, Sweden, Hungary, Poland, the Czech Republic and Ireland. How powerful this resistance is can be imagined from the Irish sample: a lone Irish Labour opposition deputy, Brian O'Shea, mildly asking for protective measures for children to be included in the latest Irish broadcasting legislation. Mr Ellis's professional research was, however, undermined when he suggested that there was a significant shift to the left in present-day European politics. But his object was clearly stated: "To ensure that Sweden does not successfully introduce and secure support for an EU-wide ban on advertising to children" and to "secure maximum freedom to advertise ['responsibly', of course] . . . to all audiences, including children".

What most preoccupied me was his announcement of the establishment of a Brussels-based "Advertising Education Forum". He described this body as a neutral information system which would have six academics on board, purporting to add objectivity to its researches. My research on this "Forum" produced the information that one of the academics was none other than Dr Brian Young of the University of Exeter, whose approach to the subject of child-targeted advertising and "childhood innocence" I have detailed in an earlier chapter.

The other significant aspect of this "neutral body" was its steering committee: it consisted of executives from BskyB, the British Toy and Hobby Association, Coca-Cola, Kellogg's, Mars, Mattel (toy manufacturers), Ogilvy & Mather, Procter & Gamble, and Toy Industries of Europe, a group that predictably overlaps with the executive committee of the World Federation of Advertisers. These bodies have now an enormous war chest to fight the Swedish initiative. There is little resistance to this onslaught, and I fear the battle has already been lost. Papers by the likes of

Dr Brian Young of Exeter University and Jeffrey Goldstein of the University of Utrecht saying we worry excessively about children's advertising appear on the EU's website. Dr Viviane Reding, an EU culture commissioner with responsibility for education, culture and advertising standards, is on record as opting for "self-regulation". She even wrote me a personal letter confirming this *laissez-faire* approach.

History is repeating itself. I am reminded of what happened to a parents' initiative begun in 1968 in the US. For ten years they campaigned to persuade the FCC (Federal Communications Commission) to introduce limits to the corporate onslaught on children's television. The latter body finally recommended that

> . . . all TV advertising for any product which is directed to or seen by audiences composed of a significant proportion of children who are too young to understand the selling purposes of, or otherwise comprehend or evaluate the advertising, should be banned.

What was the result?

All the candy and toy and breakfast food manufacturers combined forces and with an estimated budget of between $15 and $30 million bombarded the US Senate and House of Representatives with lobbying. The result was the disembowelling of the FCC and the issuing of regulations at which advertisers could laugh. Exactly the same drama is being acted out now in Europe. Why? Because in 1999 the US manufacturers discovered that their home market was saturated, if not declining. In 1998, Nike's CEO, Phil Knight, had finally admitted that his shoes "have become synonymous with slave wages, forced overtime and arbitrary abuse". Hence the advice of the *Financial Times*: "As with many consumer product, the best long-term hope for US manufacturers may lie in overseas markets."

Ireland, for instance.

I was abroad for the April 1999 Authority meeting, but on the 28th of that month I heard the first cuckoo's overture to May and witnessed the annual revelation of the full beauty of Conamara. Fortified, I returned to the fray on the RTÉ Authority. The report on children's affairs, promised in February, did not materialise in May. The omission seemed to me to show how cavalier was the attitude towards my concerns. It was time to up the ante again. I informed my fellow members that I would publicly refuse to pay my licence fee until child-targeted commercials were removed from our schedules. I have not paid the licence since.

After this meeting, Professor Corcoran asked for a private word with me. When we were alone in the boardroom, he appealed to me to postpone publicly announcing my intention until after the June meeting. I deduced that broadcasting legislation was at a delicate stage. I thought it fair to assent to his polite request. But he also added a strange comment: "You know, your tactics in this have not been very good." I was so taken aback that I had not the presence of mind to ask for elaboration. But what flashed into my mind was a distant memory of Fluther's rejoinder to a British Tommy (in O'Casey's *The Plough and the Stars*) when the latter sneered that the Irish didn't fight fair: "D'ye want us to come out in our skins an' throw stones!"

However, the professor was right. I had fought too openly and fairly for the machinations and inertia of mandarins, politicians and career movers. I should have adopted guerrilla tactics. Perhaps that was what the chairman meant. Alternatively, I should have followed the sophisticated approach of DCU, his university, to RTÉ. At our March meeting they extracted from RTÉ a commitment to invest £2.5 million in a brand new concert hall for DCU and an RTÉ annual rental of £150,000! That was the equivalent of two years of Christmas toy advertising income. The chairman correctly absented himself from the relevant Authority discussions.

It was too late for tactics. In June 1999 there was a heatwave in Conamara. The small pond fringed with wilting yellow irises dried out. It was possible to retrieve the miscellaneous toys and bric-a-brac thrown in by children, to scrape the granite bottom clear of mud. Five days before our June meeting, I sat down and wrote a prediction. It described precisely the form our discussion on child-targeted commercials would take. I concluded my letter by asking the chairman to accept this as my resignation. My prediction of the proceedings was 99 per cent accurate; the 1 per cent was accounted for by Betty Purcell and Pat Hume, again supporting my proposal to at least abolish toy commercials at Christmas. But the mandarins executed yet another swift kick to touch: the financial implications must be examined – yet again!

I handed over my letter of resignation and left the boardroom for the last time. After three days the chairman cashed my cheque.

And that was that. I did not even stay for the free lunch, of which mythical repast there was as usual one for everybody on the RTÉ Authority. The Lone Ranger galloped off into the setting sun with his usual stirring farewell.

The new chairman of RTÉ, Paddy Wright, has recently written to RTÉ staff: "There is no place in the future of RTÉ for those who are not 100% committed to the new ideals we are setting ourselves." And what might those ideals be? Better programmes, more investigative reporting, decent programmes for children, an expansion of RTÉ to reflect reality beyond the Pale? No. With the childlike simplicity of the new barbarians, Wright's philosophy can be summed up in his first words on taking the job: "RTÉ must become more commercial."

The Lone Ranger is now a creaking man of sixty-five and has finally admitted that decrepitude of mind and body are creeping up on the ego and libido that he once fancied were indestructible. He has realised that his tastes and opinions are passé, that he should channel his remaining energies into wrestling with trees. As he stomps and splashes over his six acres of bog in Conamara, the process of whose reafforestation coincided with his naive efforts to reform RTÉ, he is capable of nothing more energetic than contemplating Shakespeare:

> And this our life exempt from public haunt,
> Finds tongues in trees, books in the running brooks,
> Sermons in stones, and good in everything.

And about time, too, he agrees.

EPILOGUE

On 27 January 2000, six months after I resigned my position on the RTÉ Authority, there came from the Supreme Court the echoes of an ancient battle. RTÉ, the attorney general and the Broadcasting Complaints Commission lost their appeal. Coughlan was vindicated. If I had been Donal McCann, I would have put money on the outcome and made a fortune. The decision confirmed to me that I had been right in at least one of my altercations with RTÉ. But it was a mere moral victory and also pyrrhic, for two reasons: firstly, I was no longer a member of the Authority. Secondly I had failed in my prime object: to stop RTÉ making an ass of itself again – and in public.

Specifically, what the Supreme Court ruled was that a lower court was right in finding RTÉ at fault and that Anthony Coughlan was perfectly justified in his complaint against the station. It was some consolation for spending most of 1998 desperately trying to get RTÉ to withdraw its – our! – appeal against the High Court decision, and to get us for once to defy our political masters and do the right thing by a single citizen.

The Supreme Court judgement reassured me that neither Coughlan nor I were simply obstructionists.

The penultimate note is that, in a kind of postscript to his judgement, one of the Supreme Court judges recognised some ambiguity in RTÉ's position in relation to political party broadcasts. But that issue, he said, was no business of the Supreme Court. Only one of the five judges, Donal Barrington, disagreed with his colleagues and said RTÉ was right. But he based his opinion on the "responsible people" analysis. Thus: "There is no constitutional device which will ensure their [the people's] ultimate decision will be infallible *or even that it will be prudent, just or wise.*" (Implying, it seems to me, that politicians decisions are invariably prudent, just and wise!)

Justice Barrington also said, "To play down or neutralise the role of political leaders in favour of committed amateurs would be, to say the least, unwise." He said, "Citizens may have differences of capacity, physical and moral." And politicians do not?

Lastly, he said, "The special position of political leaders should be recognised." Though the judge had trenchantly pronounced that a referendum is the ultimate act of sovereignty of a people, he now suggested that, in a referendum, political leaders should be granted privileges "dissimilar to those granted to private citizens".

Fortunately he was only one of five, and his elitist views had no effect on the outcome. He may have given some cold comfort to RTÉ. That is all.

I could find no formal statement, much less a discussion of the matter, on the RTÉ airwaves. They did issue a very brief press statement. But Coughlan was interviewed on RTÉ's competitor, Today FM.

On the morning on which RTÉ's appeal had been originally listed for the Supreme Court, I had looked up Anthony Coughlan's number in the phone book. He was just about to leave for work. I wished him luck. That was when he mentioned Joe Mulholland's remark. During the saga it was my only conversation with Mr Coughlan. Eighteen months after the affair, I checked the details of my account with Mr Coughlan. It transpired that the plot was even thicker than I had guessed. According to him:

> It was not that political party broadcasts were so important in themselves, for they are not, except in a very tight referendum such as the divorce referendum was; but in fact such close results are rare. The real importance of the legal battle with RTÉ was that if the Supreme Court could have been persuaded to accept that fairness required inequality rather than equality – if in other words, it accepted that the political parties were so important as organisers and articulators of opinion that they were justified in having free broadcasts in a referendum, even when most of them were on the same side – that would have opened a legal path to giving public money to political parties, and to non-party bodies, on these occasions. That in turn would have been a way around the McKenna judgement, and readmitted the principle of inequality by the back door when it had been shut out at the front door. The government, the political parties, the European Movement and europhile opinion in particular were extremely anxious to bring that about, mainly because of the implications for future EU referendums.

Coughlan added that Michael McDowell, his counsel for the first hearing of the RTÉ appeal, had said in court that what the appellants, including the then attorney general, were looking for was "a licence to loot the exchequer for the benefit of the political parties".

Such are the vagaries of the legal and political professions that Mr McDowell was himself soon appointed attorney general and had to continue that office's formal association with RTÉ's appeal *against* Coughlan.

In forty years of tension between RTÉ and government, the national broadcaster never went to war, but always relied on diplomacy to maintain its status quo. In July 2001, a little late, it finally lost patience when, in response to its plea for a £50 increase in the license fee, the Fianna Fáil government awarded it a contemptuous £14.50. This signalled the clear political intention to let the public broadcaster wither away over the next few years. The workers held an impromptu meeting in the RTÉ canteen to express their anger, and this feeling overflowed into RTÉ's programming. Even Joe Duffy and John Bowman could not conceal their outrage on air. But, the minister, Síle de Valera brazened it out. On *Questions and Answers* she said that it was RTÉ's original idea to sell its transmission network. This was a disingenuous presentation of the original scenario. She had previously claimed in the Dáil that RTÉ was "happy" to sell its Cablelink shares. This was far from the truth as I saw it.

Muiris Mac Conghail called – for a second time – on the RTÉ Authority to resign. At the time of writing they have not done so. That body merely expressed "deep concern" and quibbled about figures. Political appointees are inclined to stay appointed. The RTÉ workers have final proof of how ineffectual is the RTÉ Authority; they must now realise that it is up to themselves alone to salvage the remnants of public broadcasting.

RTÉ never had swords to turn into ploughshares. But it has audience shares. Perhaps it is not too late for it to turn these into a sword with which to cut the Gordian knot of its dual mandate. It must try to escape, once and for all, from either its political or its commercial subservience. Having it both ways never worked.

For Ireland's national public broadcaster and especially its programme-makers – whose views tend to be asked for, then ignored – it is, as *Opportunity Knocks* host Hughie Green used say, "make-your-mind-up time".

INDEX

Index

Index

Index

Index